COMPASS

PATHS TO EFFECTIVE READING
SECOND EDITION, REVISED

Roumpini Papadomichelaki, J.D., M.A., MEd
Lash Keith Vance, Ph.D., M.A., MEd

The Write Press, Inc

"A capacity and taste for reading gives access to whatever has already been discovered by others." Abraham Lincoln

☐ **Copyright Statement**

The Write Press, Inc

COMPASS
Paths to Effective Reading
Second Edition--Revised

Photos provided by The Write Press and istockphotos.com.

ISBN-13: 978-0-9820005-0-2
ISBN-10: 0-9820005-0-2

Table of Contents

Chapter 1: Ethics and Philosophy 1

Essay Title	Skill Level

☐ Table of Contents

Chapter 3: Government   113

Essay Title	Skill Level

would be far more accurate—the word itself indicating to students and historians alike that there may be a thousand stories connected to a subject."

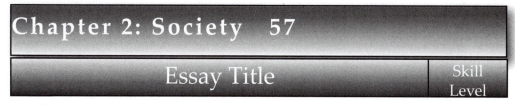

Chapter 2: Society 57

Essay Title	Skill Level

Chapter 3: Government 113

Essay Title	Skill Level

Chapter 6: Identity   263

Essay Title	Skill Level

☐ Table of Contents

Note on Essay Skill Levels

***The essays in this book have been broken down into three levels of difficulty:

Easily Accessible (A), Intermediate (B), and Challenging (C).

The Easily Accessible (A) essays, as the term implies, are more straightforward both in the complexity of the ideas presented and in the rhetorical devices used in the writing.

The Intermediate (B) level utilizes more rhetorical and writing techniques to deploy a wider range of ideas within each essay.

The Challenging (C) level indicates essays that often include more than one major idea, include more analysis and evaluation, and deploy many different writing and rhetorical techniques simultaneously.

Acknowledgements

As anyone who ever completed a large project knows, there is a host of unseen hands that secretly contribute to its completion and success. Such is the case with this book. First and foremost, we would like to thank Prof. John Briggs, Dr. Linda Strahan, Dr. Michael Moreno, Kristin Brunnemer, Dr. Kathy Moore, Paul Beehler, and Devon Hackelton for their enthusiastic support and assistance. Dr. Michael Moreno and Devon Hackelton, who tested parts of the book with various student audiences at other college campuses, are owed special thanks for their participation in the project and their constructive remarks. Their students as well as those at UCR also require special appreciation for their kind words and their encouraging welcoming of the text.

Of course, this book would have remained on the drawing board if it were not for each other's investment and dedication. We are greatly thankful to each other for this partnership which has been extremely rich, incredibly interesting, and superbly fulfilling. It has been an absolute joy to work with each other.

About the Authors

Roumpini Papadomichelaki began her education at the National Kapodestrian University of Athens, Greece, where she completed her degree in law as well as a Masters in Administrative Law. She earned her Juris Doctorate and practiced law in the prefecture of Chania, Crete, where she became a full member of the Bar Association and served as an official representative of the judicial authority for European Union and national elections. Because of her extensive language background that includes German, Latin, Classical Greek and culminates with state licenses to teach English and French in Greece, she was designated by the Ministry of Foreign Affairs as an official translator of English and French. Her interest in language development led her to complete a Masters degree in Education with an emphasis in Teaching English to Speakers of Other Languages (TESOL) at California State University, San Bernardino. For the last seven years as a Lecturer of English at the University of California, Riverside, she has taught at every level of the composition and developmental writing programs. In addition, she has worked extensively as an official representative of the University of California in the High School Outreach Program. Roumpini Papadomichelaki has served as an official reader and English as a Second Language (ESL) specialist for the Educational Testing Service (ETS) and Pearson Testing Services. Lastly, she has worked as an Administrative Analyst for the Inland Area Writing Project (IAWP), a member of the National Writing Project, which serves the Southern California area. Roumpini Papadomichelaki has co-authored two textbooks: *Compass: Paths to Effective Reading, 2nd Ed Revised*, and *Compass: A Guidebook to English Grammar, 2nd Ed Revised*.

Dr. Lash Keith Vance has completed a double major in English and German, a Masters and Ph.D. in English from the University of California, Riverside and an additional Masters in Education from California State University, San Bernardino. With fourteen years of teaching experience, Dr. Vance has been deeply involved in all levels of freshmen composition pedagogy at the University level; he has taught a wide range of classes, from developmental writing courses to advanced composition. He has also worked as a specialized grader for the Educational Testing Service (ETS) and Pearson Testing Services, as a third reader, and as an English as a Second Language (ESL) specialist. In addition, he has conducted scores of presentations at area high schools as an official representative of the UC System's High School Outreach Program. For the last four years, he has been the Director of Computer-Assisted Instruction for the Department of English at UC Riverside and the University Writing Program, has served on numerous writing committees, and has participated in student placement files. While overseeing and administrating a program with 3,000 students annual enrollment, Dr. Vance has co-authored two textbooks: *Compass: Paths to Effective Reading, 2nd Ed Revised*, and *Compass: A Guidebook to English Grammar, 2nd Ed Revised*.

Preface for Instructors

This book derives from the kernels of conversations with English Department colleagues who time and again rhetorically stated, "somebody should write a book that focuses on the process of reading with many short essays that employ all kinds of writing strategies; the essays should cover a wide variety of current issues and be short enough that students could read them in class if necessary. The readings should have in-class questions, discussion questions, and follow-up questions for writing assignments at home. They should be simple enough that students can understand but complicated enough to warrant further research at home; the essays should be accompanied by online reading comprehension tests that can be graded by the computer on Blackboard or some other system, so instructors can assign student quizzes before class to ensure they read." This book is the answer to these desires.

Essay Configuration

This book is very easy to use because of its consistent organization. Each essay is two to three pages in length on a theme of some current or social issue. It is followed by a two-page section of questions for use in and out of the class. These questions are focused on three primary tasks: 1) reading comprehension of the main points of the essay; 2) recognizing writing strategies that are modeled in each essay and evaluating their effectiveness; 3) learning a discrete set of ten vocabulary words for each essay and utilizing these words in context. All essays are roughly the same length, which allows teachers to easily estimate the amount of time students require to critically read them and begin responding. Furthermore, they can certainly be used in class for reading exercises as well as group discussions about the topics of social importance. Follow-up homework and writing assignments as well as full-fledged responses, argumentative papers, or research papers are also quite feasible with these essays.

There are a number of important features of this book that set it apart from the average anthology:

- First, the length of each essay was chosen to allow teachers to thoroughly read and discuss at least one essay per fifty-minute class session with a possibility of a pre-writing, post-writing, or discussion activity. The essay format, in essence, facilitates many more "teaching moments" in the classroom, for instructors can utilize the book to spontaneously respond to particular student needs.

- Second, the length of the essays militates against an exhaustive development, which allows a lot of possibilities for development by students in their own essay responses. Many of the essay topics discussed in the book could easily be (and have been) expanded into longer papers or chapters in other books. These essays present, in many ways, an overview of the main issues for these topics, providing along the way some significant data which students can think about.

- Third, essays are written in such a way that there may be a plurality of responses. Students are not required to agree with the authors, and the essays are sufficiently open-ended that many kinds of student responses are possible.

- Fourth, these essays do not require special knowledge or cultural background that students might not have, which sometimes hampers the reading success of some students. If a new concept is introduced, then it is explained sufficiently that students of all levels, including ESL or EFL students, can access the material.

The Reading Process

Reading is not a natural process, and there are particular skills, strategies, and techniques that students need to develop. As most teachers of English already know, reading tasks compete with all kinds of other media such as cell phones, TV watching, computers, online games, and any number of other outlets, so most students don't read enough. But even if students read more on their own or are required to by a class syllabus, it doesn't immediately mean that they automatically become better readers. This book focuses on the reading process by laying out step-by-step skills and strategies that students need to develop to become effective readers:

- First, the introduction outlines a tripartite process for reading that is clearly comprehensible. This includes specific tasks for pre-reading, during-reading, and post-reading activities. Furthermore, the questions at the back of each essay promote these tasks, which aid the teacher in developing these skills.

- Second, the introduction includes material for recognizing different writing and rhetorical strategies the authors use in each essay. The theory here is that through successive modeling and recognition of the deployment of these techniques, students will be far more likely to utilize them in their own writing. Such active reading makes them better readers and writers.

- Third, each reading or writing technique includes a definition and example, so students can clearly understand what it is and how to use it. These culminate with short paragraphs where the specific techniques are deployed in context. Furthermore, each technique is accompanied by suggestions for "strategic" uses or tips for use in the real world.

- Fourth, the essays have different shapes and organizational patterns within an argumentative or analysis essay framework. Some employ far more examples than others. Some have standard classification patterns. Some bring the thesis to the fore while others wait until the end. In short, the various formats used for these essays require students to pay careful attention to not only what is written, but also how it is written.

Beyond the Classroom

No text book exists entirely in a vacuum, for inevitably issues of assessment arise. With this book, students can be assessed in a number of ways:

- First, the book is accompanied by an online quizzing system with a pool of over one thousand quiz questions. Thus, each essay has a fifteen-question quiz that includes sections on reading comprehension, identifying writing strategies, and on vocabulary use in context. The online quiz component can be uploaded to any school system and can be easily used by instructors. Teachers simply login to their regular school account and then select the quiz they want students to take. This feature is important for ensuring students read before class, and it is practical for being automatically graded by Blackboard.

- Second, each essay is followed by an in-text series of questions that revolve around reading comprehension, identifying writing strategies, and vocabulary development. Furthermore, there are interesting questions for class discussion as well as essay topics that could be turned into longer student essay responses.

Overall Book Organization

The book is divided into nine distinct chapters that cover a wide variety of topics: Ethics and Philosophy, Society, Identity, Education, Family, and Government, Culture, Science and Technology, and Relationships. While the essays are designed to "stand alone" in an independent assignment, they can also be read as part of a conversation on a particular topic. The chapter on Government, for instance, includes a number of essays on the theme of citizenship, but each essay has a slightly different focus on the issue. Furthermore, the book is designed in such a way that instructors can easily pick and choose the essays they want to assign without having to contextualize a topic. The essays in the Ethics and Philosophy chapter don't require that the instructor give a lecture on Plato or Sartre before assigning them, for the readings are self-contained.

Student Audience

Who should read this book? The book is ideal for courses with any kind of composition component and can be useful for traditional as well as ESL or EFL classrooms. The essays are designed to aid students in the transition to reading and writing about academic subjects in an academic format. Any student who requires further training in the reading process or identifying writing and rhetorical techniques will prosper from using this text. The number of short essays, in addition, provides many modeling opportunities with varied themes designed to promote critical thought and discussion. Because of the scalable nature of the short essays and their possible application with both in class and out of class activities, this book is ideal for a range of courses with composition elements.

Preface for Students

One of the most important skills you need to learn in your education is how to read effectively. Far too often, it is assumed that if students know what the words say on the page then they will inevitably understand what the words mean. As you probably understand by now, this is far from the truth. Indeed, as you progress in your education, the reading tasks seem to get more challenging because of the various essay forms and the expectations associated with them.

This book tries to outline in a simple step-by-step format how you can improve your reading skills—and hopefully through extensive modeling, your writing skills. You face a daunting task as you progress from juniors and seniors in high school to freshmen and sophomores in college; you have to learn how to read and write at an academic level. This can be even more difficult if the types of essays you are used to have been personal narratives or journals. While these are certainly valuable essay types, they don't prepare you for the kind of "discourse" you should expect in college writing. In college, almost all of what you write is public, and the themes are typically about public or social issues. This book, then, helps prepare you for argumentative and analytical writing scenarios.

This book provides the platform for your further reading development, but it is up to you to do the work. Reading actively or critically, as you will soon learn, is much more involved than reading a pleasure book from the bookstore that you do not need to utilize later. As the formal introduction indicates, there is a big difference in how you read a text. Basically, though, you should consider the following objectives when reading through the rest of the book:

- To become more effective, efficient readers
- To follow the stages of reading
- To read actively and critically
- To recognize different essay formats
- To develop reading skills and employ reading strategies

These objectives form the basis for the book, and it is the fervent hope of the authors that your reading improve at all levels.

Lastly, some of you might wonder how it is possible to disagree with some of the essays included in the text. It is. Just because they are included does not mean they are absolutely correct. There are, in fact, many ways that you could argue for or against these essays in writing assignments given to you by teachers. You might find some of the essays lacking important elements. You might find that the topics are more complicated than at first suggested. That is good. It shows your engagement with the text. Indeed, these essays are sufficiently open-ended that a multitude of answers are possible when responding to them. So, if you do end up writing a response, feel free to disagree, agree, or problematize the ideas as you see fit. You just need make sure you clearly understand the authors' position before you respond.

Critical Reading Guide

A Short Justification for Reading

Academic research studies have consistently proven the connection of reading to better writing, the idea being the more you read, the better off you will be. Added to this plethora of voices, parents, high school teachers, and college instructors also seem to have jumped full force onto the bndwagon, each one with a bullhorn demanding that you read, read, read. Can't we just leave students alone? Why can't you just watch movies?

Well, this is not to knock movies, for they are definitely important for entertainment and education (in some cases), but they can't replace the written word. When you pick up a book, read an article, or skim an email, you are performing a complicated task of cognition that researchers with lots of degrees behind their names have been trying to figure out for some time. Part of the debate revolving around reading and its importance is that students claim to be visual learners; thus, why can't students just learn what they need know by watching Public Broadcasting Videos or seeing Powerpoint presentations in class? Well, a different perspective on this indicates that people may learn well visually, but in order to express themselves, they need a developed sense of language. If it is true that humans think in language and feel with visual images, then simply watching educational videos will be of little use in much of your academic careers.

So, the message from researchers, parents, and teachers is that you are supposed to read, but what are you to read? Does reading a comic book count? Will that improve your writing? How about a good science fiction novel? You may have even heard that there are students getting Masters and Ph.D. degrees in the literature of Star Trek or Star Wars. What if you read a thousand romance novels? Will that count? Well, you might just be turned into Don Juan or Scarlett O'Hara, but it doesn't necessarily mean that you'll *automatically* read better or write better. You will, however, certainly understand the conventions of romance novels.

The Function of Reading

Reading for academic purposes is very different from reading a pleasure novel on the beach, not so much in terms of the content but more so in terms of the function of the reading. Critical reading can be done on almost any kind of text, whether they are blogs (web logs) on MySpace or scholarly essays in prestigious journals. Though there is a difference in the depth of research, the genre, and the sophistication of the writing, all these "texts" can be approached critically to be mined for a host of information. It just depends on the function of the reading task and the focus of the reader.

Researchers in language development and acquisition have focused in recent years on the deployment of Cognitive Academic Language Proficiency (CALP) within secondary education and college systems. Although this sounds a bit like a debilitating disease, this fancy terminology differentiates between casual speech and writing versus the demands that are placed on students in high school and college. Don't be fooled by anyone who says, "you can write however you want in college. There are no rules anymore." There are certainly conventions about reading and writing in an academic setting. This does not mean that you should adopt a totally different way of writing papers or reading texts or lose your personal voice; however, the acronym CALP is meant to show that interacting with texts in an academic way is quite different than when you simply read something for pleasure.

One of the main differences in the function of reading is how you do it. Today, academics often use terms like critical, focused, or active reading to more or less denote the same idea. In layman's terms, this kind of reading means that you are actively trying to interact with the material on the page. Let's take the example of *The Matrix* comic book series. There are a few different "ways" of reading this series. If you read it for pleasure on vacation, you get involved in the plot and the pictures, accompanying the main characters in their development. You read the comics mostly for the enjoyment, and you can't put them down. However, the same series could be read critically or actively. As an active reader, you read with pen in hand in order to underline or annotate important stylistic or thematic elements. You might examine the gender roles people occupy in this futuristic world. You might begin thinking about one of the thirteen major philosophical questions that the series proposes. You might observe dialogue patterns and strange use of sentence constructions for some characters. This is not to say that the comic series is still not pleasurable to read; no, this means that you read these texts with your full attention, that you look for structural patterns, that you…analyze.

You may do many of these things—consciously or unconsciously—when you read because of your training. Already you have been trained in watching movies; when you make a determination that a certain movie stinks or as in the case of *The Lord of the Rings*, **was the best series of all time**, then you are making judgments based on some criteria. The problem for many students, both in high school and in college, is that the criteria for what to look for in a text, how to organize thoughts about the text, and how to write in "academic" discourse are confusing or unknown. In terms of reading, Cognitive Academic Language Proficiency (CALP) is simply the term for how to actively read texts by looking for more levels of meaning. In terms of writing, CALP applies because students need to know what kind of writing is expected. In this way, reading and writing are intimately linked. If you read well by closely observing organization, structure, stylistic devices, thematic elements, then it is far more likely that you will be able to employ these same things when you write as well.

Learning to read and write at a top-notch academic level requires that you know about different *discourses*. Let's say that you get together with your friends to "hang out." How would it sound if you approached your friends, who were busy shirking their homework to play X-Box 360, and said, "Your continued malfeasance and dereliction of scholastic duty will be penalized at dawn tomorrow." It is likely that the friends who were playing a boxing game might decide to make the game more real by tackling your pretentious…thorax. This is a certain type of discourse that would be more appropriate to the military, not with a group of close friends "hanging out." Now, if you were to analyze *The Matrix* in a college composition course, the same knowledge of discourse is significant within this setting as well. For instance, in your analysis you would probably not tell the instructor, "Woe, man, the battle scene in *Resurrections* was phat." An academic discussion would utilize the appropriate conventions for the expression of ideas. The discourse(s) would be the type and way of speaking, writing, or communicating under different social circumstances. One would not expect the Queen of England to start rapping in an interview in Buckingham Palace even though she now posts material on YouTube! The discourse of royalty and the interview would not allow it although it would be pretty funny.

Part and parcel of what you need to do as students is to develop your CALP by engaging in focused, critical, and active reading. As with most things, this does not happen over night. You have to train yourselves in proper academic reading techniques, which will eventually become second nature to you. Indeed, what you learn in high school and college is only partly about the background knowledge of your field. One of the most important skills is how to read effectively, for with this in place you will be able to pick up almost any document and begin working through it systematically.

How to Read in Three Stages

Developing a systematic approach to reading is essential, for with this you can tackle almost any text—and the skills can be expanded to "reading" other media such as television shows, movies, or websites. A similar set of critical features can be employed. For our purposes, the reading task has been divided into three separate stages.

Stage One: Pre-Reading

As the name implies, these are the tasks that you should consider before you even start reading a text. By considering some of the pre-reading questions, you can garner a great deal of information about a text before you even begin reading. Although you may not know it, you already have some background information about a text before you flip to page one because of your earlier training. For example, if you picked up a journal in the library called *Advanced Engineering Review*, you would have certain expectations that may or may not be fulfilled, but you would have them based on your experience or background of academic writing. You would think that this is likely a scholarly journal with high tech articles submitted by scholars. Because it is a journal, you expect research papers of fifteen or twenty pages in length that have been reviewed by an editorial committee. You could easily expect each essay to include an extensive bibliography and each journal publication to include five to seven articles along with book reviews. So, already, you have a great deal of information about the text and its *likely* organization. You might also be able to tell from some of the titles whether your engineering expertise is sufficiently developed to understand the articles.

Tasks During Pre-Reading
1. **Determining Bibliographical Material:**
   Review the who, what, when, and where about the text's production. It is often quite helpful to know what kind of source you are dealing with before you start reading. This already provides many clues about the possible authority and rele-

vance of the content.

2. **Reviewing Content Expectation:**
Examine the chapters, organization, and genre of the text, which should tell you what kind of discourse to expect.

3. **Acquiring Background Knowledge:**
Determine what background knowledge you have and what would be desirable to have before reading the text. In this way, you rehearse what you know, and you ascertain what you should learn.

4. **Evaluating Possible Assignments:**
Establish what your purpose is in reading the text and how the reading might be used. If you already have a writing assignment given to you by a teacher, look carefully at the question to see how you should focus your reading.

Pre-Reading
DETERMINING BIBLIOGRAPHICAL INFORMATION

Description

In its most basic form, these are the who, when, and where questions. Examine the text before you. Is it a book or article? Look for the author(s) and publication information. You can find this at the front of the book near the Table of Contents.

Purpose

You can tell a lot about a text by the authors, date of publication, and the press who publishes it. For academic works, for instance, you look to see the qualifications of the authors, whether the work is recent or not, as well as the press that publishes the work. This ensures that—at the very least—there was an editorial process that the text went through. This is part of the evaluation of your source material.

Specific Elements to Review

- Author(s)
- Date of Publication
- Place of Publication
- Type of Press

Reading Strategies

Use a computer to create a Word document. Write out a complete bibliography for the text at the top. This will come in handy when and if you ever want to use your notes in a paper.

DISCOVERING THE ORGANIZATION

Description

Examine the overall construction of the text to see its organizing principle. Does the text have chapters or is it broken down into sub sections at all? What are the titles for these sections and how long are they?

Purpose

How a text is organized can greatly increase your understanding of what you are likely to read even before you start reading. Once you notice chapter or section headings, think about the way the text is organized and whether there is a guiding principle.

Specific Elements to Review

- Table of Contents
- Chapter Headings
- Length and Type of Chapter Headings

Reading Strategies

Quickly jot down an overall outline of the major subject headings. This will help you if you get stuck in a confusing section to see how it fits in with the overall theme.

REVIEWING CONTENT EXPECTATION

Description

Examine the themes that recur in the chapter or section headings. Look to see if there is an identified reader and/or a purpose for the text. What kind of text is it? Is there an abstract or statement of purpose?

Purpose

Even before reading, knowing the types of themes that will be covered helps orient the mind. Knowing the possible intended audience is also helpful to discern how the text might be written and/or organized. Furthermore, you have all developed an acute sense of genre (the likely set of conventions that will appear). Thus, if you read a James Bond book, there are certain conventions you expect to see (girls, gadgets, and guns).

Specific Elements to Review

- Themes
- Audience
- Genre
- Discourse Type

Reading Strategies

Think of the intended audience for the text and determine the possible genre expectations you might have.

ACQUIRING BACKGROUND KNOWLEDGE

Description

Does the text require certain background knowledge for understanding? Is it a text designed to provide an overview of a concept? Is it a specialists' text or for the lay reader?

Purpose

Finding out what you know about a subject is pivotal before proceeding with an investigation of it. For instance, if you pick up a text on Martin Luther King Jr., it would be very helpful to know something about the era in which he lived and the civil rights movement he helped to lead; otherwise, you might be lost when reading.

Specific Elements to Review

- What you know
- What you want to know
- What you need to know

Reading Strategies

In a short paragraph, review what you know about the topic. Then list what you should know or want to know.

Do a quick search on the Internet (or access your own books) to get a broad overview of the salient topics.

EVALUATING POSSIBLE ASSIGNMENTS

Description

Consider carefully the reason for reading the text to begin with. Is this for a class assignment? Are you to write a paper or discuss the work? How should you focus your reading?

Purpose

Knowing the purpose of a reading assignment can help orient your reading. If your class has a particular focus, this may impact the type of assignment you can expect. Even if the instructor hasn't assigned a test or essay yet, consider what such an assignment might be.

(continued)

Specific Elements to Review	Reading Strategies
• Purpose • Follow-up Writing	*Write down possible topics that you would assign if you were the instructor.* *Review the course syllabus to see what other reading assignments will follow and how the current one fits into the overall design.* *Write down a list of possible topics that you could pursue.*

Stage Two: During Reading

Once you have completed the pre-reading activities, you should have a pretty good idea what to expect in the text. In this way, the text itself should be less complicated or difficult, and completing the proper steps in reading will make it even more accessible. Now let's take an example. Your English teacher asks you to look up an essay on *Hamlet*, so after serious research in the library you find an article in *Shakespeare Review* about the revenge motif in the play. You've effectively completed the pre-reading by finding an adjudicated (judged or edited) journal, by finding an article submitted by qualified people (professors, graduate students, or Ph.Ds in the field), and by having some background knowledge (you read the play and a short history of the Elizabethan period). So, you are ready to read the article. At this point, you have a few tasks before you.

Tasks During Reading

1. **Determining Content:**
   Figure out what the author is saying by carefully reviewing the organization and annotating in the margins the main points. You have to know what is said before you can respond to it meaningfully.

2. **Connecting Content:**
   Discover what you think about these points by making connections to other works you've read in or out of the field, the historical period, or simply ideas about the piece. Of course, not everything you read will require that you write a paper, but this second part trains you to make connections with the text to *possibly* develop your ideas in an academic setting.

3. **Recognizing Writing Techniques and Style:**
   Examine the writing for rhetorical features, style of writing, and the particular writing techniques employed. As with many things in life, the package something comes in is important, so you'll want to analyze the language, organizational features, and style of the text.

During Reading
DETERMINING CONTENT

Description

One of the first steps in reading is to determine what is said and to record this information in the margins of your text (if appropriate). You can summarize and paraphrase major points of the texts in the margins by using keywords and underlining key statements.

Purpose

Annotation really consists of putting material in the margin of the text (or in some cases on note paper). This helps in the memory process, and it will definitely help you when you review the text for any paper or exam later in the quarter or semester. Underlining or highlighting further draws attention to points of interest or great lines in the text that could be used for quotes.

Specific Elements to Review

- Annotating
- Summarizing
- Paraphrasing
- Underlining
- Highlighting
- Vocabulary

Reading Strategies

Try writing keywords in the margins.
  Underline and circle the important sections of writing where an important claim has been made.
  Look to annotate and underline statements of the author's position, not long examples.
Look up unknown vocabulary words.

CONNECTING CONTENT

Description

Once you know what the text said (Determining Content), you have to figure out what you think about it. You need to evaluate the text based on your critical training, relevant personal experience, and other readings you've done about the text.

Purpose

Connecting to the content is an essential aspect of reading. You have to determine what you think about issues within the text, which typically takes place on three levels. You use your critical skills to determine the relevance or interest of the argument and/or thematic content. Then you connect to the text with particular personal experiences or other texts you've read.

Specific Elements to Review	Reading Strategies

• Evaluating the Text
• Connecting
    1. Personal Experience
    2. Articles/Books Read
	Use a different color pen to write your ideas, connections, and possible paper topics in the margins of the text.
	
	You may want to put your evaluation in parenthesis to separate it from summary annotations.

RECOGNIZING WRITING TECHNIQUES

Description	Purpose
This involves looking at specific writing techniques by first examining the organization within the text. Next, you look at specific writing skills deployed.	How something is written is almost as important as what is written. Thus, as a critical or active reader, you should pay close attention to section organization as well as the writing techniques used. Some evaluation papers may even be written about the specific use of these writing techniques.

Specific Elements to Review	Reading Strategies
• Organizational Features • Definition • Classification • Compare/Contrast • Classification • Cause/Effect • Process Narration • Evidence • Refutation *Definitions for these techniques are available later in the introduction.*	*Use short hand to mark really effective writing techniques in the margin. You can return to these techniques to try to emulate them in your own writing.* *Label the principal function of each paragraph of the text (if appropriate) along with a short blurb about how it fits with the rest of the essay.*

ACQUIRING BACKGROUND KNOWLEDGE

Description	Purpose
Writing style is complex to define, but in essence it is the amalgamation of all the writing techniques that are used in author specific ways.	Recognizing style features helps you place the text within a community of texts. If the author utilizes a very angry tone, this may indicate something about the position (and objectivity) of the text. Furthermore, looking for consistent themes helps isolate overall issues of importance in the text.

Specific Elements to Review	Reading Strategies
• Rhetorical Features • Sentence Features • Tone	*Annotate for rhetorical features in the margins.* *Circle peculiar, successful, or unsuccessful sentence features for later review.*

Stage Three: Post-Reading

Most students assume they are done once they read the last page of the text, patting themselves on the back if they did some annotating or underlining. However, one of the most significant parts of the reading process is yet to come, and you don't want to short change the effort you already put in by abandoning the process now! One way to think about this third stage of reading is that you have to record what is written, what you think about it, and what you can do with it. Reading in and of itself, though wonderful at times, is not much use in an academic setting when you are expected to utilize the reading in some way, either in the form of a discussion, a quiz, a test, or ultimately a paper. In this way, you have to be able *to effectively use* the reading. Another reason to complete the Post-Reading stage is that it significantly helps you organize and remember the material. If you don't do the work of trying to shift the material from short term memory to long term memory, your effort will be wasted. The transition from short term to long term memory, after all, requires that you elaborate on a subject, organize the material, and have effective recall of it. In short, you've got to use it or lose it!

Tasks During Post-Reading

1. **Synthesizing Content:**
    Succinctly summarize the essence of the article in written and verbal formats. This does not mean that you've memorized every detail of it, but you should have a general understanding of the main points.

2. **Connecting Content:**
    Make formal connections to the content by recording your evaluations, observations, and associations with other works you've seen or read.

3. **Anticipating Assignments:**
    Train yourself to work strategically. This means that you pretend that you are the instructor of the course, and you'll be better prepared in all aspects of the class. Think about how you would use the material in a discuss.

POST-READING
SYNTHESIZING CONTENT

Description	Purpose
While you might know what the essay or text is about, it is often helpful to write the main points in a coherent paragraph. This section deals with recording the author's main points through outline, summary, and note taking.	The real test of understanding of a subject is whether you can succinctly relay the ideas. Writing out an essay outline, a summary, and taking notes on overall ideas is pivotal in this process, for you can then utilize this information. If you are confused writing the summary, then probably you misunderstood parts of the reading. You should reread your annotations, paraphrases, and underlined sections for greater clarity.

Specific Elements to Review	Reading Strategies
• Outlining • Summary • Notetaking	*Try writing an executive summary (a 4-5 sentence summary that covers the main points).* *See if a friend can read your summary and understand the main points of the text.* *Write a longer summary that covers more in depth material as well.*

CONNECTING CONTENT

Description

This section involves determining what you think about the text you read, interesting observations you made, and connections to events within your life or other books or articles you read that apply.

Purpose

While determining what the author says is important, it is no less important to know what **you** think about the text. You should consider—especially in the case of argument or analysis papers—what ways the author is correct (or not), whether there are important points the author missed, and what additional connections you can make to the text. After all, much of what is important with reading is what background you bring to the text.

Specific Elements to Review

- Short Critique
    1. Pro Issues
    2. Con Issues
- Observations
- Personal Connections
    1. Personal Examples
    2. Books
    3. TV Shows
    4. Other Ideas

Reading Strategies

Write a short overall critique of the text. If it is an argument or analysis paper, write out a list of pro or con arguments.

Record any significant observations you made while reading; you might mine the annotations you made during the reading the text stage.

Write down a list of connections that might be used for your own response to the essay.

ANTICIPATING ASSIGNMENTS

Description

This section looks to the possible uses of the reading and the knowledge contained therein. Most academic reading requires some kind of "beyond" activity that tests or utilizes the text in some way.

Purpose

By anticipating the possible uses of the reading, you put yourself in the position of the instructor, and in the process you become superior students. If you pretend that you assigned the reading, you can anticipate what quiz, test, or paper assignment might come from it. What are the main points that should be emphasized? This task is greatly eased if you already have a specific assignment from the instructor.

Specific Elements to Review

- Quote Taking
- Paper Topics
- Test Sections
- Note Cards

Reading Strategies

Review your underlined sections from the text and write down the quotes that illuminate important ideas from the text. Be sure to record the page number in parenthesis so you can use the quote later in a paper.

Make a list of possible paper topics that utilize the theme of the reading.

Create some test questions that you would ask if you were the instructor.

Essay Fundamentals

There are at least a hundred different ways to organize an essay, so it would be disingenuous to tell you a rule that absolutely determines how to read an essay or how to write a response. Indeed, part of the problem that many students have when reading and writing in an academic setting (CALP) is that they have very limited essay expectations. This means that many students expect to see a particular format in an essay. When those expectations are not fulfilled, it can be confusing. Many of you, for instance, may have been taught using the Jane Schaffer style of writing while in high school. This is the five paragraph model that typically includes an introductory paragraph, three body paragraphs, and a conclusion paragraph. This is an incredibly helpful beginning model to writing that assists students in isolating some of the main points they want to discuss in their own writing or in recognizing these points when they read. Perhaps you even trained in this formatting style as well? However, when any format is taken too far, it becomes fossilized. This means that the form itself limits the expression of thought; it becomes the mold that cannot be broken, and in academic reading and writing there are loose conventions that might not be followed exactly.

This fossilization is particularly distressing for students when they read essays and texts that don't correspond to the five paragraph format, which most professional writers don't use because of its limitations. While you (the reader) should not forget or ignore the five paragraph method, you should definitely not rely on it or expect to see it when reading texts. Instead, you should utilize the pre-reading, during reading, and post-reading stages, which will work for just about any type and length of text. Even so, despite the differences in length, type, genre of an essay, text, or book, there are some common elements and organizational patterns that you can look for to aid you in understanding sometimes complex texts.

Keep in mind that there are *many types of essays*, and the following list of elements that many essays contain is not supposed to be exhaustive. These elements are used primarily in argumentative or analytical writing (i.e. when an author argues or analyzes a position) and should help orient you in what to expect when you read such texts. Even if the text is incredibly difficult, knowing the main features can help you wade through the difficult parts and find the meaning. Incidentally, the same important elements that you read for, you also utilize when you write!

Overview of Essay Fundamentals
SUMMARY (overview)

Description

Most authors try to orient the reader on the topic, which the reader may know little about. The overview does not provide a direct summary of every one of the author's points, but it often includes a description or historical background of the central concept to be discussed.

Parts of an Effective Summary

1. A clear idea of the topic
2. A clear reference to the major issues of the topic
3. A short review of authoritative sources about the topic (if warranted)

Example

Say you are assigned to read a paper on raising the minimum wage. You would need some contextualization of the topic. What is the current minimum wage? When was this implemented? Why was it implemented? What are the typical issues pro and con about the topic? You would expect that the author used good sources for the text, which would imply a certain level of research; you would trust data from the government census or a business newspaper much more than that from a web log.

Application Across the Curriculum

Abstract:

Many academic journals require a 50 word or less synopsis of the focus of the article, including the author's argument.

Survey of the Literature:

This is the term used to describe an overview of the research completed on a topic.

THESIS (position)

Description

The word thesis comes from the Greek word, position, which is exactly its connotation today. The thesis asserts a point of view or position, which should be supported by evidence.

Parts of an Effective Thesis

1. A clear position
2. Be discernable among the text
3. Tell the reader what to think or do about a topic
4. Include support reasoning

(continued)

Example	Application Across the Curriculum
In a concept essay (i.e. simply explaining an idea), the author would explain the concept of minimum wage. In an argument or analysis paper, the author must go further by taking a position. To continue our example, once we have a background for minimum wage, we need to know what the author proposes. A powerful thesis might be, "Minimum wage should be increased across the U. S." Now, this is all well and good, but why should this be done?	***Hypothesis:*** In scientific circles, they rename the thesis "hypothesis," which in the Greek means an uncertain position. The hypothesis assumes an outcome, which has to be validated through research. ***Thought and Belief:*** Essays outside the scientific realm have theses and support reasoning, especially in cases of moral uncertainty.

CLAIMS (support reasoning)

Description	Parts of an Effective Claim
Claims are assertions that support the author's main position (thesis). Their function is to ultimately provide the reader with rationale and serve as links between the evidence and the thesis.	1. Consist of clear statements 2. Be discernable among the text 3. Tell the reader how the evidence proves the thesis 4. Connect solidly to the evidence

Example	Applications Across the Curriculum
There is almost always support reasoning or rationale that props up the thesis. Think of the thesis as the frame of a house. It's nice, but without support pieces of wood, it will certainly fall apart.	***Section Headings:*** Rationale that connects the thesis with the evidence often appears in science and business writings as part of section headings within the paper.

EVIDENCE (examples)

Description

No argumentative or analytical essay would be complete without the presence of evidence, for a position alone does not convince an audience. There must be convincing evidence as well.

Parts of an Effective Example

1. Contain pertinent, developed material
2. Clearly relate to the thesis and support reasoning
3. Utilize solid and relevant information
4. Include concise information or anecdotes, not rambling commentary

Example

Remember that examples don't take the place of a thesis or its support reasoning, which is a common error that people make. So, as a reader of the text about minimum wage, you would expect to see some data indicating how the low minimum wage affects people. You might even see a few personal examples of how workers can't survive even at poverty level on such low funds. The point is, though, that no one will go along with increasing the minimum wage unless there are substantial reasons (i.e. example material) to do it.

Application Across the Curriculum

Data and Studies:

Good research techniques utilize data, whether that be in the form statistics (the quantitative approach) or in the form of systematized observations by researchers (qualitative approach). Data are often displayed in charts and tables.

Personal Examples:

While not as "authoritative" as factual data or data based on research, personal examples can provide an effective source of evidence through the writer's personal perspective.

CONCLUSION

Description

There is a common misconception that conclusions are all about writing fluff that vaguely restates the overall thesis. Conclusions should do more than that. They often look toward the future for possible repercussions; they may try to problematize the issue even more or bring up elements that could be pursued in another paper.

Parts of an Effective Conclusion

1. *Concisely* restate the thesis
2. Look toward future problems if action is not taken
3. May employ if / then statements
4. Refrain from introducing completely new ideas that have no argumentative support in the paper

(continued)

Example	Application Across the Curriculum
A suitable conclusion to the minimum wage essay might be to take into consideration the trends in the data as well as some personal examples. The argument might be—if the data clearly support it—that "if the minimum wage issue is not addressed now, then the U.S. economy will be significantly damaged in the long run." At this point, you would not introduce an idea about the spending habits of minimum wage workers	***Results and Outcomes:*** Adequately explaining the results of research and thus the need for action is an important part of many research papers. In science, the result section functions as a conclusion that proves or disproves the hypothesis. ***Prognosis:*** Another common conclusion tactic is to indicate the prognosis or likely outcome for something.

Identifying Writing Techniques

Closely examining how someone writes can help the reader better understand the distinct connection between form and content. Knowing the most common writing techniques will not only significantly help your reading skills and your ability to understand even complex topics, but it will also directly assist you in developing your own writing. Again, these techniques are most commonly used in concept, argument, and analysis papers, but they are fairly representative of what techniques you should be looking for when reading.

Writing Techniques
DEFINITION

Definition and Purpose	Example
Defining or explaining terminology and concepts in a paper is an important writing technique to identify and utilize. Two techniques are most typically used: 1) **renaming** the term or concept by employing a dictionary-type explanation; 2) providing a more in-depth and longer explanation in the form of an **extended definition**.	Cryptography, the hiding of information in secret code, has become an important component in transmitting documents among government agencies (**renaming**). Evidence for use of cryptography can be dated back to Roman and Greek times. Julius Caesar, in fact, was famous for employing his own cipher/cryptography code (**extended definition**).

CLASSIFICATION

Definition and Purpose	Example
Classifying is the art of breaking up ideas or concepts into logical, component parts. This technique can be especially important the more complicated the idea. It also helps orient the reader as to the pertinent sections of the overall concept.	Reading is an important activity that should not be underestimated. The process of reading can be classified into three stages: pre-reading, during reading, and post-reading.

COMPARISON/CONTRAST

Definition and Purpose	Example
The common misconception about comparison/contrast is that these techniques are necessarily performed at the same time. Actually, an essay could be written in which you simply compare how two or more things are alike. Another essay could contrast how they are different.	Comparing Los Angeles and Las Vegas is easy. Both are metropolitan centers with over a million residents and a diverse population. However, that's where the comparison ends (**comparison**). The two cities are different in the taxes citizens pay and the legalized gambling in Nevada (**contrast**).

EXAMPLE

Definition and Purpose	Example
Effective use of examples is a great writing technique. There are three primary types to consider here: 1) **process examples** explain how a concept came to be or how something works; 2) **data examples** utilize masses of statistics to help prove a point; 3) **anecdote examples** usually include personal material that is designed to cater to an emotional appeal or be representative of a group.	Editing a book requires many stages; it is not engendered over night. There is the concept, the written proposal, the meeting with publishers, the draft of the book, and the editing (**process example**). Over 80% of authors have to review 95% of their work (**data example**). In one instance, a friend was asked to rewrite a section ten times before it was finally accepted for publication (**anecdote**).

REFUTATION

Definition and Purpose	Example
Many good essays employ a refutation or counter argument. In this, the author considers what the opponents say about the topic and often includes reasons why their points are not valid. This anticipates possible objections to an argument and strengthens the essay.	Guns are good. Many people will argue that the availability of guns causes deaths, but they are misinformed. Statistically, guns sold legally are rarely, if ever, involved in shootings. It is the *illegal* sale of guns that should be looked at.

CAUSE/EFFECT

Definition and Purpose	Example
As the name implies, there is a central cause to a problem that the author argues will have a necessary effect. You should be very careful when considering how logical the author's statement is, for many times there may well be more than one cause or effect to an issue. Watch for over-simplification.	The low minimum wage has made people discontent as can be seen in the statistics on property theft. Indeed, if the minimum wage is not augmented (**cause**), then there is the likelihood of a corollary increase in the crime rate as the years go by (**effect**). Notice the logical gap between the cause/effect here.

Example Paragraph Identifying Writing Techniques:

Minimum wage, the minimum amount of money an employer is required to pay an employee by law, wasn't always 6.75 dollars an hour (**definition**); in fact, before 1938 and the passing of the Fair Labor Standards Act, employees were paid what they could get. Indeed, it wasn't easy determining the definition of a minimum wage, for many parameters had to be considered (**extended definition**). Living standards, food prices, average mortgages, and the ability of businesses to pay all had to be weighed as factors (**classification**). At the time of its implementation, not all workers were covered by the minimum wage statute, for the legislation specifically targeted workers dealing with interstate commerce. Everyone else was left out (**contrast**). For those who were covered, however, the effects of much needed wage reform were felt instantaneously (**cause/effect**). Those receiving minimum wage were guaranteed that amount of money while their co-workers in other industries were left out. Although some businesses argued that the new minimum wage guidelines would put them out of business, it was thought that the public good would be served through such regulation (**refutation**). Workers of the period, including those who later worked on the interstate highway system, were ecstatic. One worker of the period, John Smith, commented how the minimum wage gave him enough money to buy a small house and raise three children (**anecdote example**).

Identifying Rhetorical Techniques:

There may be some confusion as to the difference between writing techniques and rhetorical techniques, and in some sense they do blend. *Again, the answer boils down to how you use the technique for what effect.* Writing techniques are the tools that you have at your disposal. Rhetorical techniques are how you use those tools. Just because you have a screwdriver, for instance, doesn't mean that you have to use it in one way. You might want to use it to pry open a can or chisel out a hole in the wall or even to take a bike tire off the rim. *Rhetoric is the way we use the writing tools and techniques available to us.* In addition, to the writing strategies above, there are additional rhetorical techniques of note that you should look out for in the readings.

Rhetorical Techniques
STRATEGIC US OF FRAGMENTS

Definition and Purpose	Example
Technically, a fragment is an incomplete sentence that lacks a subject, a verb, or an independent clause. Most English teachers will mark fragments as errors; however, selective use of fragments (usually short and pithy) can draw attention to the point. Many experienced writers use fragments selectively as part of their prose.	Many people envy cats for their pampered lifestyle. Just look in their eyes and you see the expectation of devotion or the requirement that they be worshipped as gods as the Egyptians once did. *Noble, somnolent, worldly, aloof, watchful.* These are the adjectives of the cat.

RHETORICAL QUESTIONS

Definition and Purpose	Example
These are questions that writers pose which they don't really expect answers for. In other cases, writers utilize these questions to draw attention to particular problems that need addressing. Many writers will strive to answer these questions in the body of their text.	The government tax system consists of thousands of tax codes that the average American can't understand. *Do you understand your tax return? Should one have to complete a degree in accounting to file taxes?*

FIGURATIVE LANGUAGE

Definition and Purpose	Example
Everyone knows that the language we use when speaking or writing counts. Many writers employ what is called figurative language, a type of vocabulary that "figures or stands for" other words or concepts. In many cases, figurative language can get a point across quicker and easier than simply using declarative statements. Three types of figurative language include: **metaphors**, where two terms are equated; **similes**, where two terms are compared using like or as; **synonyms**, where a term is described through a word of the same meaning.	The cat is the king of the house, strutting about as if he doesn't notice his human servants (**metaphor).** Is the cat literally a king? No. The car passed us like a bat out of hell (**simile).** The topography of the *landscape* shows an *environment* under stress (**synonym).**

SENTENCE STRUCTURE REPETITION

Definition and Purpose	Example
In most cases, it is wise to use varied language and sentence structure to make the writing more interesting. However, sometimes writers employ devices of similarity to draw attention to a particular set of points. This is true in the case of **anaphora** where the first set of words is the same in the sentence or with **sentence structure** where the overall structure is the same.	All know that the education system is in trouble. *It is time* for an education revolt. *It is time* that parents demand more. *It is time* that funding levels are raised **(anaphora)**. Education is incredibly important to our well being. Learning is a necessity for our continued economic growth **(similar sentence structure)**.

WORD REPETITION

Definition and Purpose	Example
Sometimes, writers employ traditional "poetic" devices to draw attention to a set of words, which may make them more lyrical. **Alliteration**, employing the same first consonant, and **assonance**, employing similar vowel sounds, are two such techniques.	**G**one was the **g**olden **g**ate that **g**uarded the **g**arden **(alliteration).** The submarine **fleet** rose from the **deep** as the ocean was **creeping** into the iron tomb **(assonance).**

Example Paragraph Identifying Rhetorical Techniques:

Minimum wage (**fragment**). How much money would you need to survive (**rhetorical question**)? According to one popular writer, minimum wage is like a slow self-cannibalism where the worker's body is consumed (**simile**), for there simply is not enough money for shelter, food, and clothing. How do people eat? How do people pay rent? How do people live at all? (**sentence structure: anaphora**). Statistics show that millions of Americans do. These are the gods of penny pinching (**metaphor**). These people take **parsimony** for more than a word, living **cheaply** by cutting coupons and buying items with a **frugal** eye (**synonyms**). Many of them **j**uggle two **j**obs, **j**oining the millions of unlucky

"Joes" who can't make it on one income (**alliteration**). Despite their hard work, they can never **reap** the rewards, for without **deep** pockets, the **street** always threatens (**assonance**).

Sample Example of Critical Reading:

Students often learn through modeling activities, and the essay below provides a thorough example of critical reading. Important parts of the essay have been underlined throughout the text, which indicate the points of focus. You should carefully review these underlined sections to see not only what has been deemed as important. In the margin on the right hand side, you can observe two types of annotations. The first type in block letters includes both information about summary and paraphrasing of the content as well as identification of various writing techniques. The second type of annotation in italics includes connections of the content to other readings, ideas, interpretations, or personal examples of the reader.

Classical Rhetoric in the Modern World

For many people today, rhetoric has become a distasteful word synonymous with politicians who lie to constituents and salesmen who cheat their customers. The commonly thought of notion of rhetoric is that it <u>connotes the ability to misuse words to prevaricate, hide the truth, obstruct true meaning, and generally convince audiences into believing in a position that perhaps they normally would not have adopted had they not been tricked.</u>

The problem with this as that <u>many of us don't understand how important rhetoric is to the modern world. Rhetoric should be praised and thought of in terms of the broader use of the term</u>: a concise method used by orators and writers to present material in an understandable way to audiences. Indeed, <u>rhetoric has not lost its place or usefulness in our modern day</u> if one

> Definition—rhetoric viewed as negative, masks truth
>
> *Example of Pres. Clinton using tricky terms about Monica Lewinsky; Pres. Nixon called "tricky Dick"*
>
> Thesis—rhetoric should be praised not condemned
>
> New Definition—concise method to present material to audience

takes the number of speeches given by public figures or the number of reports provided for the public good. From the State of the Union Address to weekly press conferences by public officials to debates in the local school boards, people use rhetorical skills without really acknowledging their importance or their origin.

Example—modern day with speeches

Without knowing it, <u>rhetoric has a great deal to do with the development of democracy and the function of citizens within a society</u>. Indeed, speaking and writing well have been an incredibly important component of civic participation for a very long time. From the time of Aristotle, who first formulated a rhetorical method still in use today, to Cicero in Rome, to President Lincoln in America, classical rhetoric has informed civic life and civic policies within the polis of the community. Indeed, the rhetorical tradition has been a constant for over two thousand years, and nearly every great orator or writer we remember studied classical rhetoric in order to perfect their public speaking and writing prowess.

Claim #1—rhetoric contributes to our function within democratic society

Historical background of rhetoric

Public speaking was/is very important

How about rhetoric now? Does it have the same importance?

<u>Of course, the art of rhetoric, the specific training in how to present one's ideas to convince an audience, can be corrupted, but this is no reason to condemn rhetoric itself.</u> Even as long ago as 320 BC Aristotle argued against using rhetoric in the pejorative sense to convince or prevaricate for selfish gain as did the Sophists of that era. For teachers like Aristotle and Plato, sophists were merely itinerant scholars who would sell their skills (speaking and writing strategies) to the highest bidder without the ethical component of instruction, which was that rhetoric be used for the public good. The ability to organize ideas and to present them effectively to an audience by using logic, emotion, or ethical ideas was thought to be incredibly powerful—as it is today.

Refutation—people condemn rhetoric out of hand even back in 320 BC

Example—the sophists taught ways to trick others

Would lawyers constitute the modern sophists?

Because of this dichotomy between sophists and traditional rhetors, <u>Aristotle broke his method of rhetoric down into three main components: ethos, logos, and pathos.</u> Ethos connotes the character of the speaker, his ethical background, and today also considers the moral or ethical dimension of the argument. Logos, on the other hand, deals with the logical aspects of the argument and that there be a logical progression in the thought process that avoids the use of logical fallacies. The third component, pathos, is often referred to as the emotional appeal. A speaker who understood the pathos of his audience had great power that must be handled carefully, for he understood then how to manipulate his audience using emotions rather than using logic. This advanced form of psychology required that would-be rhetors understand the circumstances of the address and the constitution of the audience so as to better move the audience to a suitable position.

> Classification of different parts of rhetoric: ethos (ethical), logos (logical), and pathos (emotional) appeals

> Definition—rhetoricians had an understanding of psychology

> *Emotional appeals very common in TV commercials and in advertising*

Given these three broad components, according to Aristotle's method, <u>there were also five stages to developing and presenting a speech: invention, arrangement, style, memory, and delivery. Each stage was significant in the process of formulating material and would be impacted by the particular appeal(s) that were to be used.</u> Indeed, this method taught students how to formulate an argument, how to arrange its parts, what style would be appropriate to the audience, memory devices to remember the speech, and proper delivery techniques for public speaking.

> Classification—five stages in developing speech/writing

> *The same elements I had to consider for my Valedictorian speech*

This five-step program for speech development formulated by Plato and Socrates and set down by Aristotle was added to by Latin scholars such as Cicero, Quintillian and the anonymous author of the *Ad Herrenium*. It was this survival of classical rhetoric that came to America with the colonists, but which under-

> Continued historical background. In addition to the ancient Greeks, Romans also used rhetoric

The tradition found its way to 19th century America— i.e. Lincoln

The Gettysburg Address

Claim #2: Rhetoric should be rehabilitated. It's key to a "civil society"

Claim #3: Rhetoric is integral part of being a citizen in democracy

Why would the average citizen need rhetoric? Should it be only for public figures?

Claim #4: Without rhetorical training, people become part of a mob

went a significant change and adaptation by American rhetors in the 19th Century. While still using parts of classical rhetoric, there was a change to a more "common sense" approach which included far more personal experience that operated as exempla for audiences which would "excite understanding and imagination"

It may seem that the skills of rhetoric died with the ancient Greeks or Romans a vague, ancient theory, but rhetoric is no less important today. The very principles of argumentation that form the backbone for many college text books are based on classical rhetoric. Today, though, rhetoric suffers a negative aura as something that dirty politicians practice when they learn to speak for hours without saying anything. However, we should not condemn rhetoric, for at its base it is the glue that holds our civic society together. Proper speaking and writing techniques allow citizens to act when an injustice has been done; they allow citizens to formulate arguments for or against new laws; rhetoric helps people clearly organize their thoughts. The problem is not that people are trained in rhetoric. It is that not enough are. In addition to teaching people the methods of argument, rhetoric also teaches them how to argue in a civil way, which is absolutely essential for a civilized society. Without rhetoric, people won't have the skills to be proper citizens and participate in the democratic process, and we become slowly just a mob of people screaming invectives, not debating civilly.

Reading Log: An Outline Approach

Following the post-reading strategies, the reading log below contains some of the major elements that you should be looking for and recording systematically. These logs could be part of your portfolio for any course that requires the critical study of reading materials. Furthermore, systematically engaging in post-reading activities can aid you in remembering and utilizing the material later, especially for exams and writing assignments.

READING LOG (example)

BIBLIOGRAPHICAL INFORMATION

(Cite the source according to the MLA guidelines. this will allow you to quickly cut/paste into a bibliography should you wish to use the essay in a paper of yours.)	Papadomichelaki, Roumpini & Lash Vance. *Compass: Paths to Effective Reading, 2nd Ed, Revised*, 2008.

DATA

(Type of publication, position of chapter within publication, genre, length of essay, type of press)	"Classical Rhetoric in the Modern World." This is an essay illustration in the introduction of a text book.

SUMMARY

(Give a concise synopsis of the thesis, the main points, the evidence)	The authors provide a short overview of the traditional meaning of rhetoric versus the modern connotation. Rhetoric, as formulated by Aristotle, was a way to organize one's thoughts and make coherent arguments. Today, rhetoric is too often thought of as the slick tricks of politicians. The authors argue that this could not be further from the truth. Instead, rhetoric is an integral part of the democratic process, for citizens need to have the skills to present their ideas and argue their position. Without rhetorical training, citizens can become simply part of the mob.

OUTLINE OF THE ESSAY

(Follow the basic paragraph structure of the essay to identify the strategies and goals of the writer)	**Intro**—new definition of rhetoric today (negative) **Thesis**—Rhetoric is misunderstood 1. Old definition of rhetoric as training device for communication 2. Rhetoric should be praised, not condemned 3. Rhetoric is useful in the modern world 4. Rhetoric assists in the function of democracy

(continued)

OUTLINE OF THE ESSAY

Extended Definition
1. Rhetoric is a method including ethos, logos, pathos appeals
2. Rhetoricians must know their audience and have a knowledge of psychology
3. Greeks and Romans used it in public life

Conclusion
1. Rhetoric should be rehabilitated because of its connections to civil society
2. Rhetoric gives people the skills to participate in Democracy without becoming part of a mob

(Follow the basic paragraph structure of the essay to identify the strategies and goals of the writer)

PERSPECTIVES/THOUGHTS

Too often politicians don't say much in their speeches, so the stereotype of rhetoric seems to be true there. However, I saw the effectiveness of rhetoric in a student government meeting. We were debating about funding a new club on campus, and it was a pretty hot issue. However, the president of the ASB kept the discussion on track and each side presented ideas in a logical and civil way. I can see how this mini example of democracy in action is true. If no one had any training in argument and rhetoric, then each group would simply be yelling to get their position passed.

(Insert comments and thoughts of your own in regards to the essay)

VOCABULARY AND IMPORTANT QUOTES

Pejorative, Rhetoric, Cicero, Aristotle, Constituents, Prevaricate, Sophists, Dichotomy

(Write down new words or terms as well as important quotes)

CONNECTIONS TO OTHER ESSAYS AND EXAM TOPICS

*Remember the book on speech I read in high school that listed a number of ways to organize a speech or writing.
*The student government handout on how to conduct meetings.
*Review the book for English class that has parts of "rhetoric."
*Look at Republican and Democratic platforms for rhetorical uses.

Possible Paper / Exam Topics
Examine the role rhetoric plays in today's democratic system.
Explain the idea of sophists. Are there any modern examples of this?
What do the authors mean that people without rhetorical training can become part of the mob?

Guide to the Online Quizzes

A Short Justification for the Online Quizzes

Your teacher may assign supplementary online quizzes, which are designed to help you, the student, in multiple ways. Therefore, it is important to understand that the completion of these quizzes is significant not just for the points you will earn toward your grade in class, but primarily for your practice in reading effectively. The following sections contain a brief explanation of the main aspects of each quiz that you should keep in mind, so you ensure the best results.

Quiz Characteristics:

All quizzes are consistent in the number of questions (fifteen) and in the sections they include (Content, Technique, Vocabulary, and Feedback Section). More analytically, each section has the following particular objectives:

- to help students improve their critical skills by reading in a careful and focused manner (Content Section, Seven Quiz Questions)

- to familiarize students with a host of other authors' writing and rhetorical techniques that they can also employ in their own writing (Technique Section, Three Questions)

- to help expand students' vocabulary (Vocabulary Section, Five Questions)

- help students become meta-cognitive about their own skills and strategies. (Corrective Feedback for all Questions)

How to Take an Online Quiz

Content Section (Seven Quiz Questions)
1. Before taking the quiz:

- Follow the steps in the Critical Reading Guide as well as the Sample Example of Critical Reading with Glosses of this introduction.

- Make sure you understand the *author's main points*; for this you can run a preliminary assessment of your reading comprehension by trying to answer the questions in the "Understanding the Text" section which follows each essay in the book.

- Make sure you have no unknown words, especially those that are in bold or those that may impede your understanding of important sentences or sections of the essay.

2. While taking the quiz:

- Keep in mind that there is (typically) only a limited amount of time you have for the quiz.

- Keep in mind that the quiz may not allow you to go back and change your response to a question, so think well before answering.

- Keep in mind that there are different types of questions: a) *Multiple Choice* with only one correct answer, b) *Multiple Answer* with one or more correct answers, and c) *True or False* with either true or false as its correct answer.

- Make sure you have access to the book at all times and turned to the section of the particular essay. You cannot complete a quiz successfully if you only rely on your memory of the essay because the questions often require focused re-reading of specific sections of the essay.

- Make sure you read each question and each possible answer very carefully before you respond. The correct answer may well lie in one key word either in the question or the answer.

- *Make sure you understand whether the question asks you for the author's opinion or somebody else's opinion as stated in the essay. Remember the quiz will never ask you for your own opinion or prior knowledge on the topic; these quizzes strictly assess your reading comprehension, so they only involve what is presented in the text of each essay.*

Content Section (7 questions)

From Essay #1 "Nature Through the Looking Glass"

Multiple Choice: *This question has one answer.*

According to the authors, for the Bureau of Land Management up until the 1940s, the Grand Canyon was:

a.   **an exploitable source of water and energy.**
b.   a source of infinite admiration and respect.
c.   an impediment to further explorations.
d.   a possible natural museum for Native American rock art.

Correct Answer(s) Feedback:
* the answer "an exploitable source of water and energy" is correct because the Bureau of Land Management had a proposal to turn the Grand Canyon into a huge water reservoir (paragraph 2).

Incorrect Answer(s) Feedback:
* the answer "a source of infinite admiration and respect" is incorrect because it is not mentioned by the authors in connection with the Bureau of Land Management (paragraph 2).
* the answer "an impediment to further explorations" is incorrect because the Grand Canyon was an impediment to the explorations of the conquistadors and not the Bureau of Land Management.
* the answer "a possible natural museum for Native American rock art" is incorrect because it relates to the Glen Canyon Dam which actually submerged Native American rock art in 1964.

Multiple Answer: *This question may have one or more answers.*

According to the authors, the Grand Canyon experience:

a **entails the understanding of the canyon's colossal size.**
b   includes exploring the Colorado River and the natural formations.
c   can be simulated through photographs and films.
d **can be a spiritual one.**

Correct Response(s) Feedback:
* The answer "entails the understanding of its colossal size" is correct because in the first part of paragraph one (1), the authors describe the Grand Canyon in terms of size and measurements, the typical way of understanding it (paragraph 1).
* The answer "can be a spiritual one" is correct because the authors mention that "visiting the Canyon is about experiencing the sublime" (paragraph 1).

Incorrect Response(s) Feedback:
* The answer "includes exploring the Colorado River and the natural formations" is incorrect because the authors never discuss the exploration of the Colorado River and the natural formation as part of experiencing the Grand Canyon.
* The answer "can be simulated through photographs and films" is incorrect because the authors only claim that one should experience the Grand Canyon "first hand" and not just through photographs and film (paragraph 1).

True or False

According to the authors, suburbia offers most Americans a good compromise between tamed and untamed nature. Answer is **False**

Correct Answer(s) Feedback:
* The sentence "According to the authors, suburbia offers most Americans a good compromise between tamed and untamed nature" is false because the authors think that suburbia is only a form of tamed natural environment and not a compromise between tamed and untamed nature (paragraph 5).

Incorrect Answer(s) Feedback:
* The sentence "According to the authors, suburbia offers most Americans a good compromise between tamed and untamed nature" is not true because the authors think that suburbia is only a form of tamed natural environment and not a compromise between tamed and untamed nature (paragraph 5).

Writing and Rhetorical Techniques Section (Three Quiz Questions)

1. Before taking the quiz:

• Study the various techniques explained in the "Identifying Writing Techniques" and "Identifying Rhetorical Techniques" sections of this introduction.

• After you carefully read and annotate the essay for content, you should try to focus on the primary writing and rhetorical techniques employed by the author in each paragraph. You can run a preliminary assessment of your understanding of these techniques by trying to answer the questions in the "Analyzing Writing" section which follows each essay.

2. While taking the quiz:

• Make sure you have access to the book at all times, at the section of the particular essay. You cannot complete a quiz successfully if you only rely on your memory of the essay because the questions often require focused re-reading of specific sections of the essay.

• Keep in mind that there are different types of questions: a) *Multiple Choice* with only one correct answer, b) *Multiple Answer* with one or more correct answers.

• Make sure you read each question and each possible answer very carefully before you respond. The correct answer may well lie in one key word either in the question or the answer.

Rhetorical Techniques Section (3 questions)
From Essay #1 "Nature Through the Looking Glass"

Multiple Choice: *This question has one answer.*

In paragraph three (3), the authors use the following writing technique to discuss Las Vegas and Death Valley:

a.   Simile
b.   **Compare/Contrast**
c.   Process Analysis
d.   Classification

Correct Answer(s) Feedback:
- The answer "Compare/Contrast" is correct because the authors present the preservation of the desert in Death Valley as antithetical, contrasting to the subjugation of the desert in Las Vegas (paragraph 3).

Incorrect Answer(s) Feedback:
- The answers "Simile," "Process Analysis," and "Classification" are incorrect because the authors present the preservation of the desert in Death Valley as antithetical, contrasting to the subjugation of the desert in Las Vegas (paragraph 3).

Multiple Answer: *This question may have one or more answers.*

There are no Multiple Answer Questions in this particular quiz section, but some other quizzes do include them; again, one or more answers may be correct, so a process-of-elimination technique is required.

□ **A Guide to the Online Quizzes: Vocabulary Section**

Vocabulary Section (5 Quiz Questions)

1. Before taking the quiz:

- After you carefully read and annotate the essay for content, you should try to focus on the vocabulary that has been put in bold. Five or more of these words will appear in the quiz. To best prepare, you can complete the exercises in the "Developing Vocabulary" section which follows each essay.

- Try to consult a reliable and expansive dictionary. Do not assume that an electronic thesaurus or a pocket dictionary will contain all the words in question or any substantive in-context explanation of their meaning.

2. While taking the quiz:

- Make sure you have access to the book at all times with the section of the particular essay available for consultation, as well as to your dictionary and/or annotations on the vocabulary. You may not complete a quiz successfully if you only rely on your memory because the questions often require focused re-reading of specific sections of the essay.

Keep in mind that there are different types of questions in this section:

A. **Multiple Choice** with only one correct answer
B. **Multiple Answer** with one or more correct answers,
C. **Compatible/Incompatible** questions that ask you for synonyms or words that are irrelevant to the ones selected
D. **Word Replacement** questions that ask you to replace a certain word in text with a synonym
E. **Correct/Incorrect Usage** questions that ask you to verify whether the use of a certain word in a sentence is correct or incorrect
F. **Fill in the Blank** questions that ask you to fill in the missing word in a sentence by choosing one of the words in bold.

Make sure you read each question and each possible answer very carefully before you respond. The correct answer may well lie in one key word either in the question or the answer.

Vocabulary Section (5 questions)

From Essay #1 "Nature Through the Looking Glass"

Compatible/Incompatible (also Multiple Choice: *This question has one answer.)*

Select the word that is synonymous to **antithetical**:

a.   similar
b.   compatible
c.   opposing
d.   antitrust

Correct Answer(s) Feedback:
- The answer "opposing" is correct because "antithetical" means something that is contrary to something else.

Incorrect Answer(s) Feedback:
- The answers "similar" and "compatible" are incorrect because they have the opposite meaning to "antithetical."
- The answer "antitrust" is incorrect because "antitrust" deals with the regulation of banks and trusts.

Word Replacement (also Multiple Answer: *This question may have one or more answers).*

Select the terms that *can replace* the word in bold: "In the American **psyche** there is a schizophrenic relationship with nature

a   soul
b   psychotherapy
c   history
d   consciousness

Correct Response(s) Feedback:
- The answers "soul" and "consciousness" are synonymous to the word "psyche."

Incorrect Response(s) Feedback:
- *The answers "psychotherapy" and "history" are incorrect.*

Correct/Incorrect Usage (also Multiple: *This question has one.*

Select the sentence that exhibits *the correct usage* of the word **schism**:

a A separation within the Christian church is called a schism.
b He tore a page out of his book, creating a schism.
c The schism on his knee required that he take medication.
d His relationship ended in a bad schism.

Correct Response(s) Feedback:
* *The answer "A separation within the Christian church is called a schism" is correct because "schism" refers to a separation into factions.*

Incorrect Response(s) Feedback:
* The answer "He tore a page out of his book, creating a schism" is incorrect because "schism" is not synonymous to "a gap" which would be the correct term in this case.
* The answer "The schism on his knee required that he take medication" is incorrect because "schism" is not synonymous to "a cut or a scratch" which would be the correct terms in this case.
* The answer "His relationship ended in a bad schism" is incorrect because "schism" is not synonymous to "divorce or break-up" which would be the correct terms in this case.

Fill in the Blank.

From the ten vocabulary words selected in your book for this reading, fill in the blank with the appropriate word:

The _____ about John is that he professes to love nature, yet he never re-cycles.

paradox

Correct Response(s) Feedback:
* The word "paradox" is the correct answer because it refers to a contradiction in terms, the only vocabulary word of the ten that means this.

Incorrect Response(s) Feedback:
* The other nine vocabulary words either have the wrong form (adjectives, verbs, etc.) or they do not imply a contradiction in terms.

CHAPTER
ONE

Ethics
&
Philosophy

1 Nature Through the Looking Glass

There is something completely awe-inspiring about the Grand Canyon that mere words cannot capture. It is something that must be experienced first hand, for photographs or films, though artfully and skillfully executed, can only approximate the **grandeur** of this monumental canyon. Quantifying its grandeur with numbers can of course help us put things into perspective…but only a little. Over 277 miles long, a mile deep, and in places 18 miles wide, this gorge was carved over millions of years by the Colorado River, and it is now part of a beltway of seven national parks that spread out into parts of Utah, Colorado, Idaho, and Arizona. The Grand Canyon is aptly named, for it dwarfs other natural formations in its colossal dimensions. However, the Grand Canyon is far more than the sum of its size. Visiting the Canyon is about experiencing the **sublime**, about connecting with our own spiritual selves—and for some this is a connection with God—but perhaps above all it is about re-learning that humans are but a part of nature. 1

It wasn't always so. Indeed, in his first Western account of the Grand Canyon in 1540, **conquistador** Garcia Lopez de Cardenas wrote that the landscape was devoid of both life and value…nothing but a great impassable hole in the earth. Undoubtedly, the Grand Canyon was a major stumbling block in the way of Coronado's expedition for the fabled seven cities of gold, the main reason for traversing the countryside to begin with. However, it wasn't just the greedy conquistadores searching for gold that thought the Grand Canyon was simply a hole in the ground. As late as the 1940s, plans were under way by the Bureau of Land Management to build a series of dams near the Grand Canyon, effectively turning this "hole" into a huge reservoir. In fact, part of a large canyon complex nearby was filled in with the building in 1964 of the Glen Canyon dam, which effectively submerged 266 square miles of rock formations and Native American rock art. 2

These **antithetical** perceptions of the Grand Canyon—and nature in general—would seem to be mutually exclusive. On the one hand, Americans seem to have developed a passion for their national parks, with an estimated 277 million visits to the national park system alone in 2004, which doesn't include state and local reserve or park areas. Indeed, Americans eagerly leave their busy, work- 3 worn lives and drive hundreds of miles to bare witness to the majesty of nature. The **paradox** then is that these self-same Americans, who spend their ten days of annual vacation in a national park in awe of this untouched nature, return home to areas like Las Vegas that represent the absolute subjugation and conquest of nature. So obvious is this antithesis in the U.S. that one can find it in just neighboring areas. Lying on one side of the mountain range that borders Las Vegas, Death Valley National Park, a vast preserved landscape with interesting rock formations, huge vistas, and dry lake beds, bears testament to the existence of a prehistoric lake millions of years ago. **Ravaged** only by the hand of time, this place has remained untouched and protected. Then, on the other side of this same range lies Las Vegas, a city of millions developed in the same, arid desert. Despite the intense heat and lack of water, houses boast lawns, hotels feature golf courses, air conditioners work at full power, and the famed strip of Las Vegas lights up the night sky for miles—all millions of light bulbs powered through the once mighty Colorado River, tamed now by the construction of Hoover Dam in the 1930s.

4   In the American **psyche** there is a schizophrenic relationship with nature. On the one hand, Americans seem to revere the Grand Canyon, Zion National Park, Yosemite, Sequoia, Yellowstone, and a host of other areas; on the other hand, Americans insist on living patterns that are not **conducive** to preserving the natural environment. This goes beyond building in places where nature didn't seem to have humans in mind, like Las Vegas or Phoenix, Arizona or other arid and hostile places in the desert. Overall, there seems to be a desire—perhaps ingrained from the time of the frontier days—to conquer nature, to subdue it, and to make it serve mankind. However, this desire for conquest often comes with vast needs and wasteful consumption that threaten natural resources. For instance, uncontrolled housing projects can be seen in the Southern California area, covering vast stretches of land with suburbs, swallowing whole mountain ranges and **gulping** down water reservoirs. In the name of growth and profit, every year extensive stretches of land are being terra-formed and completely altered. At the same time environmentalists are to be pacified with setting aside reserve areas where no one can build and people can visit on the weekends, a sad testament to what the landscape used to look like.

5   This dual mentality of *preservation and conquest* creates a strange **schism** in the experience of nature. The story of the American West, after all, has been the story not only of the subjugation of Native Americans, but also of the glorified subjugation of a hostile nature. It has been about building dams, erecting wind farms, digging tunnels, plowing fields, laying roads, and mining for gold. Therefore, today Americans are too often not part of nature; they experience nature only

on the vacation trips to national or state parks. Nature becomes for them a specialized retreat from the hectic pace of daily existence, a place for the rediscovery of themselves and their human spirit. This experience is separated and made distinct from daily life, where most of the times the "natural" environment is completely altered to fit human tastes. Indeed, the typical daily experience of nature for the average American of the city or suburbia is through manicured lawns, planted flowers, and tree-lined boulevards; again, this daily experience is through a tamed natural environment indicating Americans' need to conquer nature rather than blend with it, let alone leave it undisturbed.

Is it possible, however, to return nature to its previous state and never "touch" it again? One could easily assume that such a romantic notion of conservationism and conservatism would negate years of research and progress. After all, what business did man have on the moon? Instead, what seems to be necessary here is a compromise between these two antithetical forces of preservation and conquest of nature. Experiencing nature in its natural environment—even if it isn't on the monumental scale of the Grand Canyon—is absolutely essential to keeping us more human and more balanced, so it shouldn't be reserved just for our vacation. Nature should not be experienced through the looking glass but should rather be available and pursued on a daily basis through its integration in our everyday existence.

6

Discussing and Writing About The Text

Discussing Issues:

Make a list of the various ways you have been experiencing nature in your life. In class or a group, discuss the advantages and disadvantages of each experience.

Writing about the Text:

In a well-developed and organized essay, respond to the reading; be sure to support your views with pertinent examples drawn from your own experience and observations, as well as readings.

Topic 1: According to the authors, how does the average American experience nature? To what extent—if at all—do you agree with their observation of an existing paradox in this experience?

Topic 2: According to your opinion, how can the authors' suggestion of a compromise be best realized? To support your opinion, you need to examine relevant and specific examples from a variety of sources.

Developing Vocabulary:

The words below may appear as part of your online quizzes. Please refer to the introduction for study strategies for learning vocabulary.

1. granduer
2. sublime
3. conquistador
4. antithetical
5. paradox
6. ravaged
7. psyche
8. conducive
9. gulping down
10. schism

Understanding the Text

Answer the following questions by carefully reviewing the authors' aruguments in the short essay.

1. What does the history of the Grand Canyon prove about Americans?

2. What do the authors observe about Americans' relation to nature?

3. How do man-made interventions often affect nature?

4. What seems to be the suggestion the authors make in order to erase the paradox?

Analyzing Writing

Answer the following questions by carefully reviewing the authors' arugments and writing strategies from the short essay.

1. Examine the use of figurative speech. How does it affect the reader?Examine three topic sentences the authors use for how they effectively (or not) orient the reader.

2. Examine the use of sources in the essay. What kind of sources do the authors use (personal examples-anecdotes, statistics, etc)?

3. Do you think these sources are appropriate and convincing? What additional ones would you use?

2 Working with One's Hands

When I was growing up, every fall would come with long weekends spent at my father's village on the west side of the island of Crete, Greece. My father would take my two older brothers and myself to help him gather the olives from a copse of olive trees found on land that had once belonged to his great grandparents. At the time, those weekends were **dreaded** rather than cherished for all the hard work that awaited us all, but as I grow older, I find myself longing for those days.

1

It was not so much the one-hour drive to the village that made the village seem so far away, as much as it was the distance from what we considered normal. Even to this day, the inroads of civilization never seem to have entirely made it to this grove or the village or any place within 25 miles. In fact, the only **concession** to modern technology still remains the hastily erected poles along the single-lane road that brought electricity and telephone service only a few years ago. It is funny how displaced these poles seemed in this landscape, like debarked trees lined up in single file waiting for their yearly set of leaves. This still is the kind of place where you need to honk your car horn when going around curves of the one-lane road. This is still the kind of road where if by chance you encounter another driver going the opposite way, one of you will have to back up to let the other pass.

2

The olive trees stand like ancient **sentinels**, some of them two hundred years old or more, their boughs laden with their burden. By dawn, we would have already breakfasted on bits of bread soaked in olive oil and tomatoes, sprinkled with fresh wild oregano, and we would be standing in the orchard with a long rake-like tool. The process was not particularly hard, but there were specific steps to be taken with care. We first had to ensure that the tightly woven nylon netting was spread and secure underneath the olive trees. We then proceeded with the long rake and slowly passed the tool through the limbs and leaves of the tree, careful not to apply too much pressure for fear of breaking a branch and injuring the tree. Since I was the shortest one, I would try to get the low limbs of the younger trees while imagining that I was brushing the green hair of some giant. The ripe olives would drop like heavy rain onto the net and await collection later in the day. By dusk, our backs ached, and our hands were chaffed from combing through the foliage. Satisfied with our day's work, my dad would drive us back to the small village

3

house that was **bequeathed** to him by his father. We would have the dinner that my mom had prepared while my dad would tell us stories from his childhood.

4   My dad is a medical doctor and currently seventy years old but still takes great pleasure in harvesting the olives despite everyone's objections. The more, however, I think back to those weekends, the more I understand his persistence. Back then, he used to actually enjoy how at various social gatherings his colleagues and other intellectuals would feel awkward or be **condescending** when listening to his agricultural endeavors. They probably thought that my father was short of money for degrading himself to the level of a manual worker. In many societies, manual labor has the **pejorative connotation** of a lesser form of work, something that is not equal in some important way to the intellectual efforts of doctors, computer specialists, or any white collar type of job. Indeed, manual work was and is still thought to be the hard road to be traveled by people without any education, real skills, or alternatives. It is often disregarded as inferior, and monetarily, intellectually, and emotionally less fulfilling than the more intellectual endeavors of other jobs. However, this could not be further from the truth. Those who work with their hands often experience a deep sense of satisfaction about their work equal or even greater to that experienced by people who work with their minds.

5   There is something distinctly enjoyable and rejuvenating about working with one's hands. Of course, there is satisfaction in using the knowledge and skill about harvesting gathered from one's kin. At the same time there is a sense of completion of a job that at first seemed **insurmountable**. But it is not simply that at the end of the harvesting season—once all the olives have been gathered, collected, sorted, and pressed—that one can look back on the work and be thankful it is over. This misses the point entirely. My father could, in fact, afford to pay workers to harvest these olives for him, and perhaps he would make some money from their yield. But the real satisfaction came from working with his hands.

6   In harvesting olives, for instance, the work itself is part of the pleasure. The harvester can experience satisfaction throughout the whole process. The process of harvesting is not something that he wants to avoid as an **onerous** task, focused entirely on the paycheck at the end. While there is a finite goal, harvesting olives and producing olive oil, the man who labors with his hands enjoys the process of that labor as well as the active working towards producing something. There is an element of craftsmanship in shaping the growth of these trees and of gathering their produce to create flavorful oils.

      Furthermore, the manual worker has the ability to separate labor from the   7
rest of his life. On the contrary, work never really stops for the intellectual worker.
When my father came home from his practice, he continued to think about the office and his patients' problems, never fully shutting off work. At the village, however, when the work day was done, he could leave the nets, wheelbarrows, and
rake tool with the olives. He could go back to the old house of his childhood, and
his mind could move on to other points of interest. He felt tired but content with
the exercise of his muscles that led to a tangible result. Even while harvesting, the
cares of the week **sloughed** away from him in the moment, for nothing else existed than going from one task to the next. And when he was finished for the day,
his work stayed in the grove.

      What is more, manual work is never really "unskilled" or "mindless".   8
Quite the contrary, it exercises both the body and the mind, something that cannot be said for most intellectual jobs. Harvesting the olives, for instance, requires
that one know the right time of year, plan ahead for having the right tools and
equipment, use these tools efficiently to avoid damaging the trees or hurting oneself, and organize the whole day and process productively. In addition, in today's
era, almost no manual work is separate from science and technology. Indeed,
many modern farmers, for instance, are college-educated with a theoretical but
also practical understanding of terms like "soil", "nutrients", and "fertilizers".
Therefore, while the word manual derives from the Latin word "manus", meaning "hand", it does not entail that the mind remains passive in the whole process.
Quite the contrary, manual work can offer a balance between the mind and the
body, a balance that intellectuals often seek on the treadmill of a gym's artificial
environment.

Discussing and Writing About The Text

Discussing Issues:

Discuss the views and preconceptions about manual work within your family or community. Discuss your findings with your peers. Do you think these views are justified by reality?

Writing about the Text:

In a well-developed and organized essay, respond to the reading; be sure to support your views with pertinent examples drawn from your own experience and observations, as well as readings.

Topic 1: How does the author view manual work? To what extent—if at all—do you agree with this view point?

Topic 2: According to your opinion, should the K-12 educational system pursue a balance between intellectual and manual curriculum within courses? Examine the validity or lack thereof of such an education.

Developing Vocabulary:

The words below may appear as part of your online quizzes. Please refer to the introduction for study strategies for learning vocabulary.

1. dreaded
2. concession
3. sentinal
4. to bequeath
5. condescending
6. pejorative
7. connotation
8. insurmountable
9. onerous
10. to slough

3 Living in the Moment

There seem to be two **diametrically** opposed suggestions for how to live one's life within American and overall Western culture. On the one hand, we are told over and over again that we should learn to "live in the moment." For years, Hollywood has flooded the marketplace with films that show characters slowly **trudging** through life's weary path to eventually discover the joys of the moment. Robin William's message in the 1986 drama *Dead Poets Society* to all of his **fledgling** students, "Carpe diem—Seize the day," best epitomizes this teaching of living in the moment. Under his guidance and inspired word, his students in a prestigious and highly traditional private school rebel against the prospect of spending their lives without really living them. Transcending genres and time, this idea is then revived over and over again to guide the various audiences. Hundreds of films can be cited whose main message is to live life today. In the action film *Fight Club* (starring Brad Pitt, Edward Norton, and Elizabeth Bonham Carter) physical violence makes the main characters feel the moment in a cathartic effort to rid themselves of their mundane and conformist ways of life. In the mostly forgettable *Gone in 60 Seconds* (starring Nicolas Cage) the characters feel "most alive" and in the moment when driving with their gas pedal floored, ignoring the "what ifs" of the future. Last but certainly not least, we find this idea in romantic comedies, the most interesting of which within this context is *50 First Dates* (starring Adam Sandler and Drew Barrymore). With living in the moment as the film's main premise, the protagonist is challenged by a girlfriend whose head injury allows her only to live a day at a time, suffering complete memory loss the next day.

Though the message to live in the moment seems to be prevalent in theory, in practice many people seem to be at a loss when trying to follow it. Of course, if that is the case, thousands of self-help books and websites have directions on self-training. Even Oprah, the **guru** of pop psychology, has advice on her website about living in the moment: "just try to breathe deeply, focus attention on your body, and meditate"—a routine supposed to have therapeutic effects. However, living in the moment may just be slightly more complicated than just breathing rhythmically. Indeed, a close look at the theory and the practices of the West can lead to the realization that the living patterns and mainstream ideologies of Western civilization seem to be diametrically opposed to living in the moment. In the same movie theatres with films that preach living in the moment can be found films that argue for sacrificing the present for a better future. Again, this ideology transcends all genres. It can be found in the recent *Hustle & Flow* (starring Terrence Howard) where a pimp has to work hard, suffer through the system, and do his time (literally in prison) in order to make it as a rap artist. In *Million Dollar Baby* (starring Clint Eastwood, Morgan Freeman, and Hillary Swank), the heroine has to give over her body to the strict boxing training regiment in order to make something of herself.

3   No wonder people are confused, for living in the moment seems always threatened by planning for the future. On the same book shelf with guides on living in the moment are placed books on planning for the future, for "being prepared" is not only a value in this day and age; it seems to be a requirement in today's complex world. Taken to its logical conclusion, living in the moment is postponed in favor of planning for the future in the form of retirement. Thousands of websites offer advice on retirement and retirement calculators with which you can input your monthly contributions to see how much of a nest egg you'll have at the age of sixty five; of course, the idea is that this nest egg, if comfortable enough, will allow you to live in the moment. Even going on vacation—a time when you can supposedly relax and live in the moment— requires a great deal of planning ahead for finding the best airline tickets and hotel reservations, for prepaying utility bills, and for securing a house and dog sitter. Even for going on "permanent vacation," one ought to plan beyond the grave or at least to the grave. Actually, many **mortuaries** offer special incentives for the soon-to-be dead who select and pay for the coffin before the inevitable demise. In short, it seems ironic that living in the moment is not only hard to accomplish, but also something you have to preplan for. In our society, we are told over and over again how important planning for the future is with the exemplars of those who do not.

4   Hollywood and self-help books aside, for many philosophers this **dichotomy** has been a problem of **ontology**, the ancient Greek word for the "study of being." Since before the time of Christ, philosophers have been concerned with discussing and analyzing human existence and our way of interacting with the world. Where is existence? Is there a future? What is the best way to live life? These certainly may seem like questions that Keanu Reeves' character Neo would ask the Oracle in the popular *Matrix* trilogy. In so many ways, the Hollywood films, self-help books, websites, and retirement calculators that promote living in the moment or planning for the future are participating in this philosophical debate. Yet, what does all this philosophical discussion actually mean?

Well, the way these issues are reflected in American culture makes for a
schizophrenic, confused existence. On the one hand, our culture teaches us to live
in the moment, simply "being"; we should be happy in and of ourselves. On the
other hand, we are taught to plan for the future, to improve ourselves, to continuously analyze who we are and what direction we are heading towards. To make
things worse, advertising bombards us with messages of how much we lack and
how we can satiate our needs through purchasing products and services. For instance, many high school seniors and juniors participate in the annual prom, which
requires that they invest a great deal of time in searching for the right tuxedo or
the right gown; it requires a great deal of money to purchase the clothes, the but-
toneer, the tickets to the prom, the dinner before hand, the seemingly obligatory
rental of the limousine. So, all of this is done in order to live in the moment of
the prom with that favorite someone. How about all the other "moments" that
lead up to the **penultimate** event? How about the additional job taken on to pay
for all the stuff one is supposed to have? How about the elaborate planning with
friends? Are these times living in the moment, or are they forestalling the ultimate
enjoyment of the moment to some later time?

5

Our culture stresses living in the moment, and many of us feel like we are
failing as humans if we don't; we never stop "to smell the roses," "to seize the
day," "to suck the marrow out of life," "to live large" or "in the heat of the moment." At the same time, we are told "a stitch in time saves nine," "plan today
what you'll do tomorrow," "sacrifice today for a better future," or "chance favors
the prepared mind". In short, the **antithetical** advice to live in the moment and
plan for the future puts impossible strains on people, and it may not even be possible in its application. These strains may result in low self-esteem, health problems, irresponsible actions to live in the moment, or postponing all happiness for
a future that might never arrive. Perhaps the solution lies in striking a balance between these two contradictory philosophies. And just think; we haven't even
begun to discuss "living in the past!"

6

Discussing and Writing About The Text

Discussing Issues:

Make a chart of your daily activities. How often do you "live in the moment," and how many of those activities are for "planning for the future?" Do you think these two ideas are mutually exclusive? What problems could this dichotomy of living in the moment or planning for the future cause people?

Writing about the Text:

In a well-developed and organized essay, respond to the reading; be sure to support your views with pertinent examples drawn from your own experience and observations, as well as readings.

Topic 1: According to the authors, what are the two diametrically opposed ways of living in the Western world? Do you think the authors are correct about these two ways, or are there more ways to live life than are discussed here?

Topic 2: Develop an essay based on the limitations and/or advantages of the two ideologies discussed in the essay, "Living in the Moment." Do you think there areother approaches to living that are not cited?

Developing Vocabulary:

The words below may appear as part of your online quizzes. Please refer to the introduction for study strategies for learning vocabulary.

1. diametrically
2. trudging
3. fledgling
4. guru
5. mortuary
6. dichotomy
7. ontology
8. schizophrenic
9. penultimate
10. antithetical

4 The World is Ending . . . Again

One evening I found myself talking with a friend about the state of the modern world while sipping on some chilled wine. In one breath I found myself saying how bad things have become. Students today don't work as hard as they should. The general education level of people has gone down. The economy is self-destructing. Millions are dying of diseases. In short, the world is going downhill fast and may soon end.

1

These complaints may sound new, but the same things can be read as far back as 2,500 years ago in accounts by Plato, or "more recently by Roman authors in the 1st centuries BC and AD respectively, Cicero and Quintilian. To be sure, the world did not end then, and it hasn't ended now as of the publication of this book. In short, every generation thinks that it is worse off than the previous one. Nothing could be further from the truth.

2

Life was far more brutal, short, and savage in the past. In the Middle Ages, for instance, the majority of the population was peasants, meaning they owed service to the land and the lord of the land. While some families managed **to consolidate** wealth, most would have spent their entire life in absolute **squalor** and poverty, especially according to our standards. Even during the Renaissance, the fabled time of rebirth, Shakespeare's London was struck repeatedly by plagues that no one could understand, let alone combat.

3

The modern doomsayers might argue of course that roughly a quarter of the world's population currently exists in poverty, the spread of AIDS, **malaria**, or the Avian Flu threatens to be new pandemics, and hurricanes, tsunamis, and earthquakes impact the lives of millions of people. Certainly these things are horrible, and I do not intend to lessen or underestimate the suffering of the individual victims. However, I believe we need to put everything into perspective and realize that doomsday may not be here yet.

4

One reason for the modern "catastrophology" is our twenty-four-hour news cycle, which allows us to witness disasters across the planet at any given time or even at real time. Thanks to the miracle of print and television sources, we can constantly keep up with problems and tragedies not only in our local communities,

5

but across the world. The misfortunes of the global village enter our homes each and every night in **jarring** images and hurried reports of **ravaged** countryside, war-torn areas, all the way down to the local car accident or child caught cheating on an exam.

6   The world nearly ends every night on our local television and is not totally reborn in the morning paper. But this is an **erroneous** impression. Indeed, who would have known or comprehended the consequences of the 1500 BC eruption of a volcano that blew up the island of Santorini (Thera), caused a massive tsunami which nearly wiped out the Minoan civilization, and drastically reduced the world's temperature? There was no Red Cross or UNICEF waiting to fly in supplies and set up infrastructure to aid victims of the disaster. Today, catastrophes receive remarkable coverage as well as the resources of the citizens of the world in the rebuilding efforts that usually follow. The **pandemic** of HIV/AIDS and malaria in Africa are being fought with the donations of millions of dollars from countries and private individuals alike. Does this show that the world is ending or that people are cooperating more than they ever have?

7   On a more personal level, people often complain about education levels dropping or students becoming lazy and **apathetic** or money being really tight these days. Things were so much better in some golden age of the past. Was it better in the past? The United States didn't have a common, public education system until the 1800s, when a trial system was set up for education so that people could more fully participate in Democracy. Recent statistics show that 97% of the U.S. population is literate, eighty five percent has graduated high school, and 27% has completed a Bachelor's degree or more at a four-year university. This level of education further implies a population that has enough of the basic needs covered to ensure that its citizens have the time to complete their educational tracts.

8   As for the money complaints, people nowadays, in the U.S. at least, have far more material prosperity and access to food than at any time in history. While some may complain that the economy has become "tight" or "money is too hard to come by," is it really? No. The truth is that we have too many **perceived** needs that require ever more cash to satisfy. For example, people in the 1950s, that golden time of opportunity that is so idealized in print and film, would be considered poor by many standards today. Houses on average were 1,400-1,500 square feet, whereas currently signs in many parts of the United States advertise houses of 3,000 square feet or more. People did not have a car for every teenager in the house, a TV for every room, or even a room for every child. In the not too distant

past, there simply was not enough wealth to go around for newly married couples to move out on their own. Families lived together, which meant not only the married couple, the so-called **nuclear** family, but also the grandparents, grandchildren, uncles, and aunts. When in history was it possible for the average person to have their own private space?

What has changed? The mass of people is materialistically the wealthiest that they have ever been in history. More people have access to health care, food, shelter, and material goods than at any time in the past, yet many complain that things are getting worse and worse as time goes on. It wasn't true for Plato or Cicero, and it isn't true now.

9

Discussing and Writing About The Text

Discussing Issues:

Try to think of any examples of doom-saying or doomsayers you are familiar with. Compare them with those of your peers as well as of people older than you (parents, instructor). Do you find that each generation or era has its own fears about the future?

Writing about the Text:

In a well-developed and organized essay, respond to the reading; be sure to support your views with pertinent examples drawn from your own experience and observations, as well as readings.

Topic 1: According to the author, why are doomsayers wrong today? To what extent—if at all—do you agree with this view point?

Topic 2: According to your opinion, is it part of human nature to predict the worst? If yes, how could that tendency be moderated? To support your opinion, you need to examine relevant and specific examples from a variety of sources.

Developing Vocabulary:

The words below may appear as part of your online quizzes. Please refer to the introduction for study strategies for learning vocabulary.

1. to consolidate
2. squalor
3. malaria
4. jarring
5. ravaged
6. erroneous
7. pandemic
8. apathetic
9. perceived
10. nuclear (family)

5 In Defense of the Written Word

There can be no denying that the importance and popularity of the written word have been systematically shrinking over the last fifty years. How do we know? According to the U.S. Department of Labor statistics for 2004, men read on average for 30 minutes per day while women read for 42 minutes. This systematic decrease in readership over the last 20 years is evidenced again with the 1.9 % decline of newspaper circulation of 814 of the nation's largest in 2005. Although there are various factors that contribute to this systematic decline, the latter can be certainly **correlated** with the introduction and wide adoption of television over the last half century, and especially with the **proliferation** of cable channels beginning in the early 1980s. Thus, while the time devoted to reading gradually shrinks for the average American, TV seems to claim more than four hours from the day of that same average American.

This is not necessarily a phenomenon with cataclysmic consequences for the nation, the culture, or the future of our kids, as the avid opponents of TV may try to argue. Especially in the field of news reporting, TV has often proven to be a valuable medium not only for **conveying** information but also for connecting people. Indeed, the images of the Vietnam War did much toward waking up a **somnolent** American populace to the horrors of war. These images, beamed into the houses of American households every night, fueled the platform of anti-war activists and created an atmosphere of awareness. More recently, TV helped to bring attention to the ravages of New Orleans and the misery of people suffering in the wake of hurricane Katrina. However, even in such cases what is more important is that TV has a beneficial effect for all the wrong reasons.

Unlike the printed word, TV is by its very nature an emotive medium. Even when it comes to news reports, TV relies heavily on stirring images while **curtailing** words and commentary, and the constraints of the 24-hour news and reporting cycle hamper true reflection and research. Typical news programs, for instance, may offer a two-minute story about tsunami victims and then awkwardly and abruptly **segue** to local or regional news. This standard pattern shared among most TV news broadcasting programs allows almost no time for reflection. Actually, critical thinking on the reported news does not even appear to be on the agenda of news broadcasting. Viewers simply have to find out about the stories and "feel" the stories, as Stephen Colbert satirizes in his *Colbert (News) Report*. And to "feel" a story, all the viewers need is **evocative** images and catchy headlines in bold lettering.

4   Print media, while by no means complete or perfect, is a far more reflective medium of publication. If TV metaphorically targets the heart, printed media targets the mind. Printed stories are, for lack of better words, simply more complete than their TV counterparts. Newspaper stories, for instance, because of the medium, have more time and space. While deadlines certainly loom, they are not the hourly deadlines of the 24-hour TV world. News stories have to be written, and mostly they require a greater degree of craft and care. With the clock ticking and blank airtime looming, TV journalists are under continuous stress to fill massive amounts of time. CNN, for instance, airs news twenty four hours a day, and some news programs last three hours. Ironically, it would appear that this increased space would allow for greater exploration of material, but it doesn't end up this way. Even in shows with debate as part of the structure, the debaters have very little time to explore complex ideas and are usually rushed through the process or interrupted by commercials. Thus, ideas are boiled down to "**sound bites**" that can be aired without reflection or greater exploration. The viewer is lost.

5   For the printed word, there are far more opportunities for the writer to examine both sides of the story and to adequately research the facts. This is not to say that there can't be bad writing or **salacious** reporting. Certainly there is. However, the medium of print provides some safeguards against a simple emotional response not only by the writer—and the editorial apparatus involved—but also by the readers who can more easily analyze the facts. Readers can work through an article at their own pace, digest its contents, and then think about whether the conclusions or facts are valid. With TV, the image and the comment are gone with the blink of a photon, and the critical-thinking process of the viewer—if there is one— is transferred to the next image and story.

6   For a recent example, we must only look to Mike McCurry, the former press secretary to President Clinton, who in a New York Times article lamented the decision in 1998 to have live briefings from the Presidential Press Office. According to McCurry, this significantly altered the way questions were posed, the transfer of information to the press corps, and the routine of the press room. According to McCurry, this whole process became "a theater of the absurd" (*NY Times*, Feb 27, 2006). But the most interesting thing about McCurry's comments is that he wanted the written filter of the press even if he had little control over what

would eventually be written. He wanted the writers to return to their desks and **formulate** their stories, thereby putting in the necessary context, background, and source material that readers could then process in their own way. He trusted the writers to perform their jobs effectively, efficiently, and fairly. Therefore, if material is aired directly, there is no effective filter to put the subject into context. The viewer is, essentially, lost or limited to emotional responses.

The idiom "a picture is worth a thousand words" is literally true. It comes from the days of William Caxton, one of the first printers of the 15th century whose practice of placing picture woodcuts into documents could literally take out a thousand words from the text. If we continue on the road that we are currently traveling, all the words will be gone. We'll be left with a seemingly meaningless montage of images where viewers make up their own stories or not.

7

While no one has yet written the epitaph for words or replaced them with the picture of a burning dictionary, there is clearly a threatening trend. Reading rates have been in steady decline while TV consumption rises year by year. Critics may disagree why people don't enjoy the written word as much—social changes, overload of work, a mountain of entertainment channels on TV—but the point remains that the written word is simply the best venue to convey stories to people and have them truly reflect on their substance. And that's the word.

8

Discussing and Writing About The Text

Discussing Issues:

Make a list of all the recent news stories that you remember and where you gathered that information. Did you watch the stories on TV or did you read about them? Did the way you learned about the story make a difference in your understanding of it? Why or why not? How do you think websites that have both text and pictures complicate this sce-

Writing about the Text:

In a well-developed and organized essay, respond to the reading; be sure to support your views with pertinent examples drawn from your own experience and observations, as well as readings.

Topic 1: According to the authors, what are the advantages of the written media over pictures or TV? To what extent—if at all—do you think the authors are correct about this assertion?

Topic 2: Compare and contrast the same news story that airs on TV and can be read in a major national newspaper. What are the similarities or differences in the approaches? Do you think the authors are correct in their assertion about the benefits of the written word?

Developing Vocabulary:

The words below may appear as part of your online quizzes. Please refer to the introduction for study strategies for learning vocabulary.

1. correlated
2. proliferation
3. conveying
4. somnolent
5. curtailing
6. segue
7. evocative
8. sound bites
9. salacious
10. formulate

Understanding the Text

Answer the following questions by carefully reviewing the authors' aruguments in the short essay.

1. The title, "In Defense of the Written Word," indicates that words need to be defended. Why so?

2. Why is television termed an "emotive" medium?

3. In what ways do the authors believe that the printed media are better than pictures or videos?

4. Why are the authors concerned about the "threatening trend" of TV watching?

Analyzing Writing

Answer the following questions by carefully reviewing the authors' arugments and writing strategies from the short essay.

1. Examine the use of comparison and contrast in the text.

2. Find three transition sentences and analyze how they work and how effective they are.

3. Examine how the authors employ refutation in the text. Can you cite the specific paragraphs?

6 The Meaning of Words

One problem with words is that they don't exactly say what we mean; they only **approximate** what we would like them to mean. Now, this **disjunction** between thought and verbal language has been well-known in philosophical circles. As far back as the 4th century BC, the philosopher Plato argued that things—and certainly words—were but pale representations of their original idea. John Locke in his work "An Essay Concerning Human Understanding" of 1690 explored among other things how we understand our **contemporaries**. More recently, two philosophers, Charles S. Peirce and Ferdinand de Saussure, argued that an inherent break exists between words (the signifiers) and the physical object or abstract idea they are supposed to represent (the signified). Hence, according to their conclusions, in order for any communication to occur, people have to agree upon the specific meaning of words.

1

All this fancy terminology and philosophical debate can be **exemplified** in the use of a word as simple and common as love. One can surely love chocolate as well as liberty, their child as well as their spouse, their cat as well as their car. A single clumsy word is intended to represent an array of emotional nuances although one can assume a fundamental difference between the love for a child versus the love for an office chair. A need arises then for even more clumsy words to further define this rather complex feeling. In this way, words become part of a linked system that is highly interdependent, a web of knowledge that allows us to at least approximate meaning through a plethora of words and actions.

2

Although the above limitation might be frustrating, this does not lessen the importance of words not only for the expression but also for the existence of thought. Words are essential not just for conveying a thought but also for generating it. In its reversed form, this interdependence of language and thought can prove rather interesting; especially when it comes to abstract meanings and ideas, words or their absence can actually limit thought. George Orwell's *1984* is a prime example of a society in which people's thoughts are systematically limited because words are **expunged** from use or even from the dictionary. If a person or a whole community for that matter does not have the vocabulary to express an idea, the idea will eventually vanish unexpressed, or in the best case scenario both words and

3

ideas will become fossils in some dusty archaic dictionary. And it doesn't take a radical Big Brother to cause this extinction of ideas; rather this process of language loss can be illustrated through the case of educated people trying to survive in a foreign country with only a limited command of the country's language. Unable to fully express themselves in the new language, they are rather likely to suppress many of their ideas and subject them to this danger of extinction for a mere lack of the requisite language tools. If the words are not used, they eventually die out along with the ideas they approximate. If the average person of a society uses 1/3 of the existing vocabulary to express themselves, the remaining two thirds of the available words together with the ideas they approximate might eventually become extinct or fossilized.

4   But even in the case of a person who has command over a language and has read the dictionary back to front, words—by their very nature— can limit the outline or the scope of one's thoughts, if not the thoughts themselves. For example, a colleague at the university recently described the birth of his son as a miracle, a wonder, a divine, **sublime** moment. This, one would suspect, would be an accurate description of his emotional state and overall experience. However, from previous discussions, I had come to know my colleague as an **agnostic** rather than a religious person. Yet the words he chose to use and their associations naturally framed the discussion in religious overtones, ushering in connections to another child born long ago in Bethlehem. Did he mean to draw references to God, the Immaculate Conception, or the birth of Jesus? None, I suspect, but the words themselves carried these connotations and thus limited his frame of reference.

5   A non-religious example might demonstrate these limitations even further. When looking for work in the current job market, one has to "market," "sell," "package," "form," and "advertise" oneself; in even more upscale language, one should **leverage** one's personal characteristics and assets to secure a profitable platform for position attainment. This is obviously the language of the marketplace and of **barter** and trade in which the worker becomes what is traded. The workers thus fashion themselves as chattel to be sold to the highest bidder.

6   All of the above is not to imply of course that studying to become a wordsmith is of no value or hopeless. On the contrary, trying to approximate ideas in the clothing of words is what we should try to do. If we simply give up on the act of communication because words are too slippery to nail down, then we will have opened ourselves up to systematic miscommunication. Proper word choice that leads to real understanding is more important than we know. How many times in history and politics has miscommunication led to conflict? If anything, we must be as careful as possible to at least *approximate* with words the message that we

wish to convey.

The second thing we must do is to be constantly aware and critical of the way a certain individual or community uses words for what this usage indicates of their own culture and preconceptions. After all, it wasn't too many years ago that most definitions of the word "black" in the dictionary were **pejorative** with connotations ranging from soiled and dirty to dark and evil while at the same time anything white was deemed as clean, pure, holy. These connotations, however, helped to frame interactions among white people and African Americans; these seemingly innocuous definitions contributed to making racism tolerable, if not acceptable both linguistically and socially. Therefore, a study of the lexicon can aid us in our own self-discovery as a people and a culture. This knowledge of words, their usage, the cultural values they contain, and the way they frame interactions may help us break out of the mold, challenge, and discover what we really mean.

7

Discussing and Writing About The Text

Discussing Issues:

Try to think of your experience with learning another language. Make a list of the main difficulties you encountered in this process. Did they include the use of vocabulary? Have you encountered problems in the use of language by you or others similar to the ones the author describes?

Writing about the Text:

In a well-developed and organized essay, respond to the reading; be sure to support your views with pertinent examples drawn from your own experience and observations, as well as readings.

Topic 1: According to the authors, what is the interconnection between words and thought? What do you think of the authors' views and suggestions?

Topic 2: According to your opinion, are processes such as the standardization of a language necessary or helpful for communication? To support your opinion, you need to examine relevant and specific examples from a variety of sources.

Developing Vocabulary:

The words below may appear as part of your online quizzes. Please refer to the introduction for study strategies for learning vocabulary.

1. **to approximate**
2. **disjunction**
3. **contemporaries**
4. **exemplified**
5. **expunged**
6. **sublime**
7. **agnostic**
8. **leverage**
9. **barter**
10. **pejorative**

Understanding the Text

Answer the following questions by carefully reviewing the authors' arugments in the short essay.

1. What have been the various theories about words that the authors refer to?

2. What are the problems the authors see as inherent to words and their meaning?

3. According to the authors, how can words limit thought?

4. What are the authors' suggestions in regards to the use of words?

Analyzing Writing

Answer the following questions by carefully reviewing the authors' aruguments and writing strategies from the short essay.

1. Examine the various examples and their effectiveness in supporting the authors' arguments.

2. Examine the transitional words, phrases, sentences used by the authors and try to find alternatives.

3. Examine the use of sources in the essay. What kind of sources do the authors use (personal examples-anecdotes, statistics, etc)? Do you think they are appropriate and convincing? What additional sources would you use?

7   The Plurality of History

The **adage** proclaimed by Napoleon in the early part of the 19th century that "history is a fiction agreed upon" is presumed no longer true in today's world. With the Internet, thousands of publishing houses, and the advent of home-publishing software, it has become easy, fast, and inexpensive for everyone to have a voice in the construction of history. No longer is history written only by the victor, as Stalin was reputed to have said. The myriad voices that exist today in the form of blogs (web logs), news letters, TV news programs, and a host of other venues for reporting provide a thorough, yet **convoluted** memoir for historical reference. Yet, are so many voices productive for a better understanding of history? Could too many historical viewpoints only create a **cacophony** of confusion?

Undoubtedly, having more voices in interpreting events can provide for a more thorough understanding of history and historical events. The time has long since passed where **stodgy** academics proclaim history from the heights of ivory towers, or dictators force members of the intelligentsia to write events as the dictators see them. There is not one history of World War II, but thousands. There is not one web site with background about the history of slavery, but thousands. These various sources can comprise a more complete picture of the concept.

Arguably, these thousands of sources provide academics and lay people interested in history with a gold mine of source material, and these sources allow for a more complete historical record. On the other hand, it is simply not possible for any historical text to include the plethora of voices into one single narrative. Inevitably, the presumed **salient** features have to be found, revised, and included in the text, and more importantly the "lens" that historian uses to view the material shapes both the editorial process of what events or people are included as well as how these events or people are interpreted. Historians inevitably view history through their own peculiar lens, and their experiences, background, and insights alter the portrayal of history.

One safeguard that has been developed by academics has been to "situate" the narrative, which basically allows historians to include their own "subject" positions in the preface of the text. In this way, readers can always be aware of the writer's possible **preconceptions** that might color the material and its presenta-

1

2

3

4

tion. For example, an atheist writing about the history of the Catholic Church might have a different "lens" than would a devout Catholic writing about the same material. The reader can be constantly aware of how these subject positions affect the story. Thus, the effort of creating, reciting, and interpreting history may become more self-conscious.

5   However, given the number of historical accounts, the archival material available, and the particular viewpoint of the historian, what constitutes history now? At an even more practical level, how is history to be taught and what materials should be included? What "version" of history is to be taught to students at schools? The easy answer is to teach all the versions, but there is only so much time in any lecture class and so much energy students have in order to explore the majority of material. Even more so, how do we incorporate the **subtleties** and complexities of historical events so that history becomes more than memorizing important events and less than a thousand books and websites with different views of that event? For instance, for many, the American Revolution was the rightful and necessary action called for by the oppression by the British monarchy. We learn that the Boston Tea Party involved a group of heroes risking their lives for the cause of freedom. However, one man's revolutionary is another's terrorist; one's hero is another's rebel. Things are often far more complicated than what we first suspect. What was the role of France in support of the war? How were Native American tribes used as mercenary armies? For the British soldiers of the period, American fighters were little more than terrorists who didn't understand the rules of engagement for war. American **militia** didn't rush up to British forces to meet them on the field of battle. Instead, they engaged in quick ambush attacks of the superior force. To the British this was cowardly fighting; to the Americans this was the only way to survive.

6   History is complicated, just as present day life is, and it becomes even more difficult to write textbooks that will **encapsulate** the complexities of historical events. One part of the solution is to carefully scrutinize the editorial and content decisions that are made in the production of historical textbooks. In this way, different viewpoints of the same event or character are likely to be included in the text. The second—and perhaps most important—part of the solution is to teach students the skills of critical reading. Too often today students are only tested on their ability to **regurgitate** what they have read. They are too often not asked what they thought about it. Introducing critical discussions of readings into the curriculum is absolutely essential for students to understand that a multitude of voices is present within any historical event. This kind of discussion trains students over time to question the "lenses" the authors use and to realize that there

may be multiple interpretations to any story.

The problem may lie in the word itself: history. The singular form is used to denote a single story line that can be memorized and then retold. The use of the plural, "histories," would be far more accurate—the word itself indicating to students and historians alike that there may be a thousand stories connected to a subject. There will always be issues about historical content, especially for history textbooks to be used by impressionable youths. History has, after all, been a fiction agreed upon and used to promote a particular world view. The history of World War II told by the Russians will certainly focus on different elements than that told by the U.S. or by Germany. There is no denying that the content choices, organization, and presentation of history are incredibly important, but one of the best ways to ensure that students recognize that historical accounts are almost always incomplete is to learn the skills of critical reading. In this way, students will examine history textbooks with a host of questions in mind, and instructors will require them to go beyond the sterile memorization of the material into an actual critique of the material.

7

Discussing and Writing About The Text

Discussing Issues:

In groups, select a historical period or event you would like to investigate, and allow each student to brainstorm on possible sources they would like to research. Discuss your results and their implications about your training in studying history.

Writing about the Text:

In a well-developed and organized essay, respond to the reading; be sure to support your views with pertinent examples drawn from your own experience and observations, as well as readings.

Topic 1: According to the authors, what seems to be the most effective way to both teach and evaluate history? To what extent—if at all—do you think the authors are correct in their suggestions?

Topic 2: What do you think should be the instructional objectives of any history class in high school?

Developing Vocabulary:

The words below may appear as part of your online quizzes. Please refer to the introduction for study strategies for learning vocabulary.

1. adage
2. convoluted
3. cacophony
4. stodgy
5. salient
6. preconception
7. subtleties
8. militia
9. encapsulate
10. regurgitate

Understanding the Text

Answer the following questions by carefully reviewing the authors' arugments in the short essay.

1. What are the benefits of the plurality of voices in today's accounts of history?

2. What does "to situate" the narrative mean and how does it contribute to the interpretation of history?

3. What are the practical challenges teaching history poses today?

4. What are the suggestions offered by the authors in better understanding and teaching history?

Analyzing Writing

Answer the following questions by carefully reviewing the authors' arugments and writing strategies from the short essay.

1. Examine the use of classification in the text.

2. Examine the development of the essay. What is the goal of each paragraph, and how does each paragraph relate to the suggested solution proposed in the latter part of the essay?

3. Underline the transitions from paragraph to paragraph, and examine their effectiveness.

8 The Value of Life

Imagine for a second that you live in a neighborhood that is inhabited by hard-working, law-abiding families in pursuit of the "American Dream." Slowly, however, the neighborhood begins to deteriorate when a few "bad seeds" move in. Pretty soon, crime goes up in the area; there are more burglaries, more assaults, and more "suspicious" traffic on the local streets. One man in particular becomes quite busy selling drugs on the street corner, exchanging small dime bags of crack a block down from the local high school. You call the police, but the drug dealer is crafty and ditches his stash every time before the police show up. The police are frustrated because they can never nail him for anything, nor can they rely on any informants, for there are "repercussions." Anyone suspicious of calling the police hotline is beaten up and left with broken bones; after that, no one dares press charges. This goes on for years. Finally, in the middle of the night, you hear yet another siren, and you think this must be another overdose from the drug house down the street. This time, however, the police come for the murdered body of the drug dealer, shot through the chest with seven bullets.

After a **meticulous** investigation, the police eventually arrest the principal of the local middle school. At first you are shocked thinking this is some kind of horrific mistake. Would a person in such a position—a former teacher with a doctorate in education no less—have committed this crime? However, on the steps of the courthouse, the principal steps up to the sea of microphones and exclaims in a clear voice, "I shot this known drug dealer, this known **menace** to society. I do not deny it. In fact, I celebrate that I did it. I acted on behalf of the community to preserve our way of life when the police would not or could not act. This **scourge** to the community infected our children with his poison, sowing only death and destruction." To this, the principal's lawyer rushes to add that "the defendant will be pleading not guilty."

The first impulse might be to stand up and shout support for the principal, for his act cut down drug sales by 70% in the neighborhood. Not only that, the act itself may have prevented some of the middle-school-age children from becoming addicted to crack. Indeed, the families who had been victimized and threatened by the drug dealer come out in support of the principal, organizing a defense fund and writing letters to the prosecutor for dismissal of the charges. However, what might appear at first to be "poetic justice" for the drug dealer does not equate to justice within the law. While the lay person's reaction may be of support and grate-

45

fulness to the school principal, the law, on the other had, is black and white. **Premeditated** murder (murder one) only means many years in prison, if not the death penalty even for the wayward principal. So the whole case brings up an important **conundrum** in **jurisprudence**: should the value of the life of the victim be a factor in deciding whether a crime was committed or in imposing the penalty for the crime?

4   Current laws allow for some affirmative defenses in which defendants admit to committing a crime, but they claim to have **mitigating** reasons for doing so. For instance, a schizophrenic with a documented medical condition could claim not guilty by reason of mental defect (an insanity defense). A husband who finds his wife in bed with another man might claim not guilty by reason of extreme emotional disturbance (he was out of his mind when he killed the offending couple). A police officer who kills a suspect brandishing a weapon could claim self-defense (an imminent threat to a person). In certain occasions, then, the law recognizes these mitigating factors in determining either whether a person should be **indicted** or what penalty is warranted, should a defendant be found guilty. However, the value of the victim's life has traditionally not been considered as one of those mitigating factors, a principle that often finds its expression in the phrase "the victim is not the one under trial."

5   Therefore, in our current example, the principal's **culpability** or punishment would not be decided on the value or lack thereof of the drug dealer's life even though the latter was apparently a really terrible person, a very dangerous individual. The question then is whether this is fair and just. If most people consider the principal's act as heroic rather than criminal, then shouldn't the law take that into consideration? Shouldn't the value of the victim's life be taken into account in judging the murderer? Furthermore, should the principal-murderer of a drug dealer be punished equally to the murderer of a dedicated doctor? After all, it seems like the principal did society a favor while the murderer of a dedicated doctor deprived society of one of its most needed members.

6   Some would say that if the law holds the value of each individual's life to be the same, then there should not even be a debate on this issue; however, this is not an **axiom**. Indeed, the laws in every society represent the values that society holds, and these values are not absolute, for there is a constant negotiation between the law and the value system people in the community hold. Therefore, even this principle of "each life is equally valuable" is open to negotiation and reevaluation. However, if such a negotiation is to occur, there are many factors to be taken into account. Indeed, if we were to admit such an argument in imposing a penalty in a murder case, then we should consider what criteria should be adopted for estimating the "value of life." What determines the "value of life"? Certainly, the drug dealer-principal example seems like a simple one, but even in this case one could argue that by examining the drug dealer's life, this person never had a chance in becoming something better because he grew up in absolute poverty and

was turned into a drug addict and dealer by his crack-addict parents. On the other hand, one could argue that the dedicated doctor of the reverse example grew up in a middle-class family with the privileges of caring parents and the finances to pursue a higher education. Even if one were to say that the value of one's life should be judged independently from societal factors, then what about society's shift in standards? What would be the standards for "life value": age, kindness, money, education, fame, what? It would be pretty complex then to estimate this value and to make a law with a chart of specific life-value criteria.

Of course, society could leave this decision up to the judge of each case, which seems to actually be the current trend in the legal system. Actually, in its most recent "negotiation" the criminal system has implicitly given judges the discretion to factor the value of an individual's life in imposing penalties. This has taken concrete form with an important recent Supreme Court decision, U.S. v. Booker, January, 2005, which, by repealing mandatory federal sentencing requirements for some cases, it gave federal judges much more discretion in deciding what penalties to enforce based on the specific elements of the case; the decision now allows judges to consult the penalty statutes as mere "guidelines," not as mandatory requirements. 7

The Supreme Court decision U.S. v. Booker is, therefore, having important ripple effects throughout the criminal justice system by granting much more authority to sitting judges. This indicates that there is a shift in the criminal justice system towards evaluating the situation rather than the black-and-white violation of the law, a veritable situation ethics dilemma. In judging a murder case, then, the victim could be "put on trial" to have the value of their life determined by a judge. Initially, this might sound like an excellent idea, for the principal of our example might be even set free. However, this may lead to a slippery slope of adjudicating cases fairly. If there are no standard criteria set by the law and not the judges as to what is the value of life of each individual, there could be many discrepancies. If one defendant, for instance, draws a liberal judge while another defendant draws a more conservative judge, there could be substantial differences in their evaluation of otherwise similar cases. One should then wonder about the extent of judicial discretion: simply put, should it be the judges or the people through their legislators to decide which life is more valuable? 8

Therefore, the issues of evaluating "life" are quite complex if we are to admit that each person's life is not as valuable as another's. Should there be a difference in the value of life of individuals and even if there should, who would determine the criteria for value? Those are pertinent issues that society should consider before granting anyone with the power to distinguish between valuable and valueless lives. 9

Discussing and Writing About The Text

Discussing Issues:

Make a list of cases you are aware of or of hypothetical ones in which you think the "value of life" should be a mitigating factor in the court's decision. Discuss your findings with your peers, and try to determine whether there are common criteria for the "value of life" among the cases discussed.

Writing about the Text:

In a well-developed and organized essay, respond to the reading; be sure to support your views with pertinent examples drawn from your own experience and observations, as well as readings.

Topic 1: What do the authors believe in terms of the value of life? To what extent— if at all—do you agree with their suggestions?

Topic 2: According to your opinion, which route should societies choose in determining the "value of life"? If the life of individuals is to be valued differently, what should be the criteria for this evaluation? To support your opinion, you need to examine relevant and specific examples from a variety of sources.

Developing Vocabulary:

The words below may appear as part of your online quizzes. Please refer to the introduction for study strategies for learning vocabulary.

1. meticulous
2. menace
3. scourge
4. premeditated
5. conundrum
6. jurisprudence
7. mitigating
8. indicted
9. culpability
10. axiom

Understanding the Text

Answer the following questions by carefully reviewing the authors' aruguments in the short essay.

1. Is the "value of life" a mitigating factor in imposing a penalty to a defendant?

2. What do the authors think would be the problems with determining the "value of one's life"?

3. What seems to be the effect of the U.S. v. Booker Supreme Court decision?

4. What are the authors' concerns about the above case?

Analyzing Writing

Answer the following questions by carefully reviewing the authors' aruguments and writing strategies from the short essay.

1. What is the authors' thesis and where is it situated in the text? Explain how this thesis is different or similar to other theses in argumentative essays.

2. Find the focus-theme of each paragraph, and write it in the margin. Is each paragraph organized around a specific focus or not?

3. Examine the role of questions in this essay; how do questions affect the authors' argument and overall rhetoric?

9 In Defense of Superstitions

Imagine you are on your way to the airport when you cross a black cat, trip underneath a ladder, think you saw your dead grandmother when you step on a crack in the concrete, flag down a taxi with the cab number 666 and a trip **odometer** that reads 13.00 dollars, and mistakenly open your umbrella inside the airport, which you only brought because you saw a dog eating grass the day before. As if all this weren't enough, your flight is on Friday the 13th. Will you still take the flight with all the omens screaming you shouldn't? Well, maybe if you stuffed your suitcase with rabbit paws, it might be safe. Or perhaps you could phone your aunt from the airport to have her remove the evil eye from you because you are sure you've been hexed. Or maybe the bell you just heard tinkle means the angel that just got its wings will help protect you on your flight. If knocking on wood doesn't help ward off what is coming, you could remove the horse shoe from your luggage and try to bring it as carry-on. Hmmm…. Perhaps there's a four-leaf clover in the grass by the terminal entrance?

1

Although it isn't politically (or scientifically) correct to admit, most of us share one **superstition** or another, despite the fact that superstitions have no basis in science. In fact, science has sought to discredit superstitions as the **drivel** of ignorant masses who simply don't know any better. Anyone, they say, who has ever heard of **empirical** data or the scientific method, could not believe in superstitious nonsense. Yet a startling number of Americans engage in superstitious activities. Just ask the local athlete who always wears the same shoes before a game, or the lawyer who has a lucky pen, or the gambler who blows on the dice for luck. Plenty of people believe in superstitions despite the **mounds** of scientific evidence indicating that these notions are bunk.

2

Almost all superstitions boil down to the central **tenet** that signs, ritualistic actions, augurs, charms, incantations, or medallions can influence the future either for good or ill. According to superstitious belief, it is possible through the recognition of signs or through some kind of intervention to alter or influence causality. One can, in essence, change bad luck to good or create even more possibilities for **fortuitous** events to happen. Sitting in unlucky row 13 on an airline, for instance, might be inciting ill luck and should be avoided whenever possible;

3

but this bad luck might be avoided by carrying some kind of good luck talisman such as a medallion or a rabbit's foot. Does it sound ludicrous? Well, the airlines Air France, KLM, and Continental Airlines don't even have a row 13 because passengers never want to sit in these seats; plenty of hotels across the country don't have room 13 or 666. People are especially sensitive about Friday the 13th so much so that The Stress Management Center and Phobia Institute in Asheville, North Carolina estimates that stress induced by fear of Friday the 13th costs businesses around $900 million in lost time due to lost worker productivity or sickness.

Science explains these effects as "psycho-somatic." Basically, the mind is a powerful force on the body, and it creates the symptoms due to increased levels of stress and fear. This can weaken an immune system, causing people to get sick. Likewise, a host of other superstitions and their effects can be explained scientifically through the tricks the mind plays on the body. The athlete who forgets to wear the same shoes for a game may not be able to concentrate fully on the performance. The gambler might blame a losing streak not on statistics and probability, but on the lack of adequately blowing on the dice. For every superstition, there is a scientific reason for its **debunking**.

But are all superstitions necessarily meaningless and worthless as science would have us believe? No. Superstitions fulfill a cultural function and sit at the crossroads between science and religion. Whereas science seeks rational, human-oriented explanations for worldly phenomena, religion seeks answers through a higher power. Superstitions sit somewhere in between. They show a common human concern with the supernatural and the seemingly human need to attempt to understand and influence it. Ironically, even as science progresses and more about the operation of the universe is discovered, people seem even more interested in things supernatural. Just look at the success of shows like *The Twilight Zone* or more recently *The X-Files*. Both of these shows investigate **paranormal** activities, invoking along the way an array of superstitions. Moreover, these shows cater to a seemingly human need to believe in something other than the straight facts science can offer.

Not all superstitions are silly. Plenty of superstitions have roots in folk traditions and had practical value to those who believed. For instance, in folklore tradition garlic was thought to ward off the evil eye and keep away harmful demons and spirits. Although this sounds ludicrous to many, science has since proven the real medicinal effects of garlic, which can assist the immune system in warding off the common cold, treat symptoms of acne, manage high cholesterol levels, and even act as a mosquito repellent—a natural prevention of malaria. While folklore codes the use of garlic in supernatural terminology, garlic is scientifically proven to have actual health benefits.   7

    Besides practical importance, superstitions also function to remind us of important historical events, a kind of a common memory device ingrained in folk's minds. For instance, Friday the 13th, of which so many harbor some kind of fear, originally probably dates back to the arrest and slaughter of the Knights Templar in 1307 by Philip IV of France, which reflected at the time a major shift in power and economic resources to the King of France. While over the last 700 years specific memory of the event has been lost by most, the **vestige** of the event remains in our cultural memory. Terrible things may happen out of the blue on Friday the 13th just like they did to the Knights Templar.   8

    The point about superstitions is not that they should all be believed, practiced, or condemned out of hand. While they may not have a direct scientific value and taken too far they can paralyze personal action and endeavor, they do serve cultural, practical, and historical functions. People are far too likely to summarily condemn superstitions without first considering what caused them to come to exist in the first place or what their social significance is. Think about that the next time you boast about your brand-new car and then you knock on wood. The lesson here may not be about the wood preventing a car accident; it may be a cultural lesson about bragging.

Discussing and Writing About The Text

Discussing Issues:

Try to think of superstitions you have or you are familiar with. How much do you allow superstitions to affect your life? Discuss your finding with other students and construct a list of the most common or popular superstitions in your class. Then try to find if there could be a logical explanation behind them.

Writing about the Text:

In a well-developed and organized essay, respond to the reading; be sure to support your views with pertinent examples drawn from your own experience and observations, as well as readings.

Topic 1: Why does the author believe superstitions should not be absolutely debased? To what extent—if at all—do you agree with this view point?

Topic 2: According to your opinion, how could an absolute belief in superstition or science benefit or harm a society?

Developing Vocabulary:

The words below may appear as part of your online quizzes. Please refer to the introduction for study strategies for learning vocabulary.

1. odometer
2. superstition
3. drivel
4. empirical
5. mounds
6. tenet
7. fortuitous
8. debunking
9. paranormal
10. vestige

CHAPTER
TWO

Society

10 The McMore Factor

Americans are plagued by the McMore Factor, the 1
desire for and the ability to get more of everything.
From fast food to shoes, Americans seem to have an
insatiable desire to buy more of what they don't need.
The most **visceral** example of this can be seen in the
fast food industry. When Americans order a hamburger meal at McDonalds or virtually any other fast
food joint nowadays, there is always the option to
have it super-sized for an extra dollar or two. This "value" provides the consumer
with a substantial additional amount of food for comparatively little extra money.
Who wouldn't want that kind of deal? The problem is that the estimation of the
"more" has been all fouled up. For example, in the 1950s McDonalds offered one
size of french fry; now, the same size is considered small while the "large" fry **su-
persedes** the 1950's version by over two thirds. The bargain super-sized fries are
even bigger. This size disorientation is not limited to french fries. **By the same
token**, today's large sodas are nearly one third larger than the previous "large,"
and stores like 7/11 advertise the cost/benefit of super sizing. A 16-ounce drink
costs the consumer about 5 cents per ounce whereas a 32 ounce drink costs only
2.7 cents per oz. The economic advantages of "more" are clear even if more is not
needed. Buy more, save more. Well, the marketplace has fully honored this trend.
According to a 2002 study in the *American Journal of Public Health*, food portion
sizes have exploded in nearly every capacity, which **obscure**s the standards for
average, normal, or healthy. Americans don't seem to even know what an average portion is, especially when they can always buy "more" for less.

For the average American "more" has become synonymous with better and 2
quality synonymous with quantity. The examples that bear testimony to this are
abundant, and it isn't only the food portions that have grown larger. Since the
1950s, normal house sizes have ballooned from the average 950 square feet for a
single family residence to a monstrous 2,300 square feet by 2004. Many advertisements **vaunt** the possibility of buying more house for less money with upwards
of six or seven bedrooms in 3,000 square feet or more single family residences.
These huge houses are then accessorized with the standard three to four garages
in anticipation of the family's car needs. Indeed, according to the Federal Highway Administration, the number of cars per household increased by 70% from

1969 to 2001. In addition to the number of cars per household, the size of the vehicles has grown exponentially as well. Leading the "more" pack for the last ten years is the best symbol of the "McMore Factor," Sport Utility Vehicles (SUVs). Advertisements brag about their power, their ability to haul tons of supplies, and their increased horse power. SUVs have consistently led the market, accounting for most of the growth in automobile sales in the last ten years although increased gas prices have put a dent into these numbers.

3   These are only samples of the McMore Factor, for the latter is certainly not limited to fast food, houses, or cars. This new consumerist ideology is present in nearly every aspect of the American society. Super deals and super sales **lure** Americans in droves to the mall on a weekly basis, regardless of our actual needs; advertisements for virtually anything invariably offer something "more" or "bigger" than the competitor. "Buy one and get one half off" has become a sales flyer favorite. We buy and buy, desiring more and more. This greed then translates into interesting phenomena such as obese people, obese houses, or the 75% increase in the number of Americans who use storage facilities since 1995, for even their oversized houses cannot hold all their "stuff."

4   The McMore Factor has severe and detrimental consequences in nearly every walk of life. Because the desire for more has unbalanced and **skewed** any hierarchy of needs, few people actually bother to evaluate what they need. Instead, the primary focus is on what kind of deal can be had and how much can be saved by buying in bulk. Across the board, consumers forget to ask or evaluate what any actual needs might be because the whole system is skewed. Who asks whether a bigger hamburger or more fries are needed when the cost is a few extra cents? In their bid for more of everything, Americans are doing irreparable harm to themselves and their environment.

5   Our bodies don't need super-sized meals as the caloric intake far exceeds our energy requirements, and the results of this over-consumption are disastrous. Obesity rates have never been higher. Houses for families of three or four don't need to be 3,000 square feet. No one asks if the second pair of shoes listed for 50% off is good or needed. Furthermore, Americans buy SUVs with tons of hauling power when there is nothing to haul, just in case it might be necessary. Americans buy the PC with all the extra features that will never be used, again just in case….We all end up purchasing far more than is needed because the entire idea of need has been warped by over-consumption.

6   What is even more worrisome is that our expectations have risen to **unsustainable** levels for the environment. If every household in the world had the same consumption patterns and living arrangements as households in the U. S., the

effects on the environment would be disastrous, according to a 2003 article in the journal *Nature*. Although environmentalists and scientists have become hoarse warning us that the environment simply cannot sustain the burdens that are placed upon it, especially if development for countries like China and India comes in the shape and form of the American over-consumptive lifestyle, who is listening? This is not to say that Americans are the only ones to blame, nor should McDonalds or SUVs be scapegoated as the primary sinners. Increased consumption in China, in particular, as evidenced by their plan to install a new coal-fired power plant every week for the next seven years shows the adoption of consumption lifestyles by many people abroad. The Chinese are simply symptomatic of the desire for more that can be observed in nearly every industrialized nation, where similar growth patterns develop when "more" becomes socially desirable.

To what seems an **ominous** reality, there is no easy answer, for Western industrialized societies, especially the United States and countries in the European Union, have been organized around consumption both economically and socially. Consumers have been taught by advertisements, systematic sales, and social valuation that buying more is simply better and economically beneficial. Indeed, the McMore Factor **pervades** every part of modern society, and it won't be easy to change, despite the warnings by health officials and environmentalists.

For a small minority, the pendulum swing may already have begun, the motion of which may be evidenced through the popularity of books and films that criticize the culture of more. The message is finally getting out about fast food and the dangers of over-consumption with books and movies such as *Fast Food Nation* or *Super Size Me*. Some people have even founded organizations such as the small house movement that is dedicated to building smaller houses that don't sacrifice a quality existence. This group contends that a small house has the further benefit of not allowing much space for collecting superfluous stuff. These authors and groups are at the vanguard of the new trend to analyze, evaluate, measure, and redefine needs. Moreover, it is imperative that people, especially Americans, recognize that more is not necessarily better. The damage to our waist lines as well as the environment can testify to that. In fact, maybe everyone ought to learn that sometimes more is less.

7

8

Discussing and Writing About The Text

Discussing Issues:

Think of ways the McMore Factor has affected your life as a person, student, or consumer. Try to evaluate the advantages and disadvantages of this influence and discuss your conclusions with your peers.

Writing about the Text:

In a well-developed and organized essay, respond to the reading; be sure to support your views with pertinent examples drawn from your own experience and observations, as well as readings.

Topic 1: According to the authors, what is the McMore Factor and what are its effects? To what extent and why do you agree with the authors' overall condemnation of this desire for more?

Topic 2: According to your opinion, what could help the American society reevaluate its standards and needs?

Developing Vocabulary:

The words below may appear as part of your online quizzes. Please refer to the introduction for study strategies for learning vocabulary.

1. visceral	2. supersedes
3. by the same token	4. obscures
5. to vaunt	6. to lure
7. to skew	8. unsustainable
9. ominous	10. pervades

Understanding the Text

Answer the following questions by carefully reviewing the authors' aruguments in the short essay.

1. What is the "McMore Factor" and what are its symptoms?

2. What are the causes of this desire for more in the American society?

3. What are the effects of this desire for more in the American society?

4. What are some of the counterarguments the authors have included?

Analyzing Writing

Answer the following questions by carefully reviewing the authors' arugments and writing strategies from the short essay.

1. Examine the use of cause and effect analysis in the text.

2. Find the focus-theme of each paragraph, and write it in the margin next to each paragraph. Is each paragraph organized around a specific focus or not?

3. Examine the use of sources in the essay. What kind of sources do the authors use (personal examples-anecdotes, facts, authorities, etc)? Do you think they are appropriate and convincing? What additional sources would you use?

11 The Simpler Life

Paris Hilton has never been one to shy away from media attention or to utilize her **notoriety** in her four-teenth-minute of fame for **self-aggrandization**. But her TV show "The Simple Life," co-starring Nicole Richie, shamelessly capitalizes on and exploits a new popular movement in the United States: the return to a simple life. In the series, Hilton and her co-star Richie inexpertly perform work of various kinds in racy overalls and halter tops. The appeal of the program, of course, is not to learn how one milks a cow, cleans a horse stall, or builds a carburetor, but it is to **juxtapose** Hilton and Richie's otherwise lavish lifestyle to the modified daily routine of laborers. What is most interesting about the show, however, is its contribution to the evolving debate in the U.S. and other developed countries over lifestyle choices, over-consumption, and the return to a less-demanding and complicated life often synonymous to a life closer to nature.

While the appeal of returning to an unbounded nature has inspired famous philosophers and writers such as Rousseau, Thoreau, or Emerson, for most of human existence people have been striving for the more "complicated" life of abundant consumer goods and technological advances that alleviate them from la-borious chores and make their lives easier. In short, people have dreamed of the Hilton lifestyle or at least of one that is relieved from the cares of everyday exis-tence. The dream of progress has been for ages to create technology that would simplify daily tasks and create an environment of ease in which people control machines that do most of the work. Therefore, how is it that despite irrefutable technological achievements, there are people that crave this return to a life that negates these achievements? Although technology and consumer goods have cer-tainly improved our lives on an exponential scale, they have also made it undesir-ably complicated.

This is where people like Dave Wampler, founder of the Simple Living Network back in 1985, come in. According to those ascribing to the "simple life" framework, computers, TVs, PDA organizers, GPS systems, new cars, Ipods, and any number of new inventions, and especially material goods above people's pay grade, simply complicate life and force them to work increasingly harder to main-tain the things they own or loan. Furthermore, because people work harder, they

1

2

3

have less time for themselves, for family, for friends, for exercising, for traveling, for overall enjoying life; however, they compensate for this lack of fulfillment by purchasing more stuff to fill their already stuffed closets. When the closets and garages are not enough, people look to other places for storage solutions. To this attests the **proliferation** of self-storage facilities in the United States with approximately 44,000 facilities encompassing 1.5 billion square feet.

4   To avoid falling victim to these trends, simple life **advocates** argue that we should reorient our lives with three principles in mind: 1) Reevaluate our hierarchy of needs; 2) Work less, earn less, buy less; 3) Live in a manner that will not impact the environment negatively. These seem like reasonable suggestions to adjust one's lifestyle, yet there still remain certain issues with the movement and its wider portrayal in society.

5   The first problem is that the kind of simple life that is promoted is often so antithetical to the average lifestyle that people may not even try to simplify. For example, the 1997 PBS special entitled *Affluenza* depicts the life of a family of four who suffered from **affluenza**, a social malady that has over-consumption as its main symptom. Determined to recover from this "disease," the family underwent a lifestyle adjustment and became able to survive on one income, grow their own food, make most of their own clothes or buy them from thrift stores, and also rid themselves of unnecessary "gadgets" such as a TV, a computer, or a car. Although their efforts and achievements are admirable and their tactics certainly cut down on monthly expenses, would this dramatic change be **plausible** to the average citizen? Is it likely that most people would even try or be able to grow their own food or make their own clothes? Even more so, the video makes the simple life look like a curse of poverty, not a conscious choice to simplify life's cares. Last but not least, this version of simple life relies on the over-consumption of others in the purchasing of second or third-hand items. There have to be consumers who throw out useable goods that can then be recycled through thrift stores.

6   The second major problem is that those in developing nations already have "the simple life," and they don't want it. How can Western residents, for the Simple Life Movement is almost entirely a movement within industrialized countries, tell citizens in traditionally impoverished countries that they shouldn't pursue a more comfortable life, they should not buy a new TV, a car, or new clothes, for they simply don't need these things? The poor in other countries see consumer goods as an outward sign of prosperity and wealth—a way to enter the global community and show off their new found success—and who are we to forbid them that? Citizens in industrialized countries, weighed down by consumer goods, have the luxury of returning to a simple life, many times with hefty savings accounts or

401Ks in case of emergencies. The simple life is seen as a possible, environmentally friendly choice, but it is, after all, a choice. On the other hand, is a financial setback, a lost job, or an injury that creates so-called new circumstances labeled as "the simple life"? Of course, people think of their reduced financial capacity as a significant blow to their family's future. Overall and to a great degree, people in developing nations may currently lead a "simple life," but they definitely don't entirely want it. Many among them don't want to wake up at dawn and milk the cow; they just want the bottled milk.

In conclusion, many of the representative examples of the simple life movement are too extreme. What is needed instead is a "simpler life" movement, one that seeks to moderate our current over-consumptive lifestyles. This modified approach has a number of advantages. First, since the U.S. economy relies heavily on consumer spending, the economy won't collapse because of a consumption halt. Second, people will be able to reevaluate their needs and gradually adjust to more moderate consumption habits. If not getting rid of their car and throwing away the key, they could buy a new car every eight or ten years rather than every two. A simpler life does not mean that a person should have no pleasure goods or new clothes. It means there should be a rational limit. A handbag should not cost $200.00 to purchase, and a person earning $30,000 a year should not purchase a $35,000 BMW. Third, adjusting our lifestyles has to take time. Going from mega-consumers to growing our own food and buying third-hand sofas cannot work as a solution, nor can it be appealing to the average person in the U.S. or other industrialized countries.

7

The family in the PBS *Affluenza* special represents one extreme in which the family almost appears **impoverished**; Hilton's and Richie's Simple Life represents the other extreme, an exaggerated version of Western **hubris**. Indeed, it's easy to have a simple life if we can leave it at any time and return to an extravagant and **opulent** lifestyle. Living simply should not be about one extreme or the other; it should be about moderation, common sense, and the consideration of our actions' impact on the environment.

8

Discussing and Writing About The Text

Discussing Issues:

Do you think you or your family suffers from "affluenza"? If so, in what ways? What do you think are the effects of affluenza on you or your family? Should you try to moderate your life style and make your life simpler? If yes, how can you achieve this moderation?

Writing about the Text:

In a well-developed and organized essay, respond to the reading; be sure to support your views with pertinent examples drawn from your own experience and observations, as well as readings.

Topic 1: Why do the authors advocate a simpler life? To what extent—if at all—do you find this suggestion valid and plausible?

Topic 2: Watch an episode of "The Simple Life" or a show like it and try to evaluate its messages and the values that are being promoted.

Developing Vocabulary:

The words below may appear as part of your online quizzes. Please refer to the introduction for study strategies for learning vocabulary.

1. notoriety
2. self-aggrandization
3. proliferation
4. advocates
5. to juxtapose
6. affluenza
7. plausible
8. impoverished
9. hubris
10. opulent

Understanding the Text

Answer the following questions by carefully reviewing the authors' aruguments in the short essay.

1. The title, "The Simpler Life," is juxtaposed to what other ways of life?

2. What is the "simple life" movement?

3. What do the authors see as problematic with the "simple life" movement and its depiction?

4. What is the authors' suggestion in the pursuit of lifestyle?

Analyzing Writing

Answer the following questions by carefully reviewing the authors' arugments and writing strategies from the short essay.

1. Examine the use of classification in the text.

2. Examine the contextualization and integration of sources in the text.

3. Examine five word choices that seem interesting and effective.

12 Buying the Lifestyle

Imagine you are floating on your back in the pool of a cliff top house overlooking the ocean. The pool blends with the horizon, and the only sound you can hear is that of the water as it **cascades** into the nothingness beyond. There is no human presence around you, other than your exotically tanned husband who is sipping on his margarita while adoringly looking at you through the spotless windows of your whitewashed house. An 80-inch flat screen TV hangs on a wall above an equally imposing fire place, a modern leather sofa nestles a white Persian cat with piercing blue eyes, and a pile of art books is scattered on the marble coffee table, displaying your knowledge and appreciation of the arts. There is nothing to disturb this **idyllic** scene. Nowhere in the picture are there maids lurching through the living room with a mop and bucket; nowhere is the pool maintenance guy with a skimmer and a container full of chlorine to disrupt your day dream; nowhere is there a sense that any effort is required to daily maintain—let alone acquire—this house on a cliff top above the ocean.

1

Images like this abound on TV and in magazines to sell not just specific products, but mostly a specific lifestyle; the issue, of course, is how one can attain and maintain this lifestyle? Is this lifestyle for the masses, as the ads are? For every couple in a fancy house on a cliff top overlooking the sea, there are thousands of others who live modest lives in small houses. Yet films and advertisements make it seem so easy for the viewer to "buy into" the dream because the dream is so pervasive. Interestingly enough, no one works in the dream, for there would be a danger for the viewer to mistake themselves for the workers at the scene rather than the owners of the house. The fantasy advertisements never show anyone actually doing any work, for there is a total disconnection from reality. Wouldn't it be slightly disruptive to see the couple getting up early to commute from the cliff top to a **hectic** job? Or see how impractical it is to keep all those magazines and expensive knickknacks all over the place when someone tries to dust them? The advertisements are not selling reality; they are selling dreams and illusions to the masses through a lifestyle accessible only to the very few and the very wealthy.

2

Indeed, buying the lifestyle is much harder than it looks, and this is one of the cruelest tricks of all, for it appears so easy—just a little hard work and presto,

3

house on a cliff. Few if any advertisements ever include any indication of the difficulties or steps a person has to take in order to achieve the lifestyle, for it is always already achieved. The average reader and viewer of these advertisements, who sees up to 3,000 ads per day, rarely thinks of the issues involved in having such a life. Take for example a recent student who in an essay detailed her attempt at becoming a "super model" because she wanted to be "filthy rich and famous" and own a million dollar house. Born and raised in average middle-class circumstances, she was initially obsessed with the idea, so much so that she enrolled herself in a pricey modeling school and bought all kinds of expensive designer clothes. The first classes went well because she got to wear some really fancy pieces and to learn to strut like models on the runway. However, she soon grew tired because later courses included intensive material on nutrition, dieting, financial planning, and the techniques of photography. She dropped out because the courses became too difficult and "boring."

4   This student is not alone in her dream of becoming rich and famous via the easy and fast lane. The proliferation of shows like *American Idol*, *Survivor*, *The Apprentice*, *Fame Story*, or *Who Wants to be a Millionaire*, just to name a few, offer normal people the chance to step from rags to riches without the inconvenience of working like a slave or marrying into old money. Is it by chance that *American Idol*, for instance, is one of the most watched shows on television? What is the source of its popularity? Part of the allure is certainly seeing the "unsuccessful" contestants who perform despite not having any talent. Even the judges sometimes **cringe** when hearing or seeing such performances. The other side, though, has to be the possibility of a big pay-off in money and fame without the struggle real life would impose. If anything, these shows are proof of the desire even desperation for these achievements.

5   Movies and TV shows are equally as **culpable**, and there are hundreds to choose from that promote, directly or indirectly, the lifestyle of the rich and famous even when it is not important to the story at all. Take for example the **imminently** forgettable movie, *Rumor Has It*, starring Kevin Costner, Jennifer Aniston, and Mark Ruffalo. Aniston's character is billed as middle class, which accompanies her job as obituary writer for a local newspaper. Her fiancée is a successful lawyer (Ruffalo), and she nearly disrupts their engagement by falling in love with a big time entrepreneur (Costner), who happens to be a billionaire. The disturbing thing about this movie is not so much the implausible plot development; it is the default position of wealth. Aniston's family owns a "modest," supposedly middle class house in Pasadena, California, which in today's money would be worth 1.5 million dollars. She lives with her fiancée in New York in a large apartment that

would certainly cost a million or more to buy. She falls in love with a billionaire who has his own private jet, landing strip, super-sized villa, and apparently a lot of free time to enjoy. How did those elements find their way into a supposedly realistic story about you and me and your average person in a quest for identity and meaningful human relationships?

The fantasy of such a lifestyle is incredibly effective, but its effects carry with it a collective social price far beyond the cost of the expensive house or its **accoutrements**. The first problem is that massive wealth is considered the normal, default position, but little is ever shown as to how that wealth is attained or maintained. That would disrupt the fantasy. Advertisements, TV shows, and movies rarely show the disruption of the fantasy by including all the hard working support staff or possibly the seventy-hour per week professions required to make so much money.   6

The more **invidious** problem is that normal and average people are most likely to feel inferior for not measuring up to all the fantasy standards. Thousands upon thousands of ads every day collectively take their toll on people, burdening their psyches with feelings of lack. Sound ludicrous? The statistics don't lie. The average American household has roughly $10,000 dollars of credit card debt. The average new car purchase comes with a loan of $24,000 dollars. People are living beyond their means, buying the material items they see in the advertisements. The problem is that people want the fantasy of the cliff top house, they want the wealth, they want the private jet, and some even want the fame, but this is well beyond the reach of 99% of the population even though plenty reach for it with the aid of credit cards and numerous loans.   7

The student who wanted to be a supermodel is a good example of the effects of such a bombardment of these images of wealth without boundaries. She worked after school every day to earn enough money for the modeling classes. She sacrificed her study time **in lieu** of taking Advanced Placement courses to get into a good college. The cumulative effect was that she felt like a failure after she dropped out. Because she had paid so much for the school, she had to take an additional loan to finance her college tuition. Unfortunately, the fantasy lifestyle portrayed in nearly every media has real world effects, ranging from a constant feeling of **inadequacy** to possible bankruptcy for those who try to buy the lifestyle without having the means.   8

Discussing and Writing About The Text

Discussing Issues:

Make a list of your dreams and aspirations as well as your plans in order to realize these dreams. Discuss the compatibility between the two with your peers. How much have your dreams been influenced by ads or shows like the ones mentioned in the essay?

Writing about the Text:

In a well-developed and organized essay, respond to the reading; be sure to support your views with pertinent examples drawn from your own experience and observations, as well as readings.

Topic 1: According to the authors, what are the problems posed by the media-proposed lifestyle? To what extent do you find the authors' arguments and concerns valid?

Topic 2: Describe your dream house, its location, accoutrements, and features. Next, try to find this dream house on the Internet and provide a realistic estimate about how much it would cost and what it would take you in your chosen profession to acquire this house.

Developing Vocabulary:

The words below may appear as part of your online quizzes. Please refer to the introduction for study strategies for learning vocabulary.

1. cascades
2. idyllic
3. hectic
4. cringe
5. culpable
6. imminently
7. accoutrements
8. invidious
9. in lieu
10. inadequecy

would certainly cost a million or more to buy. She falls in love with a billionaire who has his own private jet, landing strip, super-sized villa, and apparently a lot of free time to enjoy. How did those elements find their way into a supposedly realistic story about you and me and your average person in a quest for identity and meaningful human relationships?

The fantasy of such a lifestyle is incredibly effective, but its effects carry with it a collective social price far beyond the cost of the expensive house or its **accoutrements**. The first problem is that massive wealth is considered the normal, default position, but little is ever shown as to how that wealth is attained or maintained. That would disrupt the fantasy. Advertisements, TV shows, and movies rarely show the disruption of the fantasy by including all the hard working support staff or possibly the seventy-hour per week professions required to make so much money.

6

The more **invidious** problem is that normal and average people are most likely to feel inferior for not measuring up to all the fantasy standards. Thousands upon thousands of ads every day collectively take their toll on people, burdening their psyches with feelings of lack. Sound ludicrous? The statistics don't lie. The average American household has roughly $10,000 dollars of credit card debt. The average new car purchase comes with a loan of $24,000 dollars. People are living beyond their means, buying the material items they see in the advertisements. The problem is that people want the fantasy of the cliff top house, they want the wealth, they want the private jet, and some even want the fame, but this is well beyond the reach of 99% of the population even though plenty reach for it with the aid of credit cards and numerous loans.

7

The student who wanted to be a supermodel is a good example of the effects of such a bombardment of these images of wealth without boundaries. She worked after school every day to earn enough money for the modeling classes. She sacrificed her study time **in lieu** of taking Advanced Placement courses to get into a good college. The cumulative effect was that she felt like a failure after she dropped out. Because she had paid so much for the school, she had to take an additional loan to finance her college tuition. Unfortunately, the fantasy lifestyle portrayed in nearly every media has real world effects, ranging from a constant feeling of **inadequacy** to possible bankruptcy for those who try to buy the lifestyle without having the means.

8

Discussing and Writing About The Text

Discussing Issues:

Make a list of your dreams and aspirations as well as your plans in order to realize these dreams. Discuss the compatibility between the two with your peers. How much have your dreams been influenced by ads or shows like the ones mentioned in the essay?

Writing about the Text:

In a well-developed and organized essay, respond to the reading; be sure to support your views with pertinent examples drawn from your own experience and observations, as well as readings.

Topic 1: According to the authors, what are the problems posed by the media-proposed lifestyle? To what extent do you find the authors' arguments and concerns valid?

Topic 2: Describe your dream house, its location, accoutrements, and features. Next, try to find this dream house on the Internet and provide a realistic estimate about how much it would cost and what it would take you in your chosen profession to acquire this house.

Developing Vocabulary:

The words below may appear as part of your online quizzes. Please refer to the introduction for study strategies for learning vocabulary.

1. cascades
2. idyllic
3. hectic
4. cringe
5. culpable
6. imminently
7. accoutrements
8. invidious

13 The Forged City

The Mall of America, located just outside of Bloomington, Minnesota, is **aptly** named, for it is not just the biggest mall complex in the world. The Mall of America is also a symbol of the ongoing transformation of town and city centers throughout the United States. Built in 1992, The Mall of America weighs in at a **gargantuan** 4.2 million square feet—the equivalent of seventy-three full-sized football fields of consumer space. With over 520 stores, twenty restaurants, thirty fast food joints, a cinema, seven night clubs, an amusement park, and a police station, The Mall of America seemingly has it all. Or almost all, for the building is not complete yet. A new construction phase has been initiated in order to include hotels, a conference facility, a business center, a recreation center, as well as additional stores and restaurants, which will add a whopping 5.7 million square feet to the mall's area. Soon enough The Mall of America might be renamed The City Mall of America, for one may never have to leave the Mall to find other things in other places. So, what could be so bad about that?

While the Mall of America is superlative in nearly every way, it merely represents the **apotheosis** in the shift in the organization and deployment of towns and cities across the continent. Similar inclusive multi-use mall structures have been built in suburban areas or near cities across the United States in the last two decades. Interestingly, these pedestrian area malls have taken the place of the traditional city-centers, the kind enjoyed throughout Europe, in parts of mostly the Eastern United States, and some parts of the West. In these traditional centers, laws prevented significant commercial growth in outlying areas, which forced stores and services to open up within one or more central areas, forming city-centers, downtowns, and piazzas.

Emulating these centers, places like the Mall of America boast nearly all the services that a regular city-center would have in a much more convenient package. Indeed, the 20,000 parking spaces, parking attendants, and free parking make this a snap. The climate-regulated interior keeps people comfortable all year round and saves them the definite torture of shopping outside during the freezing winters of Minnesota. The myriad stores, including a few non-chain stores, offer people innumerable options while at the same time attract millions of consumers from all

1

2

3

over the world. The theme park with all kinds of roller-coasters offers a safe and supervised playground that harbors overexcited or nagging children. The mall then boasts that there is no social need that it cannot satisfy. Indeed, one can even get married in the Mall, for there is even an affordable wedding chapel complete with a non-denominational priest to ensure an easy marriage; you can buy or rent your gown and tux in the store right next to the chapel, have your make-up and hair done, get married, sign the paperwork, and then celebrate, all in one place. There is no denying that these new articulations of city-centers, complete with all the services and shopping one needs, are often more convenient than traditional city-centers.

4   But where consumers may be content with the one-stop shop ideology, as the former governor of Minnesota, Jesse Ventura has called it, they may not have reflected on the underlying social, cultural, and personal freedoms that have been **abdicated** to the private sector in the name of convenience. These so-called city-centers have core-differences to real cities, for they have no elected officials, no responsibility to the real city, and no governance by the people. Unlike real citizens, visitors to the city-mall don't sit on boards or committees to decide the **disbursement** of resources; they are not **part and parcel** of creating a set of bylaws for behavior within the "city-center" mall. In short, the mall is privately owned, and these owners can decide to run it however they wish. Therefore, the mall's managers don't hold allegiance to nor have to answer to the "people" as would be the case with the administrators of actual cities, who would be accountable to the citizens; their only accountability is to their stock holders.

5   The realization of this ownership helps reveal the illusion most people have in malls across America: that one is truly free. This could not be further from reality. The truth is that in these so-called cities or city-centers, behavior is strictly controlled, more so than in regular city-centers. Can one, for instance, distribute political flyers in the mall or grab a soapbox to give a speech about our political leaders? Can one hand out petitions for various statewide propositions? Can one organize a demonstration in the city-center of a mall? The answer is that undesirable behavior, i.e. any behavior that disrupts the shopping process, is strictly controlled and can be banned. Therefore, people entering these malls are not citizens of these "city-centers," with the rights and privileges that accompany citizenship such as freedom of speech or even protest; they are mere visitors to a consumer space where they are expected to consume.

6   Now, supporters of such mall complexes may say that even in city-centers there are a great number of shops and restaurants, and one is "expected" to shop and dine. This is true, but it is also true that many "traditional" city-centers also

have public squares and parks where visitors can just sit down, read a book, feed the birds, or distribute political flyers. In traditional city-centers consumption is part of the environment, but it is not the whole part. So, in malls, for instance, there is an illusion that a visitor has so many options. Options to do what? Can one play hide and seek? Can one play hopscotch on the sidewalk? Can one invent one's game or way of entertainment? Probably not, for everything has been strategically designed to incite consumption in one way or another. All the apparent options one has are controlled by designers who carefully place stores and services in different areas of the mall based on the price of lease agreements for the stores.

Lastly, the new mall city-centers are not realistic or representative environments, for they filter out all elements deemed "undesirable" by the institutions that control them. In traditional downtown areas one can find the occasional homeless person, the beggar for change, the needy family. One can find a distinctly heterogeneous society, or in other words, one is forced to see the poor and the needy of society, and one may be prompted to think about these social problems, for this is reality. However, malls like The Mall of America **elide** and exclude these "distasteful" elements in the name of security, but mostly in the name of the shopping experience. The same security guards that circulate around these malls to ensure the safety of the merchandise and the customers are there to also ensure that real life will not distract consumers from the mall's artificial safe and happy **haven**. Indeed, the sight of an eight-year old child begging for change might be catastrophic for the potential buyer of that $3,000 Gucci purse. Thanks to security guards who "patrol" the mall, consumers are kept safe from shoplifters, and companies are kept safe from people like the eight-year-old beggar asking for the change from our Starbucks coffee and disrupting our view of the **impeccable** fountain in the middle of the Starbucks "piazza." Gradually and mistakenly people are **lulled** into forgetting that city malls are not real but artificial cities. Therefore, they should merely be perceived as market places. Even if they offer us a "more comfortable" environment, they cannot and should not replace traditional city centers where people don't necessarily have to buy anything to simply sit on a bench and experience the real "city."

7

Discussing and Writing About The Text

Discussing Issues:

In your class, vote for Mall city-centers or traditional ones. Each group should then list arguments and counterarguments for their thesis to participate in a debate on which city-center should be preferable and for what reasons.

Writing about the Text:

In a well-developed and organized essay, respond to the reading; be sure to support your views with pertinent examples drawn from your own experience and observations, as well as readings.

Topic 1: Why do the authors think Mall city-centers are unrealistic environments and should only be perceived as market places? To what extent—if at all—do you agree with the authors' concerns?

Topic 2: According to your opinion, what should be the elements to constitute a city-center? To support your opinion, you need to examine relevant and specific examples from a variety of sources.

Developing Vocabulary:

The words below may appear as part of your online quizzes. Please refer to the introduction for study strategies for learning vocabulary.

1.	aptly	2.	gargantuan
3.	apotheosis	4.	to abdicate
5.	disbursement	6.	part and parcel
7.	to elide	8.	haven
9.	impecable	10.	lulled

14 Public Space and Social Decorum

Cell phone usage is **rampant** in this day and age. So much so that performances, movies, and even classes regularly begin with the admonishment to turn off cell phones and to refrain from their use while doctors' offices and hospitals have signs forbidding cell phone calls within the confines of the facility. Yet, although the signs exist, one can hear their trespass with the loud voices of those talking into the ether. This seems like a minor infraction, not even worthy of a single sentence, but cell phones are just the tip of the iceberg of the increasing problem of social decorum in public spaces.

1

One disruptive person in a public space can perhaps be tolerated because he soon leaves, or it is possible to move away to another area. Now, however, too many people seem to be doing as they please when they please, which is bad news for the rest of us. This disturbing of the peace of others can be documented with any stroll down the local street to almost any public area. One of the most visible examples of this is smoking, for smokers often violate the no smoking signs in restaurants, bars, airports, lounges, and any number of other public spaces, and others are supposed to **inhale** the secondary smoke. After going out for a night on the town, a non-smoker might even have to dry clean their clothes to get the smoke smell out. Of course, trespass on public decorum doesn't stop there. One should not forget the most **egregious** threats against public decorum: permissive parents. These parents are the ones who allow their children to yell, scream, roll on the floor, and throw their toys about at the expense of everyone in their vicinity, but not at the expense of their children's so called "freedom of expression." Last but not least in this indicative list of public decorum violations come the blasting stereo systems only "cool" cars feature, which allow everyone to "share" the music even if no one likes it but the driver.

2

It would not be an overstatement to say that many people today have lost a sense of what constitutes acceptable behavior in public environments, for the trespass on others' right to peace has become the rule. It's too easy to dismiss those who complain or even speak up from time to time, labeling them as **curmudgeons** who want to return to the "oppressed" behavior fostered throughout much of the 1800s. Those who "trespass" on these supposed values ask in refu-

3

tation, "who are you to decide how I behave, what I do, or how loud I listen to my music?" Indeed, these are valid questions. Social decorum, after all, is not a hard and fast rule that was ratified by everyone on earth. In fact, some people even disagree about what the term means, arguing that different cultures, societies, and eras have different standards.

4   This may be true, but a very basic definition of social decorum can be of some assistance in determining what should be allowable. Social decorum might be termed as the commonly agreed upon standards of behavior in public that won't impede the comfort or social communication of others. To be sure, these standards have undeniably changed over time. In the 1800s, for instance, social decorum dictated that children were to be seen not heard. Children caught rolling around in a doctor's waiting room would have been punished, reprimanded, scolded, and possibly beaten for their social misdeeds if we are to believe the numerous manuals for etiquette and **deportment** published at the time. These manuals for rearing children included advice that children should only speak when spoken to, should never directly ask questions of adults, and should remain still, without fidgeting, when in the company of others.

5   Clearly, ideas about social deportment and decorum have changed since the nineteenth century, as is natural with any society that evolves. No one is suggesting that we return to the days when children could be beaten for **uttering** a sound. However, should we have gone to the opposite extreme where children in a doctor's office can scream or hide under chairs just because their happiness should not be disrupted? How can we decide on what constitutes appropriate behavior in public, or how can we judge when someone is being too sensitive to another's behavior? Indeed, it may well be the smoker, the cell phone user, or the parent who could be offended when they are asked to extinguish the cigarette, cease the call, or still the child? Who decides what is offensive or disturbing to whom?

6   One possible answer is the use of the Golden Rule: "Do onto others as you would have done onto you." This would seem like a logical way to determine social behavior. In this system, one is to behave in such a manner that if someone else in the room were doing the same thing, it would not be **bothersome**. However, the problem with this rule is that many people do not view their behavior as problematic or disturbing. They are in their own world, and they would certainly not be bothered should anyone else adopt the same behavior. Therefore, cell phone users are not annoyed with others who talk on cell phones even at the top of their voice; smokers are certainly not inconvenienced by other smokers; parents with unsupervised children are not typically disturbed by other children acting the same

way; and of course people with blasting stereo systems can hardly hear anything above their favorite song unless, of course, it comes from a more powerful sound system.

Consequently, the Golden Rule has not proven **efficacious** in determining the standard for tolerable behavior in public, for people too often do not evaluate their behavior in connection with those around them. But even if they do notice that their behavior is disturbing others, they are unlikely to stop it. The cell phone user, the smoker, the parent, all place their individual desires and needs above those of the strangers in their midst. What is interesting here is that the Golden Rule, although supposedly aimed at maintaining social relationships and social civility when people gather, is fundamentally about self-interest. Indeed, let us not forget the second half of the aphorism to do onto others, "as you would have done unto you." 7

Another option might be a much needed revision of the Golden Rule. Instead, it should read, "do onto others as *they* would have done onto them." This alteration switches the focus of proper behavior and decorum from the "I" to the "They." Where the first formulation is that of so-called "enlightened self-interest," the second is that of citizens concerned for each other. In this way, the cell phone user might think for a second about the people around him before **hollering** into the phone, not about what he would like as behavior. The smoker might consider the confined space and the likelihood that others around him might dislike the smoke. The parents might consider that not everyone is used to children. Why is this needed? What's the big deal? Well, the future of our common social spaces is at stake. If trends continue as they are, every doctor's office will be filled with misbehaving children and adults screaming on their cell phones. Every car will come equipped with a trunk full of speakers and sub-woofers, so the music can be turned up to ear-splitting **decibels**. Every public space will become a collection of private spheres controlled by the whims of individuals, regardless of the effect on anyone else. This might be fine if the number of public spaces were infinite and if it were possible to move away from offending individuals. They are not. Should a family in a public park be forced to pack up their Sunday afternoon picnic because another family is blasting music through a monstrous CD-player? Should the patient forego the doctor's appointment because she can't stand the screaming kids in the waiting room? Should the safety of passengers on an airline be endangered because a smoker just had to get a fix? No. It's time that the Golden Rule is changed to focus on the comfort of the many, not that of the few or the one. 8

Discussing and Writing About The Text

Discussing Issues:

The authors employ a number of extended examples and few statistics. Do you think these examples are sufficient evidence to illustrate a problem with social decorum? Do you have any personal experience of similar behaviors to those described in the essay? Should anything be done about the supposed "trespass" on decorum? If so, what alternative solutions might you come up with?

Writing about the Text:

In a well-developed and organized essay, respond to the reading; be sure to support your views with pertinent examples drawn from your own experience and observations as well as readings.

Topic 1: According to the authors, what are the escalating problems with social decorum in public spaces? What do they think should be done to solve the problem? To what extent—if at all—do you think the authors are correct about this issue?

Topic 2: In a short essay, formulate your own Social Decorum Constitution for behaving. What kinds of rules would you include and why? What could possible penalties be for violating these rules?

Developing Vocabulary:

The words below may appear as part of your online quizzes. Please refer to the introduction for study strategies for learning vocabulary.

1. rampant
2. inhale
3. egregious
4. curmudgeons
5. deportment
6. uttering
7. bothersome
8. efficacious
9. hollering
10. decibels

Understanding the Text

Answer the following questions by carefully reviewing the authors' aruguments in the short essay.

1. What is social decorum and why are the authors concerned about it?

2. What examples do the authors employ to show that a problem exists?

3. What is the Golden Rule and why doesn't it work for social decorum offenders?

4. What do they suggest should be done instead?

Analyzing Writing

Answer the following questions by carefully reviewing the authors' arugments and writing strategies from the short essay.

1. Examine the use rhetorical questions in the text. Where are they used and to what effect?

2. Examine the differing definitions for Golden Rule #1 and its revision. Is the same technique employed in both cases?

3. The authors switch point of view (I, you, he, she, it). Find at least five instances of this shifting and analyze how effective (or not) it is.

15 Good Manners

In every age, there is always debate about the decline of civility and the deterioration of good manners. Even Socrates back in the fifth century BC lamented that his students were growing worse, no longer showing the same respect for their teachers that students used to. In nearly every culture, the older generation laments how good manners are no longer a virtue that the young possess. This may well be a literary trope, or it may be the same progress of evolution that children and students undergo that various authors, philosophers, or average people have noted. Literary trope or not, two issues come to mind: 1) Are children becoming more impolite in general; 2) and if they are, why have they become this way? Let's start with an example. I recently walked into a freshmen college composition course I am teaching and greeted the students. Out of the eighteen students in the class, only two responded with anything approaching a greeting. The others, seemingly absorbed in their own worlds, did not bother to answer at all. At that point, I "formally" started class by commenting on a book I had been reading called *Iron & Silk* by Mark Salzman. This book **chronicles** Salzman's experiences as an English teacher in China in the early 1980s, including accounts of the way he was treated by his students. Indeed, in one section, Salzman explains how when he walked into class, all students would stop speaking, stand up, and loudly greet him as "Teacher Mark." My students did get the message, but I asked myself what exactly was the message? What form of conduct was I expecting of these students, and why did it seem rude that no one responded to my greeting?

The first issue is to determine what exactly "manners" mean. The dictionary defines manners as the mode of acceptable behavior, but whose acceptance is required for manners to be validated as "good"? Indeed, there are certainly more than one set of ideas about politeness in the United States today. Because of the nature of our multi-cultural society, peoples from various lands have settled in the U.S., bringing with them a host of cultural assumptions and norms for behavior. For some Asian cultures, for instance, entering a house with shoes is a grave breach of etiquette while in many other households a person would never think to remove his shoes before entering. In the latter cultures, people would insist on one "feeling right at home" and "helping oneself to anything in the kitchen."

1

2

3   Therefore, part of the problem here is that younger generations don't know what to learn because there is no established guide to manners. In **mono-cultural** societies and cultures where there are clear "rules" of manners, it is obvious how children ought to behave because the adults both enforce and model such behavior in a consistent way. In such societies, there is very little outside influence, so the values of that society can be transmitted to the children without complication, and this is true for any **homogenous** group. Take for example a dinner party offered by Chinese immigrants to the U. S. As is the custom in China, a dinner invitation is an elaborate affair that may include dozens of distinct food dishes. Families often display the best silverware and thoroughly clean the house in preparation for their guests. Children in these households learn first hand the manners of properly hosting others as well as the norms and behavior expected while the visitors are in the house, one of which is to keep silent while adults dine.

4   However, what happens when there is no set standard for behavior, where nearly every family hails from a different cultural background as in the case of many communities in the United States? The same Chinese-American children might be shocked at arriving at the household of an "American" family for dinner because the same set of strict rules on manners will probably not apply. The hosts will most likely not have cooked a dozen separate dishes and may even serve food on paper plates. Children will not only be allowed to speak at the table, but they will be encouraged to participate in conversations. In short, **heterogeneous** societies are disruptive to learning a common set of manners. This negotiation of multiple modes of behavior can be confusing for anyone, especially children who are in the process of acculturation and **socialization**.

5   Even the example of my own students is more complicated than it first appears. Like my literary **forbearers**, I was also ready to condemn my students for being ill-mannered. I, too, was ready to add my verse to the long **litany** of complaints by older generations that the youth of today has not been educated in proper behavior or manners. So, I asked them why they didn't respond, for I thought it to be quite rude not only because they didn't greet their instructor, but also because they didn't respond to someone who directly talked to them. Their responses surprised me. Most of the students admitted that they didn't know what to do. In high school, it was quite common to greet instructors, but in college many of the instructors walk into large lecture halls and "formally" greet the students, expecting no reply. Thus, in their confusion and unwillingness to be embarrassed in an unknown social situation, they kept silent.

It seems like a truism that every older generation eventually complains about the young. But maybe the problem is not the young, but it is the older generation. Perhaps the literary trope has gone too far, and those who complain have forgotten what it is like to be younger. Children and teenagers alike are faced with a myriad of unknown social situations, so they are far more likely to trespass on all the unwritten rules of the social graces, either wittingly or not. In time, of course, most do learn the standards of expected behavior as they observe in more instances how they ought to behave. This process is not simple and often includes embarrassment.

Even adults often suffer the same uncertainty about social behavior, and sometimes they don't even know they've trespassed on some time-honored rule of manners written in a nearly lost **codex**. The same ignorance children face, adults can face as well. It is common etiquette, for instance, that guests invited to dinner bring a small gift such as flowers, a dessert, or a bottle of wine. Where is this written and how should one simply know this? What if the social circumstance is further complicated by, for instance, a dinner hosted after a funeral of a distant relative? Would dessert or a bottle of wine be appropriate? Maybe the wine is needed to get through the funeral?

It seems that the older generation has been too hard on those just growing up. Children as well as many adults need time and exposure in order to learn how to behave and what manners are appropriate given specific instances. This interpretation of proper behavior is a complex matter and requires a fair amount of observation and training. The task of developing proper manners is further complicated by the increasing multi-culturalism in our heterogeneous society. Because families **hail** from many different cultures, it is hard for children and adults alike to determine what is appropriate and what isn't. Now, this is not to say that there aren't uncouth, barbaric, and badly mannered people loitering on the fringes of dinner parties and gatherings just waiting to commit an egregious **faux pas**. There are genuinely nasty characters out there without a doubt; however, the rest of us ought to be given a break. Life can be confusing, and no one is born with a guide to good manners imprinted on the brain.

Discussing and Writing About The Text

Discussing Issues:

Make a table of what your parents, grandparents, and your contemporaries consider good manners and compare and contrast your findings with those of your peers.

Writing about the Text:

In a well-developed and organized essay, respond to the reading; be sure to support your views with pertinent examples drawn from your own experience and observations, as well as readings.

Topic 1: According to the author, what are the issues in defining, determining, and acquiring good manners? To what extent—if any—do you find her ideas accurate and valid?

Topic 2: How can a multi-cultural society instill a specific set of rules for good manners in its members? Develop your essay as a proposed solution to the existing problems that the author analyzed.

Developing Vocabulary:

The words below may appear as part of your online quizzes. Please refer to the introduction for study strategies for learning vocabulary.

1. chronicle
2. mono-cultural
3. homogenous
4. heterogeneous
5. socialization
6. forbearers
7. litany
8. codex
9. hail
10. faux pas

16 TV Watching

Many critics of TV watching **prognosticate** the near ending of the world because people spend far too much time watching TV. Indeed, if one were to simply look at the statistics for television viewing, then there is sufficient cause for alarm. According to the A. C. Nielson Co. statistics, the average American watches four hours of TV per day. By the time a child reaches the age of eighteen, they will have seen 200,000 violent acts, including 40,000 murders. By the time a person reaches 65 years of age, they will have seen two million commercials, for overall about thirty percent of what is seen on TV is commercial sales.

Authors have commented on these statistics and have warned that TV can be incredibly **deleterious** to people's lives. Marie Winn, for instance, warned of TV addiction being as severe as the addiction to alcohol or drugs; in her comparison, Winn, drew parallels between the two that ranged from the pursuit of a "high" and the escape from reality to the detriment of personal relationships and the interest in one's work or other off-couch activities. Furthermore, other critics have argued TV can make people more apathetic to crime or more prone to violence, it may contribute to obesity in children, and it may lead to the downfall of our society through the projection of overall "immoral" material. In confessing to an addiction, forty-nine percent of Americans admit that they watch too much TV and wish they could stop. Examples **abound** in the press of those people who dedicate more than four hours daily to TV, let alone other media such as DVDs, video games, and games on the computer. In a national survey in March of 2005, The Kaisar Family Foundation found that the average child between the ages of 8-18 spends eight hours and eighteen minutes per day involved with TV, video games, and computer play. Moreover, according to the Institute of Medicine of the National Academies, obesity in children 6-11 has tripled in the last three decades.

Critics, however, also point out that in any activity there can be **overindulgence** of one kind or another, but that should not **negate** the possible value of that activity. How about, for instance, educational programs such as *Sesame Street* or programs on the History Channel? These shows provide entertainment and education and should not be made part of the overall scourge of TV watching. In moderation, they say, TV watching can be quite beneficial to the development of children and adults alike. As long as TV watching is controlled, then it can be beneficial. This can be seen in the attempt by parents' groups to introduce the "V-Chip" into all televisions in the late 1990's. This chip, which could be set to control the types of content, would allow parents more control over what their children watch when the parents are not around to police the airwaves.

4   Despite all the statistics of television abuse, the fears of parents for their offspring, and the claims that TV is not bad as long as content is monitored, all these critics are missing a very essential point. The problem does not merely lie in the kind of programs or the hours of TV we watch. The most important issue is *the way* we watch TV. For instance, the quite innocuous TV show hit, *Friends*, would have many teenagers today believe that they could move to New York, get a part time job, and live in an apartment like Phoebe, Rachel, Ross, and Chandler or be able to afford a fetish with Manolo Blahnik shoes at an average of $500 a pair on a columnist's salary like Carrie Bradshaw in *Sex and the City*. The problem here is that in the real world Rachel and Monica would have to pay upwards of $2,500 a month for that "humble" New York apartment, and Carrie Bradshaw would have to substitute food for her precious shoes in order to survive.

5   Children and often adults confuse TV reality with the real world, and this is not only in cases as obviously extreme as *Jackass*. Instead, this confusion is more likely to occur in shows that appear to be realistic or even documentary. Recently, my nephew announced his intent to attend West Point, become a Navy Seal, and then "see the world" through the military. While these might be noble goals, my sixteen-year-old nephew has no idea what these goals really **entail**. Having watched a History Channel special on Navy Seals, he was fascinated by the glorification of this military regiment through their extremely challenging training; however, apart from the demands for extreme physical and mental endurance, there was no information about additional requirements for admission at the Navy Seals or highly prestigious institutions such as West Point. Furthermore, my nephew was not able to notice that the show only focused on the Seals' training, which left the real battle scenes to other "credible" media such as "video games". So my nephew's **fervor** to join the Navy or West Point was mainly fueled by his desire for "a career that would bring some action to [his] life".

6   The solution to TV watching is actually pretty simple and more realistic than **eradicating** TV from the household or just moderating TV time through "rehab". Instead, what might be more feasible and plausible is for people to be educated in TV viewing. Currently, many school curricula include educational programs for learning car repair, for learning to type, for writing papers, or for becoming proficient with computer software. These curricula could, therefore, be

complemented by a course on watching TV actively and critically. The implementation of such a program could start as early as elementary school and continue as far as college. It's time that those avid TV watchers who spend four hours per day in front of the tube be enabled to get the most out of those hours.

To further explain the particulars of such a program, it would consist of multiple levels. First, participants would focus on the actual portrayal of the material and some of the technology involved in creating television shows. Commencing from these surface aspects of any show, people would then proceed to learn how to question what's behind the surface and the camera; more specifically, they would learn to discern or at least seek the various social, ideological, and cultural systems that may have affected the show or are reflected in it.   7

Thus, educated viewers would watch *Friends* in a vastly different way. They would reach behind the show settings and the cameras and question the values and lifestyles espoused by the characters and/or the settings. In that way, they might start wondering about simple math: how can a person who waits tables afford their half of a $2,500 a month rent, or how can a columnist afford her Manolo Blahniks at $500 a pair? They might also look for possible biases in shows that may appear realistic and objective; finally, they might discuss many more facets about the series with parents, peers, or friends, reaching a greater understanding of the show and its social dynamics.   8

While watching inappropriate content for so many hours a day *may* affect viewers (especially children) negatively, the optimum solution does not lie with **censoring** the programming or with **vilifying** its producers. Also, simply pointing out the "educational" shows in defense of television is not an adequate remedy for what may otherwise seem useless or harmful. In essence, with the right training, almost every television show can become educational, and each individual can become their self-governed censor.   9

Discussing and Writing About The Text

Discussing Issues:

Try to think of your and your family's TV watching habits and strategies, and try to examine how they affect you (and your siblings or friends) in your life, communication, and development. Compare and discuss your findings with those of your peers. At a further level, discuss whether you see any merits in the solutions provided by the various TV analysts including the author.

Writing about the Text:

In a well-developed and organized essay, respond to the reading; be sure to support your views with pertinent examples drawn from your own experience and observations, as well as readings.

Topic 1: According to the author, what is the most plausible way of TV watching and regulating? To what extent-if any- do you think their solution could be beneficial?

Topic 2: According to your opinion, how can a person or a family best use TV? To support your opinion, you need to examine relevant and specific examples from a variety of sources.

Developing Vocabulary:

The words below may appear as part of your online quizzes. Please refer to the introduction for study strategies for learning vocabulary.

1. to prognosticate	2. deleterious
3. to abound	4. overindulgence
5. to negate	6. entail
7. fervor	8. eradicating
9. censoring	10. vilifying

Understanding the Text

Answer the following questions by carefully reviewing the authors' aruguments in the short essay.

1. What are some of the arguments of the defenders and also of the opponents of TV?

2. What does the author believe is the problem with these arguments?

3. What does the author believe is the major issue with TV watching?

4. How does the author suggest "regulating" TV watching?

Analyzing Writing

Answer the following questions by carefully reviewing the authors' arugments and writing strategies from the short essay.

1. What is the role of statistics in this essay and especially in the first paragraph?

2. Examine the type and quality of counterarguments offered by the author.

3. Examine the use of sources in the essay. What kind of sources does the author use (personal examples-anecdotes, statistics, etc)? Do you think they are appropriate and convincing? What additional sources would you use?

17 Managerial Techniques

There is no doubt about it. Managing workers for efficiency has become big business. All one needs to do is consult the hundreds of graduate programs in the United States alone that offer Masters and Ph.D.s in management theory and organizational behavior. Yet despite the hierarchy among these programs and their **jockeying** for position, they all do roughly the same thing: provide theoretical background and techniques to allow managers to achieve maximum worker efficiency, productivity—and by extension—business profitability. Nevertheless, within that common goal, there is a **bewildering** array of different techniques managers can choose from.   **1**

    The traditional methodologies employed by managers can be easily broken up into two different motivational types. In lay terms, these are the "carrot-and-the-stick" types. In many traditional management situations, workers are almost solely rewarded with money or cash **incentives**, which, in theory, should allow employees to buy enough carrots to satisfy all their pet rabbits and encourage them to perform at their jobs. The theory goes that if workers are efficient and productive, they earn the reward, and in this paradigm, workers work hard because they have frequent possibilities for rewards. Another reward-based program is that of fringe benefits. Instead of a raise or a bonus, companies can secure efficiency through offering medical insurance, a company car, or an expense account. It works on the same principle, however.   **2**

    The **converse** of the reward is what is **euphemistically** called the "disincentive," another common technique employed by management. Most employees feel the "stick" at one time or another. When a boss **peremptorily** summons workers to the office to rebuke them, this is a definite form of a "disincentive." According to this system, since few if any people like to feel humiliated, degraded, or less-than-competent, verbal reprimands will eventually increase efficiency and production, and workers will be motivated to do better out of fear for a reduction in pay or for the loss of their jobs. Motivation through fear can be a very powerful force in modifying behavior.   **3**

    But do these methodologies of control really encourage efficiency? Studies from the *Journal of Labor Economics* seem to correlate worker efficiency with pay—at first glance; they seem to support the theory that workers respond to in-   **4** centives and disincentives, and like rats in a maze they work toward some eventual goal. But when examined more closely, we notice that many of these studies were conducted utilizing data collected from Henry Ford's assembly line in 1914! More recent research by numerous respected authors (Berg, Dickhaut, McCabe in 1995 and Fehr, Gachter, and Kirchsteiger in 1996) all show that there were modest gains in efficiency and productivity based on incentives. However, most interestingly, all these studies found that the most gains in efficiency were due to so-called **reciprocal** behavior. That reciprocal behavior generates efficiency gains has been confirmed by several other studies, even under conditions of double anonymity or in which participants were unaware of the experiment and the experimenter could not observe individual behavior.

5   But what exactly is reciprocal behavior? It's all about common sense. Reciprocity means giving and receiving so that all participants feel they received an equitable deal. In older days, this would have been called a barter system. But this barter system (reciprocity system) amounts to far more than giving raises and other money incentives to stimulant for worker efficiency. In a recent study conducted by the members of the business school at Stanford University, "innovative" human resources programs that included managers who listen to worker issues, flexible job design, ongoing training in skills and problem solving, work teams, information sharing, pay for performance, and employment security, experienced an incredible 6.7% increase in productivity across the board. Moreover, the study found that the more "**innovative**" the program, the more efficient and productive the workers became.

6   The study merely supports what many of us already knew. Companies have to treat their workers as human beings, not as cogs in a machine. If workers feel that work-related complaints are fairly **adjudicated** by managers, if they have flex-time to deal with personal issues, if they have the training necessary to successfully complete their job, these employees will work better and more efficiently. Monetary rewards are only one component for workers. Certainly, employees who earn $100,000 a year are likely to try to be efficient in their jobs, but what happens if the manager never listens, if employees never have a day off, or if necessary training has not been provided? Is efficiency and productivity so clearly tied to money?

7   What previous capitalist theories forgot to account for is the human element. People need their voices heard. They need to have the training in order to competently complete their jobs. They need to be more invested in their jobs than simply performing tasks in pursuit of carrots. They need to be part of a team and be responsible not only to themselves but to their fellow team members. Capital-

ist theories of efficiency for money have forgotten the human element. Management schools now label these theories of managerial control as Human Resources (HR), which clearly **delineates** the role workers "ought" to play in a business. Unfortunately, too many times workers are still considered resources that should be exploited—mined and clear cut—until the resource is exhausted, leaving angry workers who might try to directly or indirectly sabotage the company. Companies must steer clear from this theoretical orientation! Human Resources should be relabeled Human Relationships. By providing a suitable working environment—where relationships can flourish, where workers and managers can avoid misunderstandings, where workers are provided with the skills, tools, clear objectives, and personal investment in the product—employees will be more content, and businesses will reap the profits of greater worker efficiency. That makes sense.

Discussing and Writing About The Text

Discussing Issues:

Interview two professionals about their experience with managerial techniques. In class, try to discuss your findings from your interviews with those of your peers and examine whether they validate or disprove the authors' arguments and suggestions.

Writing about the Text:

In a well-developed and organized essay, respond to the reading; be sure to support your views with pertinent examples drawn from your own experience and observations, as well as readings.

Topic 1: According to the authors, what makes the technique of "reciprocal behavior" the most logical and effective managerial technique? To what extent—if at all—do you agree with the authors' assertion?

Topic 2: Try to imagine yourself as the manager at your job or if you do not have one at a student project. What techniques would you adopt and in pursuit of what specific objectives?

Developing Vocabulary:

The words below may appear as part of your online quizzes. Please refer to the introduction for study strategies for learning vocabulary.

1.	jockeying	2.	bewildering
3.	incentives	4.	converse
5.	euphemistically	6.	peremptorily
7.	reciprocal	8.	innovative
9.	adjudicated	10.	delineates

Understanding the Text

Answer the following questions by carefully reviewing the authors' aruguments in the short essay.

1. What are the objectives of most managerial techniques?

2. What has been the basis for the traditional managerial techniques and what are the problems with those approaches?

3. What is the technique of "reciprocal behavior" and how can it be beneficial?

4. Why do the authors suggest Human Resources be renamed to Human Relationships?

Analyzing Writing

Answer the following questions by carefully reviewing the authors' arugments and writing strategies from the short essay.

1.   Examine the use of definition and classification in the text.

2.   What sources of evidence do the authors use to prove his claims? Examine the quality and effectiveness of these sources.

3.   Examine the role of questions as rhetorical devices in the text.

18 Multi-Tasking Taken to Task

What would you think if you were undergoing an operation and your doctor were listening to music, checking her Palm Pilot, talking on her cell phone, and eating a sandwich? You would probably hope that she be **disbarred** from the medical profession before the scalpel hit the skin. While this is a very unlikely scenario, why do we tolerate multi-tasking in nearly every other walk of life?

1

The easy answer is that everyone does it, and in this case it may be true. Look at the drivers on the freeway who busily fiddle with their stereos, talk on their cell phones, or look at their GPS systems, despite there being laws in many states against operating any other device while driving. Against laws or logic, however, we have come to not only tolerate multi-tasking, but to hardly ever notice it anymore. This phenomenon can be tracked from the clerk in the video store who simultaneously answers the phone, helps a customer find a video, and rents a DVD to another customer, to conference participants who "listen" to speakers, check their messages, read the conference catalog, and play games on the Blackberries. Even more often, this phenomenon can be seen on people's computer screens with the ten or more windows open at one time.

2

Although multi-tasking has come to be seen as normal in our fast-paced society that **mandates** time-saving and maximum efficiency techniques, it has serious side-effects. First off, it indicates a severe shift in the social institution of manners, if not a breakdown. Examine, for instance, the student who checks his phone for messages, draws tic-tack-toe boxes on his paper while only partially—if at all—listening to the instructor. This multi-tasking shows an immediate lack of respect for the instructor, and this can be better understood if one were to imagine a whole classroom of multi-tasking students versus a single one. Simply put, the student is being extremely rude. This student places his own amusement and need for diversion above the rules of polite behavior. Even if the teacher's lecture is dry and boring, the student still has a duty to pay attention. Instead of being rude by multi-tasking, the student can still complain about the lecture but in a different and more constructive format, such as evaluations or letters to the dean. However, even a **scintillating** speaker could lecture in front of an audience and observe the same behavior from its members, for this has become common practice.

3

So it isn't simply teenagers who are at fault for not being socialized enough. Is the conference participant in the earlier example any less guilty simply because in her case there were more people in the room or she was older?

4   Nevertheless, even in more informal and less structured settings, multi-tasking contributes to a social **dysfunction** by allowing the individual to be selfish and rude. How often has it occurred that two people, even friends, are having a discussion and one of them begins checking their cell phone for messages or takes calls on the cell phone without even apologizing for disrupting the conversation with the other person? This behavior, besides being **disruptive** to interaction, clearly privileges the individual over social intercourse. The social or rather anti-social message here is that "my call is far more important than anything you might possibly have to say, so I don't even have to apologize for interrupting our conversation." And what is even more bothersome is that most people wouldn't even recognize or perceive this behavior of theirs as rude or selfish.

5   But let us take an example of someone multi-tasking in a non face-to-face context. Many people nowadays are required by their work situations to multi-task. They check email while listening to phone messages while working on spreadsheets. **Proponents** of multi-tasking would argue this is the only way for the modern professional to keep up with the demands of the workplace and become successful. However, multi-tasking is eventually not efficient. According to a study published in *The Journal of Experimental Psychology*, multi-tasking actually slows down **cognitive** processes. In psychological jargon, people utilize their executive-decision-making apparatus in more complex ways when multi-tasking, thereby relegating some tasks as more critical for brain function **allocation**. What does that mean? In simple terms, or according to common sense, one cannot switch from working on a spreadsheet problem to writing emails very effectively. Something has to give. Inevitably, there is time-loss when people have to reorient themselves to the problem, remember what they had thought about it, and then proceed with coming up with a solution. It takes time to rehearse what mental work had already been done on a problem in order to proceed.

6   Besides being counter-productive rather than time-conserving, multi-tasking also leads to work of lower quality. The person who continuously shifts back and forth between tasks will more likely miss something along the way, thereby reducing the quality of the overall project. The doctor who multi-tasks may forget to put in the proper number of **sutures** or provide for a full regiment of drugs for follow-up procedures. The student who multi-tasks may miss an important announcement made by the instructor. The plumber who multi-tasks may forget to completely solder the copper pipe he was working on. The list can go on and on.

Overall, multi-tasking and our increasing tolerance or practice of this approach to things certainly mark a new era in human interaction and in work strategies. However, multi-tasking eventually defies the rules of civility and is selfish as well as counter-efficient. Human interaction requires common, agreed upon rules of conduct for social correspondence to occur. Without these rules, our attempts at communicating with each other will be met with failure. Interaction also requires a **modicum** of civility towards others and the relegation of individual needs to a later time in favor of providing the conversation partner with one's full attention. Of course, one could argue that times change, and so do people's perceptions of good manners; something that would be considered rude in past eras can be totally acceptable today. Beyond any moralistic or ethical approach, it would be hard to argue that important messages and information would not be lost or a conversation would not be interrupted due to concentration on other things. And even in other situations without personal contact, the negative effects of multi-tasking are clear and scientifically proven. We need to rewire the way we talk with others and remodel the way we work; let's just hope that we're not multi-tasking while we do it.

7

Discussing and Writing About The Text

Discussing Issues:

Make a list of the instances that you have observed people or yourself multi-tasking. In a discussion with your peers, examine the results, both positive and negative, you thought multi-tasking had in each one of these cases.

Writing about the Text:

In a well-developed and organized essay, respond to the reading; be sure to support your views with pertinent examples drawn from your own experience and observations, as well as readings.

Topic 1: What is the authors' critique of multi-tasking? Do you find multi-tasking as damaging as the authors suggest?

Topic 2: According to your opinion, what are the conditions and elements necessary for one's best performance at work?

Developing Vocabulary:

The words below may appear as part of your online quizzes. Please refer to the introduction for study strategies for learning vocabulary.

1. **to disbar**
2. **to mandate**
3. **scintillating**
4. **dysfunction**
5. **disruptive**
6. **proponent**
7. **cognitive**
8. **allocation**
9. **suture**
10. **modicum**

CHAPTER THREE

Government

19   The Responsibilities of Citizenship

It is common when discussing citizenship to mention the rights that citizens enjoy. Of course, one of the most fundamental rights is the right to vote, the ability to voice concern in how the government is to be run and what decisions are to be made both locally and nationally. Other rights are nearly as important and have been dutifully listed by our **prescient** forefathers or amended to the Constitution at a later stage. Among the most important are the right to free speech, the right to bear arms, or the right to a speedy trial. In all there are twenty-seven Amendments to the Constitution which outline and guarantee certain irrevocable rights to the citizens of the United States.

1

But in all the fervor to ensure citizens have their just and inalienable rights secured, no one created a Bill of Responsibilities. People become citizens in this country merely through chance of birth, and they seemingly have no other responsibility except to obey the laws of the land and to pay taxes. Citizens don't have to vote, don't need to know who is President, and don't even need to speak a common language. Citizenship, however, is far too important to be granted merely by virtue or chance of one's birth; it should be earned through *regular maintenance*. Evidently, one of the fundamental responsibilities should be citizens' full participation in the political system in order to preserve a healthy body politic. However, what is the state of the state? How are citizens fulfilling their responsibilities? Woefully. Voting statistics in the U. S. hover around 50% for presidential elections, with a small spike in the 2004 election, and the statistics are even lower for local or regional elections. In developing countries or places where democracy is not secure or firmly rooted, elections have 80-90% voter turn out!

2

To be sure, the problem goes deeper than the percentage of those who vote. It is also about the "quality" of the voters who do turn up at the polls. This has little to do with class, race, or gender. It has to do with information. Plenty of voters arrive at the polls without having researched or reflected upon the main issues of the political debate. They have little if any knowledge about the candidates, usually limited to only that which they might have gathered from the **bombardment** of biased campaign advertising on TV. Indeed, the political money trail does not

3

lie. Statistics show that the price tag of political campaigns has ballooned in the last years, and consumers/citizens are affected by these often **pithy** political ads during election season. Many people vote for the most charismatic or "well-packaged" figures, not necessarily for the candidates of substance, the truth of which can be evinced as far back as the Kennedy/Nixon publicized debates. Like consumers, uninformed citizens may be manipulated into voting for the proposition with the easily-remembered or oft-repeated phrase, not paying any attention to the essence of the reform and its potential effects on society in the long run.

4   Considering this situation and its potential consequences, a Bill of Responsibilities seems like a necessity, and its First Amendment should require that all citizens not only vote but also be informed. Citizens must be aware of the major issues of the day beyond the sound bite messages **promulgated** on TV. This does not necessitate that every one can or should be a research fellow at a university; however, it does mean that through discussion with peers and a **modicum** of reading they can be reasonably informed. The irony here is that those who become naturalized citizens—immigrants from other countries who apply and receive citizenship, only do so after they have taken a "citizenship test" which includes salient points of U. S. history as well as reference to some of the previous and current political figures. Many citizens born in this country would be unable to pass this test, yet they carry the benefits of citizenship merely by the chance of their birth.

5   Furthermore, the Second Amendment to this Bill of Responsibilities should include the responsibility to be involved and engaged. This involvement does not require holding an office or being a public servant or running a political campaign. Involvement means engagement in democracy; it can range from debates with friends over important issues coming before local or national legislatures to volunteering at a local park to election to a public office. Involvement means that citizens go beyond enjoying the rights granted them by law to active participation in their communities, regions, and nation.

6   The **naysayers** may respond to this new **mandate** by claiming that modern life is so busy and work consumes much of the week. There is no time for involvement, research of issues, or almost anything else. While this is true to some extent, even a truck-load of excuses cannot **exculpate** the duty of citizens to participate in democracy, for inactivity or ill-formed votes affect the entire structure of the body politic—from local issues to foreign policy. Lack of participation in democracy does not merely affect the individual; it affects non-citizens as well, for the policies implemented in the United States always have ripple effects in the global villages of the world.

The real challenge in implementing such a Bill of Responsibilities would   7
be its application or enforcement. While enforcing penalties on citizens who do
not bother to vote is a measure that could be easily implemented, the enforcement
and assessment of people's information and knowledge would be more complicated. There would be many sensitive issues to consider in setting the standards
for the "informed citizen" to avoid the dangers of government **censorship** or any
threats to democracy. However, the first step is to recognize the need for some
changes in the way citizenship is perceived and exercised. Citizenship in a democracy should not be free; actually, it never was, and people in the past had to struggle towards a democratic state. Therefore, it should not be taken for granted but
should be **cherished** through citizen participation. These responsibilities should
not be implemented to curtail participation in the democratic process by forbidding whole groups from voting or holding office. If anything, these reforms are
designed to heal the ailing health of our political process. After all, the very word
for Democracy derives from the ancient Greek words "demos," that is people, and
"krateo-o" that means to have/hold power. If people are to hold power in a democratic state, they cannot afford to be ignorant or indifferent. Thomas Jefferson
is oft quoted as saying that the "the tree of liberty must be refreshed from time to
time, with the blood of patriots and tyrants." In actuality, Jefferson wrote these
words in a letter to William Smith as a response to just having received a copy of
the Constitution. In the same letter, however, Jefferson warns that if people remain
quiet and lethargic, it is "the forerunner of death to the public liberty." He is, in
essence, discussing the principles by which a democratic state can continue to
exist. Citizenship is not free, and with rights should come responsibilities.

Discussing and Writing About The Text

Discussing Issues:

What has been your role in maintaining or ameliorating democracy in this country? Make a list of your actions or the instances of inaction and compare them to those of other students.

Writing about the Text:

In a well-developed and organized essay, respond to the reading; be sure to support your views with pertinent examples drawn from your own experience and observations, as well as readings.

Topic 1: According to the authors, what should be responsibilities of a citizen and to what end? To what extent—if at all—do you agree with the authors' ideas?

Topic 2: What do you think has shaped your identity as a citizen of this country? Do you think there are ways people could be motivated to become more conscientious citizens?

Developing Vocabulary:

The words below may appear as part of your online quizzes. Please refer to the introduction for study strategies for learning vocabulary.

1. prescient	2. bombardment
3. pithy	4. promulgated
5. modicum	6. naysayers
7. mandate	8. exculpate
9. censorship	10. cherished

Understanding the Text

Answer the following questions by carefully reviewing the authors' aruguments in the short essay.

1. In what ways do people fail to fulfill their role as citizens nowadays?

2. Why does a Bill of Responsibilities seem necessary?

3. What should be citizens' primary and most important responsibilities?

4. What would be the arguments raised by opponents of this Bill of Responsibilities?

Analyzing Writing

Answer the following questions by carefully reviewing the authors' arugments and writing strategies from the short essay.

1. Isolate and identify the type of counterarguments used by the authors, and examine their effectiveness.

2. Underline five different transitional devices and examine their effectiveness.

3. Examine the role of the last paragraph in the authors' argumentation process.

20 Citizenship and Multi-Culturalism

The word "citizen" has its origins in the Middle Ages with the development of independent towns and cities in the late thirteenth and early fourteenth centuries. More specifically, it etymologically derives from the French *citeain-citiseain*, that is the person who hails from the city. The precursor to this is the Latin word *civitas*, which, according to the *Oxford English Dictionary*, was the Latin word for the major seats of civic government of the different regions of conquered Gaul (now France), separated by ethnic tribal origin. It wasn't until the Renaissance and the **nascent** development of nationalism and nation states that "citizen" was used to denote membership as part of a country. During the fifteenth and sixteenth centuries feudal lands reigned over by feudal lords were consolidated under the ruler ship of a centralized power. These smaller entities were forced to pay homage to the kings and queens of the period, thereby creating larger national countries. From these beginnings with kings and queens arose republican and democratic governments. 1

American Democracy is the ultimate extension of this historical development into nationhood. The idea of America, at its very core, tests the proposition that people from all over the world with vastly different cultural, religious, and personal backgrounds can come together under one system of government. Since its shaky beginnings in 1776, America has been the great democratic experiment, testing whether it is possible for peoples of such different persuasions to rule themselves. The experiment has been considered a success and a model of government for other **burgeoning** democracies across the globe…at least so far. 2

America's plurality, the mixture of hundreds of ethnic, cultural, and religious backgrounds, has been one of the secrets to its success. Indeed, immigrants from hundreds of countries have adopted the U. S. as home, deciding to settle, have families, and start businesses. This has been the strength of the U. S., drawing on the expertise and varied experiences of vastly different populations toward an overall development and improvement. The U.S. has also used the labor of immigrants to build the infrastructure, including the railroad in the 1800s or the interstate system in the 1900s just as it continues to use a vast number of immigrants in its agricultural businesses. America has indeed thrived on the constant pool of laborers emigrating to the U. S. as well as the overall immigrant population's ex- 3 pertise in numerous fields.

4   Originally, the secret for America's success lay within the idea of a created national identity, the rules by which all immigrants would want to or would have to abide. Instead of group affiliations, there was the concept of the Melting Pot, coined by Israel Zangwill in his 1908 play entitled *The Melting Pot*. According to Zangwill, "America is God's crucible, the Great Melting-Pot, where all the races of Europe are melting and reforming." The statement carried with it the connotation that all who came to U. S. shores had to melt into some new **amalgamation**, a new entity, re-forming into something else by casting off what they once were. Over the run of several decades, however, this idea was discredited as simplistic and has been gradually replaced by that of multi-culturalism. According to the latter, immigrants and residents alike don't have to melt into anything; they have the option of remaining as they are, of retaining the customs and norms of the old country, and of being selective in their adaptation to the new environment. This multi-culturalism movement has taken hold, celebrating the differences of cultures found in a multitude of forms. The secret of this plurality has been toleration and acceptance of the traditions, cultures, and **creeds** of immigrants. Actually, in many cities across the nation, it is possible to walk or drive through neighborhoods where only Spanish, Chinese, Korean, Japanese, German, or any of a number of other languages is spoken. In parts of Los Angeles, for instance, all the signs are in Chinese, and the shopkeepers speak little English. In parts of Minnesota, German is still the predominant language and cultural background while New York is the virtual Tower of Babel!

5   Multi-culturalism should be **lauded** for forcing to the forefront of our national consciousness the many and important contributions that immigrants from other countries have made. It has also alleviated people of their **xenophobia** and has rectified many of the historical inequities that existed for far too long, such as the infamous laws in the 1800s against immigrants of Chinese descent. However, multi-culturalism, taken too far, has within it the seeds of deterioration of the country's unity. For instance, today, ethnic groups in many cities have become galvanized and pursue agendas of their own, and according to Patrick West, author of the *Poverty of Multi-culturalism*, multi-culturalism encourages groups to see themselves as separate, which **foments** conflict with other groups within the society and can lead to violence. Other countries are already experiencing this fragmentation which can be clearly seen in the sectarian violence erupting in France, Britain, and other regions of the world, and beginning to be seen in the U. S. with the continuing debate around immigration policy.

America could then fall victim to its size, expansiveness, and tolerance of   6
difference; therefore, there arises a fundamental question of the constitution of a
coherent social body established on and empowered through the similarities of its
members rather than their differences. If the idea of multi-culturalism is pressed
too far, at what point does a governing body break down if the citizens that constitute it feel more like citizens of a particular group than of the overall nation?
How can the U.S. continue to function if someone identifies himself first as German, Chinese, Mexican and then as American? The danger here is that the allegiance is to the particular group, not to the overall country could at critical
moments paralyze the political process in a **miasma** of **partisan** interest.

Interestingly, the etymology of the word citizen may be of some help in the   7
difficulties that surround multi-culturalism today. "Citizen" used to mean those
people from the same city who shared not only a geographical location but also
and foremost a certain set of values. Without a common set of values or even a
common language, no country can survive, for how can it be governed? Indeed,
recent movies such as the Academy Award winning *Crash* have begun showing
these cultural and language conflicts that have been festering in our communities.
The **patina** of multi-culturalism shines as the exemplar of cooperation and mutual
existence, but the reality is that multi-culturalism, when taken too far, leads to
segmentation. The danger is quite profound: the dissolution of America. What
does it mean to be a citizen if there are no common bonds of culture or language
that hold us together?

Discussing and Writing About The Text

Discussing Issues:

Make a list of all the different clubs at school. Next, divide them up into ones based on ethnic affiliation versus ones based on activities. What would happen if a non-ethnic person wanted to attend a specific club such as the German or Spanish club? Would there be any problem? Do you feel like a "citizen" of your school or more a part of a particular clique or group? Why or why not?

Writing about the Text:

In a well-developed and organized essay, respond to the reading; be sure to support your views with pertinent examples drawn from your own experience and observations, as well as readings.

Topic 1: What is the connection between multi-culturalism and citizenship, according to the authors? Why are they concerned about multi-culturalism? To what extent—if at all—do you think the authors are correct about this fear?

Topic 2: Formulate your own proposal so that people can balance their own ethnic heritage with their duties as citizens. Are there specific issues that arise? Are there any problems with the current system that you can isolate and/or fix? What system can bring people together for the common good while allowing for separation of ethnic traditions?

Developing Vocabulary:

The words below may appear as part of your online quizzes. Please refer to the introduction for study strategies for learning vocabulary.

1.	nascent	2.	burgeoning
3.	amalgamation	4.	creed
5.	laud	6.	xenophobia
7.	foment	8.	miasma
9.	partisan	10.	patina

Understanding the Text

Answer the following questions by carefully reviewing the authors' aruguments in the short essay.

1. What is the origin of the idea of citizenship?

2. Why has do the authors call America the "great democratic experiment"? Why has America been historically so successful until now?

3. What is multi-culturalism and what are its benefits to the U.S.?

4. Why are the authors concerned about the connection of multi-culturalism and citizenship?

Analyzing Writing

Answer the following questions by carefully reviewing the authors' arugments and writing strategies from the short essay.

1. Examine the use of the extended etymological definition at both the beginning and the end of the essay.

2. Consider the use of history in the text. What information is cited?

3. Look for the thesis of the essay. Are there more than one? Do the authors make multiple claims?

21 Citizenship and Friendship Revisited

Recently, I assigned an essay by Robert N. Bellah's entitled "Citizenship and Friendship" to class of students at the university where I teach. In this **excerpt**, Bellah argues that friendship among Americans has essentially changed over time. In today's world, friendship is about being useful to one's friend and enjoying one another's company whereas it lacks a third component that used to characterize friendship in previous eras. This third component, which was first defined by Aristotle, Bellah describes as the "shared common commitment to the good." In other words, one has an obligation to ensure the friend's moral development and promote the abstract concept of "the good." In upholding the moral standards for one's friend, one not only benefits the friend, but also and in a larger sense, one benefits society. Eventually, this dedication to the good translates to the very fiber that holds communities and countries together. For Bellah, good friendship is ultimately and inextricably connected to good citizenship.

The student responses to this short excerpt were quite interesting and **indicative** of a major social shift in our value system. Indeed, most students agreed with Bellah that friendship nowadays is mostly about "having fun," "hanging out," and even "helping out" when friends are in need. The first two are easily explainable as part of the first component, while the latter connects with the **principle** of "being useful to one another." The majority of these students, agreeing with Bellah, argued that the moral commitment to one's friend as well as to the common good does not exist in today's society. Friendship, according to many students, has become entirely about fun and usefulness.

If this small sample is representative of friendships of a broad **spectrum** of Americans, it is indicative of a certain breakdown in social relationships and of citizenship in ways not even imagined by Bellah. If fun has become the essence of modern friendship, it can explain but also lead to a cultural **elimination** of critical debate from the **realm** of discussions with friends. Indeed, debates about controversial issues such as capital punishment, education, or the prison system are often avoided, for they could easily spoil the "fun" by creating tension or even animosity among these friends. After all, it is common for newcomers to the U.S. to be cautioned against talking about "politics and religion" if they wish to avoid the

1

2

3

label of "**persona non grata**." The only way to avoid the tension and keep the peace has apparently been to shift these topics aside and replace them with topics that all friends can agree on: sports, video games, movies, and so forth.

4   How often have serious issues been elided among friends? How often have political discussions been shifted aside by stating from the outset that politics won't be discussed because the debate will inevitably lead to a fight, not a healthy debate? While there are those among us who enjoy and regularly engage in debates over serious subjects, the vast majority of friends prefer to keep these subjects on the **periphery**, looking mainly for enjoyment and a good time. This systematic avoidance of serious issues or at least discussion and debate of these issues is one of the major reasons for the decline of "traditional and moral" friendship and citizenship.

5   Therefore, it is not only the elimination of the commitment to the good that harms the essence of citizenship in today's society, as Bellah believes, but it is also the limitation of friendship to the components of enjoyment and fun. Indeed, true citizenship should be far more than having the right to vote. It is the engagement with significant social issues that affect us all. While Bellah argues that the lack of enforcement of a moral code among friends—i.e. preventing a friend from committing a crime—leads to a deterioration in the moral fiber of our country (hence citizenship), there is a more troubling connection to the decline of citizenship. If we fail to critically engage in social and political issues with our friends and family members, with whom should we discuss these issues? Strangers? They end up being elided until individuals, without the benefit of others' insight, make up their minds at the polling booth. The lack of critical debate among friends can easily and gradually lead to the lack of social coherence and **solidarity**.

6   But both students and Bellah are mistaken about the lack of a moral commitment to one's friends in today's society. The moral commitment has simply changed, but it still exists! Now, however, it has morphed into the necessity to support one's friends in every case despite real or apparent guilt. It is still commitment to the friend but not necessarily to the good in a friend. Let's put it into context. In one student example, a friend shoplifted and was caught, but according to this student, it was not his obligation to prevent his friend from shoplifting or from lecturing him afterwards. His obligation was to stand by his friend when the police arrived on the scene and to provide a false excuse that the friend had simply forgotten to pay for the candy he had put in his jacket. There is still a sense of morality, but it points towards the individual not society.

This shift in values can have a detrimental effect on our society because it locates the center of our value system not among our shared commitment to each other, but only on a shared and unconditional commitment to our closest friends. This refocusing of social energy loosens the bonds that hold larger social institutions together such as local communities, cities, and ultimately countries. If the moral commitment to everyone living in our community, city, or country has been reduced to a commitment to our friends—regardless of their moral stance—then society may be on the verge of breaking apart. 7

Benedict Anderson, in his book *Imagined Communities*, has argued that it is precisely our belief in a group beyond ourselves or our close friends that creates communities in the first place. For Anderson, belief in an over-arching idea and ideal beyond the individual allows people to coexist in communities. We must, in essence, have shared values and shared beliefs in order to work together. The new **figuration** of the moral code—to support one's friends despite the laws or codes they break—is a direct attack on citizenship. Responsible citizenship requires that we adhere to a system of common laws, placing the good of the many above the good of the few or the one. In short, we all have to share at least some aspects of the same imaginary concept of community—be it neighborhood, town, city, or country—in order for us to have a peaceful coexistence. 8

We see the effects of this personal interest in one's "friends" put before the public interest with the scandals of government officials in Congress. These officials are often so committed to their "friends" that they put their personal gain above the public trust. Taken in this context, the "moral commitment" in the political realm becomes synonymous to the support of friends and political allies even when the latter break the law in order to insure there be no scandal. Would it be a stretch then to argue that support for a shoplifting friend is not so far removed from support for an embezzling ally? 9

Good friendship and citizenship require that we debate and discuss issues of importance and that we uphold certain moral standards for both ourselves and for our friends. They should neither require blind support for friends or allies who break the law or commit a moral lapse, nor should they be satiated only through having some good time with our buddies. 10

Discussing and Writing About The Text

Discussing Issues:

Try to think of your own experiences with friendship and citizenship. Is there any connection between the two in your life? Make a list of your friends, past or present, and examine the salient characteristics of each relationship. Compare and discuss your findings with your peers taking into consideration the author's perspective and arguments.

Writing about the Text:

In a well-developed and organized essay, respond to the reading; be sure to support your views with pertinent examples drawn from your own experience and observations, as well as readings.

Topic 1: According to the author, what are the elements of friendship today, and how do they threaten society's well-being? Do you agree with his expanded definition of friendship and why?

Topic 2: According to your opinion, what should be the essence of friendship and citizenship?

Developing Vocabulary:

The words below may appear as part of your online quizzes. Please refer to the introduction for study strategies for learning vocabulary.

1. excerpt
2. indicative
3. principle
4. spectrum
5. realm
6. persona non grata
7. elimination
8. periphery
9. solidarity
10. figuration

Understanding the Text

Answer the following questions by carefully reviewing the authors' aruguments in the short essay.

1.   What are the three essential components of friendship according to Robert Bel-lah?

2.   Does the author agree or disagree with Bellah's diagnosis of today's society?

3.   According to the author, what are the major consequences of the change in the definition of friendship?

4.   What should be the relationship between friendship and citizenship according to the author?

Analyzing Writing

Answer the following questions by carefully reviewing the authors' arugments and writing strategies from the short essay.

1.   Examine the role of questions in the text. Does the author answer those questions? What is the effect of answered and unanswered (rhetorical) questions in the validity of the author's arguments?

2.   Examine three words, phrases, and/or sentences that help transition from idea to idea, paragraph to paragraph. Try to replace them with synonyms or more effective ones.

3.   Examine the use of sources in the essay. What kind of sources does the author use (personal examples-anecdotes, statistics, etc)? Do you think they are appropriate and convincing? What additional sources would you use?

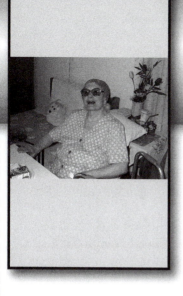

22   The Sick Care System

The United States of America does not have a national health care system; it has a sick care system. And if you are sick but not too poor, good luck to you. You may not be able to receive the kind of care that you need when you need it. This is not new, and examples are **rife** in the media of how Health Management Organizations (**HMOs**) and health insurance companies have limited procedures based on a cost/benefit analysis. Waiting times to just get an appointment with a doctor are at nerve-wrecking levels for patients, and the doctors and nurses are fairing no better. Health care professionals are increasingly pressured to see a **quota** of patients per day, which means that they only have a few minutes to treat patients like humans, make a sound diagnosis, and resolve the issue. In fact, it's only due to the dedication of these health care professionals that the system works as well as it does.

     1

But the system works better for some than others. As with most things in the U.S., there is a hidden class system at work that requires only a little attention to **discern**. At the top of the heap are CEOs, executives, and managers who have the best kind of insurance available. When they go to the hospital, they often don't have all the additional fees, called co-pays, that the rest of us have. As one would expect, their care is fully covered, including the cost of rehabilitation and medication after a bout of illness or an accident. However, as one descends down the corporate and employee ladder, the insurance typically gets worse, and the amount covered in medical expenses is also reduced. Ironically, the poorer the worker or employee is, the greater percentage of average income must go to health-related expenses.

     2

At the same time, having insurance is no guarantee that someone will keep it even if they pay for it privately out of their own pocket. For instance, a mother of three in California had been suffering from knee pain for some time, but the initial deductible of five hundred dollars, meaning she must always pay the first five hundred dollars of any expense incurred, kept her from seeing a doctor. When the pain got so bad that she scheduled an appointment and paid her fee, she found out that the knee had to be replaced to the tune of twenty thousand dollars. The insurance covered 80% of the operation, leaving four thousand dollars out of

     3

pocket expenses that she didn't have. Sounds bad enough, but the real problem started when her insurance company decided to leave California and relocate because there were too many claims in that state. Now, no insurance company will cover this woman for her knee because the latter has been labeled as a pre-existing condition. This may sound illegal or at least unfair, but justice and legality are not always synonymous; it is a perfectly legal tactic that companies can use in assessing "high risk" patients.

4   All of this may sound overdramatic, but tell that to the estimated forty-eight million people in the United States who don't even have health insurance at all. Despite the U. S. being one of the richest countries on the planet, roughly one-sixth of the population lives day to day without insurance. One accident or one illness could literally bankrupt the people in this fragile population, and bankruptcy statistics prove this. It's estimated that of the 1.7 million bankruptcies reported in the U. S. per year, fully 80% are due to medical bills and/or job loss (and hence loss of medical insurance).

5   An additional **idiosyncratic** feature of the present health care system in the U. S. is that most of the forty-eight million people who have no insurance are people that do have jobs; however, they either do not have insurance through their jobs or they cannot afford to pay for it privately. The stop-gap answer has been that the U. S. government has provided limited health care for these uninsured individuals, but this comes with a big catch: poverty. This means, therefore, that under normal circumstances a couple would have to earn less than 12,490 dollars per year to qualify for government health care through the Medicaid program. So, if a person were working and earning a very modest 25,000 dollars a year and did not have health insurance, they couldn't get assistance from the government. They would first have to run through their savings and become **destitute** before the government would step in to help.

6   All this would be laughable if it weren't true. However, it is true, and that makes the situation more tragic than comic. What's worse is that there is clearly a better way. According to the Physicians Working Group who sponsored The National Health Insurance act in 2005, the current system—in addition to its coverage gaps—is incredibly wasteful. If a national health care system were implemented, it would not only provide comprehensive coverage for every citizen of the United States; it would also save upwards of 150 billion dollars just in administrative costs. The system of HMOs, hospitals, and the newly implemented Medicare system is incredibly complicated and require forests of paperwork. As if all of these complications were not enough, these various programs vary from state to state, making the simplest transfer, for instance, of a hospitalized patient

from one state to another a virtual jungle of **red tape**.

A national health care system would not just save money on administration; it would potentially save money—billions of dollars—on health care costs, according to numerous research studies found in the *American Journal of Preventative Medicine*. As the system currently operates, one has to typically be sick before receiving care. This is obviously not only financially wasteful, it is socially irresponsible. If people had comprehensive, government health care, they could and would utilize preventative health care services. The mother of three with the arthritic knee might have received preventative care, which might have saved her the pain, the time, and the expense of an invasive operation. More people would be tested for cancer, avoiding delayed **diagnoses** with **irreversible** consequences or high reparative expenses. The scientists agree. According to a February, 2008 article in the *New England Journal of Medicine* that reviewed over 1,500 scholarly articles on the economics of preventative health care, smart and targeted preventative care could save substantial amounts of money for the mass of people.

7

What's standing in the way of this new frontier? Pharmaceutical companies, insurance providers, and bought-off government officials—that's who. The ill health of Americans is a business worth an estimated 1.7 trillion dollars per year, and these companies are unlikely to quietly **forego** profits even if it means their patients would have better care for less money. Perhaps, it's time to heal the sick care system.

8

Discussing and Writing About The Text

Discussing Issues:

Make a list of people you know who have had an illness. How did their illness affect them financially? Were they able to get adequate health care? Why do you think the government has been unwilling to create a national health care system? Do you see merit in the arguments for health care for those who can afford it.

Writing about the Text:

In a well-developed and organized essay, respond to the reading; be sure to support your views with pertinent examples drawn from your own experience and observations, as well as readings.

Topic 1: According to the authors, why do we have a "sick care" system in the U. S.? What do the authors believe should be done to remedy the problems of the current system? To what extent—if at all—do you think the authors are correct about this assertion?

Topic 2: Compile a list of average medical expenses and then subtract these expenses from an estimate yearly income of ten thousand dollars, thirty thousand dollars, and ninety thousand dollars. What percentage of this hypothetical person's income goes toward medical expenses? What might be a solution for this problem?

Developing Vocabulary:

The words below may appear as part of your online quizzes. Please refer to the introduction for study strategies for learning vocabulary.

1. rife
2. HMOs
3. quota
4. discern
5. idiosyncratic
6. destitute
7. red tape
8. irreversible
9. diagnosis
10. forego

Understanding the Text

Answer the following questions by carefully reviewing the authors' aruguments in the short essay.

1. What do the authors mean by the title, "The Sick Care System"?

2. What do the authors mean when they write that health care is class-based?

3. If a person has medical insurance, does that mean they pay no health care costs?

4. According to the authors, what should be done to improve the health care system?

Analyzing Writing

Answer the following questions by carefully reviewing the authors' arugments and writing strategies from the short essay.

1. Find three transition sentences and analyze how they work and how effective (or not) they are.

2. Examine how the authors employ data examples in the text. Can you cite the specific paragraphs?

3. Circle at least three uses of intentional fragments in the piece. Do you think these uses are effective?

23 A Third Side to Abortion

The status quo debate about abortion virtually dictates that one view it as black and white, a **binary**, an either-or choice of morality where one side must be absolutely wrong and one right. There is no straddling the fence on this issue; there is no ambiguity; there is no partial abortion or partial choice. Everyone has an opinion, and everyone knows the arguments. Pro-choice advocates argue for the mother's right to choose and the **abeyance** of government interference in a person's choices about their body. Pro-life advocates argue that abortions at any age of the fetus are the equivalent of murder and neither states nor their citizens should **condone** legalized murder; according to this view, the state has not only the right but the duty as well to regulate certain aspects of a person's body when it comes to committing homicide. The state, after all, they argue, already regulates many aspects of a person's power over their body, especially when it comes to drug use or physician-assisted suicide. Brought into this toxic mix are issues about when life begins, the point of conception, and general ethical problems involved with terminating life at any stage.

1

While abortions were illegal for virtually all of recorded history, anecdotal evidence suggests that they had been occurring for many years before "abortion" arrived on the national stage in 1970 when New York State legalized the procedure, and even more prominently in 1973 with the Supreme Court decision of Roe vs. Wade, which legalized it on a national level. After the controversial decision of Roe v. Wade, pro-life advocates stepped up their efforts to de-legalize the procedure or at least inhibit its implementation, with some radicalized groups even participating in bombing clinics that performed—among other procedures—abortions. On the other side of the aisle, pro-choice advocates formed action groups designed to fight legal threats to the Supreme Court decision of Roe v. Wade. Radicalized pro-choice groups have even offered "guerilla workshops" to train volunteers in getting the pro-choice message out in the loudest, most visible way. It is not only these specialized groups who have strong opinions about abortion. Indeed, most people in the United States have strong beliefs about the legality and morality of abortion. The only thing these groups can agree on is that this has been one of the most divisive issues in the U. S. in the last thirty-five years.

2

3   Abortion is certainly a serious concern, and the 1.4 million abortion procedures conducted every year in the U. S. is cause for necessary debate, but there is a third side to the issue, one that is perhaps just as important as the legality of the procedure itself. Abortion has caused a national **rift** that has effectively hijacked political debate over other issues that personally affect many more people. After Roe v. Wade, nearly every major election in the United States has been focused to a large degree on abortion and the representative **platforms** adopted by the Republican and Democratic parties. One wing of the Republican Party took the line that abortion would not be tolerated and thus dedicated itself to the overturning of legalized abortion. By political necessity then, the Democratic Party took the opposite position, favoring pro-life groups, feminist groups, and groups devoted to the non-interference of government with personal decisions. Thus, most elections became an either/or choice, a one-issue vote regardless of other issues of significant concern.

4   In a very interesting way, the matter of abortion has crossed class lines and has unified social groups on the basis of culture and religion rather than class and employment. Voters have been repeatedly polarized, and their ballot casting has often been determined by this one subject. At the same time, other issues, such as rising unemployment or the quality of jobs, which are inherently less black and white and could use an approach based on logic rather than ethics, have not been given equal attention. Indeed, this **polarization** and distraction from other important matters have been and continue to be the major contributions of abortion to the culture and the political stage of the U.S. This is not to say that abortion should not discussed, but should the topic almost exclude other relevant issues?

5   It is no coincidence that 1973 marks the change toward a focus on abortion as one of the central issues of our time. During the same period in 1972 around when abortion was legalized, employee wages reached their highest point and have been on a steep decline ever since. While most elections boil down to the either/or abortion decision, social analysts including Barbara Ehrenreich of the *New Yorker*, have cautioned about workers' rights being systematically **eroded**, wages (adjusted for inflation) significantly falling, and job security becoming neither guaranteed nor expected. In short, while the country has been sidetracked with abortion, the collective pockets of our employees have been rifled by new laws that support big business.

6   This is not precisely a Republican or Democratic problem. The net effect is the same regardless of who is in power. While citizens focus so exclusively on abortion, issues of incredible importance are regulated without a great deal of national debate. The standards of the clean air act of 1970 have recently been loos-

ened; there is a plan to drill in the Alaskan wilderness; reclassification of environmental hazards benefit big business. Yet it is not only environmental issues that have been neglected. As of 2006, companies can legally treat employee retirement funds as "assets," which then enables them to use these funds to pay off company debts in case they declare bankruptcy. Millions of people have already been robbed of their hard earned retirement money, yet Congress refuses to pass legislation changing this **loophole** in the law, which significantly benefits corporations. At the same time, billions of dollars in tax relief have been funneled to the upper 5% of the population without anyone saying peep; the federal deficit has grown to nine trillion dollars, nearly thirty thousand dollars for every man, woman, and child in the U.S.

All this, of course, is not to say that abortion should not be treated as a significant issue or that it is directly to blame for the host of major problems facing the country. However, it is a co-conspirator, for the net effect of the abortion issue has been to disproportionately limit the **scope** of national debate over important topics that affect many more people in the U.S. and the world. The **pundits** and advocates on either side of the abortion aisle have a right to have this matter aired for debate; however, this should not be the subject that receives the most attention and shapes the entirety of the political dialogue or the entirety of citizens' political identity, especially when there is still such disagreement about the ethics and morality involved. While the attention of the populace has been sidetracked, matters of great importance have been decided for us—many times to our detriment.

7

Discussing and Writing About The Text

Discussing Issues:

Try to think of your own position on abortion. Interview some of your peers, your parents, or friends to find out what their position is and whether it could be a matter on which they would entirely base their vote for a specific candidate. Evaluate your findings and discuss them with your peers and instructor.

Writing about the Text:

In a well-developed and organized essay, respond to the reading; be sure to support your views with pertinent examples drawn from your own experience and observations, as well as readings.

Topic 1: According to the authors, what are the consequences of polarizing issues such as abortion? To what extent—if at all—do you agree with this view point?

Topic 2: According to your opinion, how can political debates avoid such polarizations? To support your opinion, you need to examine relevant and specific examples from a variety of sources.

Developing Vocabulary:

The words below may appear as part of your online quizzes. Please refer to the introduction for study strategies for learning vocabulary.

1. binary
2. abeyance
3. to condone
4. rift
5. platform
6. polarization
7. eroded
8. loophole
9. scope
10. pundit

Understanding the Text

Answer the following questions by carefully reviewing the authors' aruguments in the short essay.

1. What are the main arguments on abortion?

    That although it is an important issue it over shadows other issues that should also be important to voters

2. What is the authors' response to the debate on abortion?

    reduce the amount of talk over it & focus on other issues

3. Why are the authors concerned about the extent of the on-going debate on abortion?

    That it over faders other issues in the political process

4. What are some of the authors' suggestions on the issue of abortion?

    Let women decide whether abortion should be legalized or not

Analyzing Writing

Answer the following questions by carefully reviewing the authors' aruguments and writing strategies from the short essay.

1.   At which point of the essay do the authors state their thesis (beginning, middle, or end)? How effective do you find this positioning?

In the middle, it's effective but I feel that putting in the beginning would be equally effective

2.   Find the focus-theme of each paragraph, and write it in the margin next to each paragraph. Is each paragraph organized around a specific focus or not?

Yes, & It is very effect

3.   Examine the use of sources in the essay. What kind of sources do the authors use (personal examples, anecdotes, facts, authorities, etc)? Do you think they are appropriate and convincing? What additional sources would you use?

The author uses all the sources discussed & they are very appropriate for the topic & convincing

24 Protesting 101

The mass demonstrations against proposed immigra- 1
tion policies of 2006 came as quite a surprise for their
ferocity and the number of people involved. In one
demonstration alone in May of 2006, over a million
opponents of the proposed law that would restructure
and restrict immigration in the U. S. set foot on
streets across the United States. This is heartening
news for a Democracy that is by the people and for
the people, for it shows how citizens (and non-citizens) take action to have their
voices heard. Similar large-scale protests took place in the 1970s with Cesar
Chavez and the Farm Workers Union, who protested the exploitation of migrant
farm labor. But who is listening and does it matter? Even with a million people
out on the streets, does this matter to those in power?

The answer is no. This will, no doubt, sound like heresy and cynicism to 2
someone who is intensely dedicated to the democratic process. However, demonstrations are ineffectual if they have no follow-up action. They amount to a semi-
organized, angry parade of people that chant short limericks made up on the spot:
"No Justice; No Peace," "What do we want? Justice. When do we want it? Now."
These may be stirring to the blood for some, but ultimately they accomplish very
little. It is a mere echo on the wind that those in power may be annoyed by, but
they won't hear. Sounds cynical?

Well, first of all, the protest may be literally too far away from anyone to 3
hear. There have been systematic efforts by the government since the late 1960s
to reduce the possible **efficacy** of protests or demonstrations. This begins with
limiting the time, manner, and place of gathering. Government officials cannot directly **outlaw** association and assembly, for that would be unconstitutional; they
just make it likely that any assembly will have limited visibility and effect. Examine, for instance, the protests that were staged at the inauguration of President
George W. Bush in 2004. Based on "reasons of security," protesters were **sequestered** in a separate area far from anyone where they could protest to their
heart's content without interrupting the inauguration or being heard by any of the
audience members. Furthermore, protests have to be registered with government
officials, who can enforce permit fees and bureaucratically dissuade protestors
from mounting anything at all. Even the design of many public areas has taken into

account the limitation and **subjugation** of protesting. The UC San Diego campus, for instance, contains only a small central courtyard where few students can rally at any given time, which was originally designed with the fear of student protests turning into riots.

4   Thus, mounting a protest is difficult enough given the restrictions of time, manner, and place, or in other words, the government hoops that have to be jumped through in order to get a permit. Even if all this is accomplished, the place can be significantly controlled by the authorities. More troubling, however, is that even if a group manages to pull-off a large-scale demonstration, such as what occurred with the protestors concerned about proposed immigration policy, what effect will their effort have? Unfortunately, those in power are not much affected by people shouting in the streets. Some might argue that this was not the case with the massive protests in France that occurred in April of 2006. Were they not effective? Did the French government not promise to provide billions of dollars of development assistance? Yes, the French did eventually offer economic support to the poorest immigrants in the area, but this was after months of ineffective demonstrations that eventually turned into wholesale riots. Cars were burned; stores were plundered; people were beaten in the streets. The French government did nothing while thousands protested. They only acted once Paris was burning.

5   Look at the large demonstrations before the war in Iraq. Look at the thousands who protest the World Trade Organization at any of its annual meetings. Look at demonstrations in local communities to see what effect any parading about has had. This does not mean that nothing should be done or that those in power should be given free reign over all, but the answer is not through protesting on the street. Such protests may only be part of the solution. No, change is wrought by the threat of consequences. This does not necessarily demand violence, as was the case in France with the immigrant protests. Demonstrations, per se, without the threat of further action that will cause harm to those in power are worthless. For any real change to occur those protesting must have some sort of **leverage**.

6   These are facts that the forefathers of civil disobedience learned the hard way, which we seem to have forgotten. Members of the Thirteen Colonies didn't march around the pier in Boston railing against the Tea Tax. They first **petitioned** the British government, listed their grievances, and attempted to change the law. When King George failed to listen, they boarded the ship and dumped the tea into the harbor. Another central figure in civil disobedience, Henry David Thoreau advocated change in laws (only once democratic means were exhausted) by withholding taxes from the government. For Thoreau, the democratic method was best, but in the real world power tends to preserve itself because of vested inter-

est. Thoreau called this "expediency," and according to him, all those in power seek to retain their power. Likewise, Indians protested British rule throughout the 1940s, but it wasn't until Ghandi and his followers began breaking what they thought were unjust laws in protest that anything was achieved. Martin Luther King believed protesters should create "tension" in a community through **boycotts**, strikes, and large-scale disruptions of community operations. His march on Birmingham, Alabama not only included a public demonstration, it also included a significant stoppage of the entire transportation system of the city, crippling its infrastructure. These figures all wanted peaceful change through non-violence, and they did not advocate taking up arms, riots, or any violent disruption of the government. However, they all realized that government and institutions have a vested interest in the status quo, for those in power refused to **budge** because it was not in their best interest despite the parade-like protesting that had occurred. Things only changed once there was an effect and the harm that the protesters were doing to the vested interest outweighed maintaining the system as it was.

We like to think that we live in an **enlightened** age when the rights of people, once aired in rational and democratic processes, will be followed. However, power by its nature, though more refined now in its practice, still holds sway. However, the true greatness of America and other democracies is that the laws protect protestors from being harmed or thrown in jail. The real beauty of democracy is that it *allows for the possibility of protesting, but it doesn't mean that the people's voices will necessarily be heard,* for without a credible threat to the pocket book or reputation of those in power, no fundamental change can or will occur.

7

Discussing and Writing About The Text

Discussing Issues:

Have you ever tried to change anything by protesting? Were your actions effective? What do you think the role of negotiation should be as an agent of change? Think of a current issue that you would like to change. How would you go about it? What means would you use?

Writing about the Text:

In a well-developed and organized essay, respond to the reading; be sure to support your views with pertinent examples drawn from your own experience and observations, as well as readings.

Topic 1: According to the authors, why are some protests ineffective? How can protesters change the system? To what extent—if at all—do you think the authors are correct about this assertion?

Topic 2: Read Martin Luther King's "Letter from Birmingham Jail." Write a compare and contrast essay in which you discuss the views from "Protesting 101" in the context of King's work on civil disobedience.

Developing Vocabulary:

The words below may appear as part of your online quizzes. Please refer to the introduction for study strategies for learning vocabulary.

1. ferocity
2. efficacy
3. outlaw
4. sequestered
5. subjugation
6. leverage
7. petitioned
8. boycotts
9. to budge
10. enlightened

25 Locking up the Population

Imagine what you might say to thousands of college graduates as a keynote speaker at **commencement**. Would it be something like this? "Your future is bright, and the world is your oyster. Your mission is to find challenging work to better this world." Right? Wrong. In perhaps what would sound like a more **cynical** but certainly more realistic message, I would tell them that if they wish for a chance at secure employment, excellent pay, exciting work conditions, the likelihood of meeting interesting people, they should get a job "locking people up." Indeed, what other industry has been more prosperous in the U.S. than imprisoning people? The business of locking people up has actually skyrocketed since the 1980s. Now, one in every 140 citizens is currently **incarcerated**; at any given time, there are more than 2 million people behind bars in the U.S., and the U.S. *has the highest prison population as well as the highest percentage of prison population in the world*. While exact statistics vary, according to *BBC News* (April, 2006), the U. S. imprisons over 700 out of 100,000 residents, which is followed by Russia at 638, Belarus at 554, Kazakhstan at 522. Even Britain, which leads the European Union, tops out at a **measly** 139, according to the UK Home Office government statistics of 2003. If you want a job in a growth industry, forget computer science or engineering: boring. Look to the U. S. prison industrial complex.

It may be difficult to understand why the U. S., arguably one of the richest and most developed countries on earth, would have the largest prison population. One explanation for the millions locked up might be that there are simply more criminals and that the prison system has had to expand to **accommodate** societal needs. After all, prisons are designed to **dissuade** potential criminals from engaging in illegal activities. Yet, even while more people are being incarcerated, crime rates keep going up, so there doesn't seem to be much dissuading occurring. One reason for the increase might be in the one demographic that has gone up—way, way up—the population incarcerated for drug offenses, which now forms the mainstay of the prison system. Overall, according to the U. S. Department of Justice, since the 1980s crime rates have gone down for serious crime, violent crime, property crime, and fire-arm related crimes, but at the same time incarcerations for drug-related offenses have gone up exponentially. Supporters

1

2

of the prison industry take credit for the crackdown as tougher sentencing guidelines were introduced in the early 1980s. The results can be seen in the thirteen million convicts who have spent time locked up (Justice Policy Institute, 2004) over the years and are now paroled.

3   If you had invested in a prison stock in 1982 when expenditures were roughly seven billion dollars per year, you would be able to retire now with the 573% increase in prison funding, around sixty billion in 2003 for just the prison system. This money, of course, does not include all the costs of the courts or the 1.1 million police officers on the street, all of which increase the annual expenditure to 167 billion per year. This is where the money is at. So, as the keynote speaker would you tell the thousands of hopeful faces to pursue advanced degrees, to become teachers, or to serve the community? Unfortunately, there does not seem to be much future in such community-based service industries, especially in terms of funding and investment. Is it **coincidence**, irony, or both that as prison spending skyrocketed, education spending has increased hardly at all? In California, for example, from 1980-2000 prison spending more than doubled while education spending went up by only 1%. Despite all the expenditures on locking up the population, which according to prison officials should dissuade people from committing crimes, California had one of the highest rates for violent crime in a national survey done in 2000 (ranked 9th out of the 50 states). With tougher and longer prison sentences, it would seem like people would get the message. Crime doesn't pay. This may be easy enough to explain. At the same time California ranked 9th out of the 50 states for violent crime, its education ranking plummeted to 48th place. California is in the top tier for incarceration and at the bottom in education. Hmmmm.

4   Certainly the factors for the rise in the incarceration and crime rates are quite complex, ranging from personal to societal ones. A direct correlation of this rise, however, to the lack of education is tempting to make. Would it be unreasonable to hypothesize that if a society builds a **draconian** prison system, then fewer people would want to break the rules? The answer to this lies not in stiffer prison sentences but in the level of education they achieve. It may seem obvious that a lower quality and level of education for people is bound to result in fewer opportunities for their development, both personal and professional. This is common sense that is born out by just a cursory glance at the statistical data. The demographic of the prison population itself proves this point, for convicts often commit crimes because they don't know any better—literally! Education rates for prison populations are **abysmal**. Over 65% of the population never graduated high school. The academic skills on reading, writing, and arithmetic are terribly

low. If prisoners do have a high school degree, many of them receive it by attaining a GED (General Education Degree) in prison. Indeed, these are some of the few courses that the incarcerated can complete while in prison, for higher education degrees are certainly lacking. The point is simple: tougher prison sentences don't stop people from committing crimes, education does.

The exponential investment in prisons and in the justice system in general is a choice that people in society seem willing to make, but it doesn't make human or economic sense. According to a 2001 UCLA and University of Rochester study published in the *Joint Center for Poverty Research* journal, only a 1% increase in the male high school graduation rate would save as much as $1.4 billion dollars ($2,100 per additional high school graduate) because those people wouldn't commit crime. They would get jobs and become part of the community. Need more facts? The likelihood for committing crimes goes down—way down—the higher the education achieved, which is particularly pronounced for minorities. Indeed, an average of only 3% of the current prison population received a college degree before being incarcerated. There is no denying that a clear correlation exists between the incarcerated and the uneducated. Becoming a criminal is usually not a matter of natural selection, nor can it entirely be a matter of personal choice. If people are not provided good educational opportunities in good and safe schools, what are their chances? As citizens, we have chosen through our votes to threaten with prison rather than prepare with education.

So, how should our imaginary commencement speech end? "Your future is bright because you are college educated and there are jobs available, especially in the growth industry of subduing the criminalized poor. You are the privileged. You are statistically unlikely to commit (or need to commit) a crime that will land you in prison. You are destined for a higher paycheck and slightly higher tax bracket. You can vote to protect your tax bracket rather than provide educational services to the poor." Instead, perhaps the message ought to be one of self-interest. "You can get great jobs in locking people up and controlling the population, but you will have to live in a secure compound yourself (i.e. a gated community). If you cast your vote to support the prison system instead of the education system, you may well prosper. But you or a family member could be the next victim. The world is your oyster until the next high school drop out takes it from you by gun point."

Discussing and Writing About The Text

Discussing Issues:

Make a list of any of the startling facts from the essay. Do you think more education would lessen the crime rate? The data indicate that many people nowadays are locked up for drug-related offenses. Do you think this is the right solution, or should something else such as drug rehabilitation be implemented? Do you favor tough prison sentences or mandatory prison sentences for three time offenders?

Writing about the Text:

In a well-developed and organized essay, respond to the reading; be sure to support your views with pertinent examples drawn from your own experience and observations, as well as readings.

Topic 1: According to the author, what are the connections between the prison system and the education system? To what extent—if at all—do you think the author is correct about this assertion?

Topic 2: Research the issue of education within the prison system. Consider what effect—if any—education programs have on the prison population and on their likelihood of committing crimes after they are paroled. Does greater levels of education create calmer prisoners who are ready to integrate into society?

Developing Vocabulary:

The words below may appear as part of your online quizzes. Please refer to the introduction for study strategies for learning vocabulary.

1. commencement	2. cynical
3. incarcerated	4. measly
5. accommodate	6. dissuade
7. aphorism	8. coincidence
9. draconian	10. abysmal

26 Privacy Under Attack

When most people think of privacy under attack, they think of **nefarious** criminals compromising their personal information by rifling their garbage or sifting through the cyber trails they make online. To be sure, identity theft is a huge problem today, with over ten million people affected in the United States in 2005 alone! But it isn't reckless behavior of computer users that seems to pose the highest risk. Ironically, it is the security systems of companies and the plethora of personal information that is available on these systems. Complete life histories, credit reports, important numbers (ID, social security, Driver's License), even preferences for products are all available for the aspiring thief, the theft of which costs companies and people 53 billion dollars a year as well as a loss of 297 million hours (*CQ Researcher*, June 10th, 2005). In a series of semi-publicized crimes in 2005, hackers broke into and compromised the systems of Bank of America, Ameritrade, Citifinancial, Time Warner, and a host of other companies. In May of 2006, the extensive personal records of twenty-six million military veterans were stolen! These are just the crimes that we know about that make us realize that our privacy and safety are undeniably in danger.

In the case of **fraud** or hackers **invidiously** securing others' information, the violation of privacy is clear and criminal. They should be tracked down by the F. B. I. and put in jail. However, people's privacy has seldom been under assault from so many different sides as it is today. This becomes particularly apparent when one examines the *legal* violation of privacy for the sake of safety and governmental control; in this case, privacy and its violation become a two-edged sword. Take the terrorist bombing in the London Underground in July of 2005. It was possible, for instance, for the police to capture the individuals involved in the crime and to prevent a similar bombing two weeks later on account of the 6,000 video **surveillance** cameras just in the Subway itself. No one even knows how many other cameras can be found in London at ATMs, as traffic cameras, and as surveillance cameras. In Birmingham, England, for example, every corner of the city is under constant surveillance, which police say has cut down on crime. The U. S. has also followed the Closed Circuit Television (CCTV) boom, which was boosted in 2005 with the advent of high quality digital cameras that can take ex-

1

2

tremely clear video at 1600x1200 pixels while continuously running face recognition software. Almost anywhere you go, someone is watching your every move. The constant surveillance is completely legal and is only half of what is happening.

3   Not only can we be seen everywhere, we can also be heard as well. Currently, in the U. S. there is an ongoing constitutional crisis over the use of "illegal" wiretaps by the U. S. government on so-called "suspects of interest" who might have a connection to terrorists. As far as anyone knows, there have been over one-thousand wire taps that were conducted by the F. B. I., and the current government is unapologetic for them, claiming its right to use them for the sake of national security. What would have been cause for a Watergate-like scandal (i.e. the bugging of the Democratic National Headquarters in the Watergate hotel by Nixon) some years ago has debatable legal grounds today.

4   As if government prying and spying were not bad enough, we are being monitored by corporations as well. While corporations and stores collect information from willing people through the use of club cards, raffles, or rebates, much of that can be and is sold to other parties. Customer name lists have been a sellable **commodity** for some time now, so when you buy a subscription to *Time Magazine*, you will soon be getting calls from similar magazines and periodicals to whom your name was sold. The law is on the side of companies, for consumers have to fight to have their names, identities, and purchasing habits protected. The **default** position for companies is that any information they collect about you can be sold, and consumers have to search for the box on any form, if available, to indicate they don't want their personal information sold to the highest bidder.

5   Last but certainly not least is the most recent issue with privacy that has arisen with the invention of Radio Frequency Identification Devices (RFIDs). These tiny microchips come with miniature antennas and are **imbedded** in the bar codes of all manner of products. From milk to high definition televisions, manufacturers are labeling their products to be able to track their use. In this way, they know when product inventory is low, where it is **en route** to a store, and how long it stays in a person's house before being discarded. If a person paid with a credit card for that product, the purchase history is routinely stored with the specific identification for that product. According to *Consumer Reports*, the forecast is for 1.3 billion RFIDs to be sold in 2006 alone, with the number going up exponentially as the price comes down to roughly one penny per tag (June, 2006). At that rate, within five to seven years nearly all products will have a tag. In the near future, even shoes will have a built-in transmitter, so if a company wanted to check on the location of a particular pair of shoes, they could access the sales informa-

tion and name on the credit card. They could even get a precise location of the person walking down the street wearing those shoes as they now have in place for the RFIDs attached to cars that use toll lanes. Despite, however, plausible allusions to and echoes of a *1984* Big Brother type of interference, there are advantages to RFIDs since companies may know when store supplies are running low, so they can ship new inventory before the shelves are left bare. Companies can know how quickly items are thrown out, so they could even conduct research to better their products. Consumers, in effect, could really win when companies are better informed.

There is no denying the advantages of foregoing some of our privacy. The police in London were able to prevent a similar subway bombing, and crime rates across the U.S. are down, and some attribute this to the estimated two million installed surveillance cameras. There is no denying the consumer advantages that we enjoy because of companies tracking our purchasing habits and product usage. At the same time that our lives are made easier and safer, it may be shortly possible that every citizen will be under video surveillance everywhere we go, and the purchases we make will be intimately connected to us, forever stored in some database that awaits an assault by a cyber criminal. The cost for these benefits of increased security and convenience is the forfeiture of our privacy. We currently are straddling the edge of the sword, balancing our values on the **honed** edge. The problem is that Congress has its head in the sand, and the only protection of citizens and consumers is the assurance by governments and corporations that they won't misuse their power **to pry** into our privacy. Can we be so sure? Privacy (or the lack thereof) is one of the most crucial issues of our time, but ironically there is a significant lack of public discussion over private rights that may already be lost without a fight. Perhaps they can be found by video surveillance or RFID tag?

6

Discussing and Writing About The Text

Discussing Issues:

Make a list of all the recent news stories that you remember on the topic of privacy. Do you think that people's information should be private, especially if there is a matter of public security? Corporations now argue that whatever information you give them is theirs to keep. Is this right? What should be done—if anything—to keep information private? What do you think is the greatest danger to the privacy of individuals?

Writing about the Text:

In a well-developed and organized essay, respond to the reading; be sure to support your views with pertinent examples drawn from your own experience and observations, as well as readings.

Topic 1: According to the authors, how is individual privacy being attacked nowadays? What are the dangers involved with the loss of privacy? To what extent—if at all—do you think the authors are correct about their concerns?

Topic 2: Try to find out any information about yourself that you can that is publicly available on the Internet. Make a list of everything you find and compile your observations into a short research paper. What information did you find and how easy was it to find?

Developing Vocabulary:

The words below may appear as part of your online quizzes. Please refer to the introduction for study strategies for learning vocabulary.

1. nefarious	2. fraud
3. invidiously	4. surveillance
5. commodity	6. default
7. imbedded	8. en route
9. honed	10. to pry

CHAPTER
FOUR

Education

27 Should Everyone Go to College?

Every November in high schools across the country, one can see seniors **scurrying** around quads, lurking near counseling offices, and running to the post office for extra postage. Why? This is the typical month when college applications are due and the task of vetting admission begins. This culminates a process of finishing Advanced Placement (AP) classes, attending preparatory courses for the Scholastic Aptitude Tests (SATs), taking the SATs (sometimes twice), filling out applications, writing letters of intent, and **soliciting** recommendations from favorite instructors or administrators. Months of eager anticipation and worry follow the circuitous path of these applications as nails are bitten, hopes are aired, and mailboxes are watched for fateful acceptance or rejection letters. The collected angst of high school students waiting for word from selected colleges could probably power a small town, for this is no small matter. According to the Department of Labor statistics for 2004, over 67% of the nation's recent 2.8 million high school graduates enrolled in colleges across America. It seems like everyone is going to college or at least wants to. But should they?

Every fall newly **matriculated** freshmen arrive at hundreds of colleges to begin illustrious (or sometimes pedestrian) careers as college students. While many already have an idea in mind of what they would like to do and have picked out a course plan for the next four years to achieve their goal, a cartload of students not only doesn't have an idea what they want, but they are also ill-prepared to pursue whatever it is they might want. In many of these cases, students have been pushed and **prodded** through the gates to college campuses by eager parents who have planned out the general life path of their offspring. "Our Johnny will be a doctor, will graduate from Stanford University, and will do a residency at Johns Hopkins." "Our Susan will be an engineer, will graduate with honors from MIT, and will be the CEO of a firm building bridges." While these examples may seem far-fetched, they are not too far from the truth when one thinks that often parents are encouraged to set up special college funds when the child is still a baby just as parents are encouraged to be part of the college process. Universities across the U. S. have even implemented orientation programs not only for students, but for parents as well. Parents, after all, carry the check book, and they want to know where their money is going.

3   Now, after the parents have left the tuition checks on the way out of the dorms, some of the students who stay behind just seem confused at what they are to do. Some don't like the choice of major or don't have the skills or background for it, but parents (or career guides) have told them a thousand times that "Bio-Med is the way to go, not Art History." And there was never any possibility considered other than attending college. Indeed, the students who don't want to be in college at all are in an even more difficult position than the ones confused about their major. However, is there any option other than college? The American high-school system is set up as a funneling instrument for college. High-school students are told by parents, counselors, and peers that attending college is "expected," and for some there is no other choice. Indeed, the 33% of high-school graduates who forego college must face the possible **wrath** of angry parents and the social status of a **pariah** who could not "hack it," "could not get in," or who will do nothing with their life. At the time, it seems that the only two things worse than not attending college are dropping out of high school or going to prison.

4   Unfortunately, the high-school-education system in the U. S. is set up as a college-prep machine, which leaves all the students who either don't want to attend college or who might want to pursue a trade-school education hanging in the wind. Sure, high schools have the mandatory wood shop, metal shop, or auto shop for those students who "don't want to strive for anything better." These under-valued, under-funded, and socially illegitimate courses are thought to be the bulwark of students who can't or won't put their noses to the grindstone of vigorous academic work. How would Johnny's parents feel if he didn't become a doctor, but he elected to become a mechanic? Would he be socially recognized for his great skill with engines when he could have been a surgeon?

5   The 33% of high school seniors who don't attend college are left with an **ad hoc** mixture of on-the-job training and vague certificate programs. There is no Advanced Placement program for high school vocational training; in most high schools, there is only a sporadic possibility for elective courses once the "real" courses of English, Math, and Science have been taken. A look at the annual *U. S. News and World Report Guide to America's Best Colleges* can prove this. In this guide, a complex equation to rank colleges nationwide is used. On the other hand, there is not a similar publication for the best vocational schools. The electricians, mechanics, plumbers, carpenters, machinery operators, landscapers et al too often receive what knowledge they have through inconsistent on-the-job-training by employers who train them not in the theoretical, historical, or pragmatic background of their vocation, but only in the tasks at hand they need to complete. If

workers do complete a certification course (and there are many available), they cannot be sure of the quality of the course, and their high schools probably will not have prepared them for this training.

One may ask why a mechanic should know the theory or history behind automobile engines. Well, this may not help in the day-to-day task of changing oil, but what if there were an unusual sound coming from the engine where analytical skills and knowledge would be required? Proper education and background in engine repair would allow for a more systematic, consistent, and efficient approach to the repair. The mechanic would probably know how to better isolate and focus on the problem, thus saving both time and money. Furthermore, even more money could be saved by taxpayers on the overall education system if students who know they like working with their hands could choose as early as the 9th grade to attend **vocational** high schools. Why should these students take Advanced Placement courses in English or Anatomy if they really want to work with wood?   6

High schools in Europe may be a model for this dual system; in many European countries such as Germany and France, high schools have been divided (not **stratified**) for a long while based on whether students wish to attend college or a vocational school, following matriculation from high school. Students decide in 9th or 10th grade what they wish to focus on, and they begin strenuous courses in either college preparation or vocational training. Furthermore, graduates from vocational high schools are not left to their own devices upon graduation. To work in almost any industry, they must complete additional rigorous certification programs that can last up to two years full time. Thus, upon graduation with a certificate, they really do know their stuff. Additionally, they are not socially **vilified** for not having attended college, for these trained professionals can make a decent living and earn prestige as competent technicians. Not everyone wants to attend college, nor should they; however, there need to be valid and socially acceptable alternatives to the dichotomy of college graduate versus social loser.   7

Discussing and Writing About The Text

Discussing Issues:

Make a list of the factors that prompted you to attend college and then compare them those of your peers. Make another list of other options you considered in the process of choosing your professional future and try to explain why you rejected these alternative options.

Writing about the Text:

In a well-developed and organized essay, respond to the reading; be sure to support your views with pertinent examples drawn from your own experience and observations, as well as readings.

Topic 1: According to the authors, what are the main problems with the current educational system in terms of students' professional orientation? Do you think the authors' views are valid, to what extent, and why?

Topic 2: When and on based on what criteria do you think people should make decisions about their professional future? What do you think should be the parents' involvement in this process?

Developing Vocabulary:

The words below may appear as part of your online quizzes. Please refer to the introduction for study strategies for learning vocabulary.

1. **scurrying** move quickly
2. **soliciting** ask for something
3. **matriculated** be enrolled in college
4. **prodded** persuade
5. **wrath** rage
6. **pariah** outcast
7. **ad hoc** particular purpose only
8. **vocational** direct training
9. **stratified** classify
10. **vilified** critizize

Understanding the Text

Answer the following questions by carefully reviewing the authors' aruguments in the short essay.

1. How does parental interference affect children's decisions about their professional future?

   Parents will often make decisions for their child. They will also plan what career their child will have, and won't take into cosideration what the child wants to do.

2. What are the problems many students encounter in making a choice of profession?

   Many students face peer pressure in selecting what proffession they want to persue.

3. What is the role of high school in the current system, and how could it change?

   The current role of high school is to teach students how to be accepted into a college, but don't prepair them for the accademics. Maybe High schools could teach what students want to learn.

4. What are the authors' suggestions for improving the education system?

   Allow students to choose in 9th grade whether they want to enter a vocational school or go to college.

Analyzing Writing

Answer the following questions by carefully reviewing the authors' arugments and writing strategies from the short essay.

1. Examine the role of questions in the text and their effectiveness.

2. Underline five transitions you thought were particularly effective and explain why they are.

3. Examine all the paragraphs and their topic sentence(s). Do the topic sentences help clarify the focus of the paragraph?

28 Traveling as Education

Few people directly connect traveling with education, but even if they do, the connection occurs primarily in the form of sightseeing, museum visiting, foreign-cuisine sampling, and, of course, souvenir gathering. The education involved is often limited to what travelers acquire from a museum docent or a guidebook. Ultimately, the travelers return to their normal routines with a set of pictures and some stories to tell about strange architecture, strange foods, and strange people. Besides and beyond these aspects, however, traveling can be one of the most important contributing factors to a person's educational development. Under the right circumstances, traveling may prove to be equally necessary, if not more enriching than schooling. 1

First things first, however, for defining this kind of traveling is of primary significance. Starting in a reverse way, we can define traveling by what it is not. To be educational, traveling does not necessarily involve a great distance to or a great length of time at the place of destination; it does not have to be a trip to Tibet or a year spent in the Australian Outback as a **hermit**. Traveling could be as simple as taking a bus trip to a nearby city to spend a Saturday morning. Thus, it mainly depends on the places of origin and of destination. Distance and time are not the issues; rather, what is more important is that travelers should be exposed to an environment and to people that are different from what they are used to. In that sense, traveling can stretch the fabric of what the travelers know, exposing them to different experiences, cultures, and people. Therefore, if one is from a particular region in the U.S., journeying to a town ten miles down the road may not count. Though some of the landscape or the facilities may be different, most likely the essence of the place and the way one interacts with the environment remain the same. The way one shops for food will be more or less the same in the local supermarket, organized in a **congruent** way, having identical products, and overall the same **modus operandi**. If the place of destination is then quite similar to the place of origin, travelers will not be intrigued to reevaluate the environment and their place within it. 2

The real traveler should pursue not only exposure to an array of new stimuli but also an understanding of the differences and similarities among places, peo- 3 ple, and cultures. Indeed, real traveling goes beyond "seeing" a place to "understanding" it. In that mode, traveling can broaden our cultural horizons, allowing us to see and seek to comprehend the ways of the peoples of the world. It can allow us to at least try to explain, if not appreciate, the multitude of lenses in living and viewing life. In that way, an act as simple as eating ice cream could be interesting and instructive. Most Americans would think nothing of purchasing an ice-cream cone from an ice-cream parlor and then strolling down the street. A similar action in Japan, on the other hand, would bring stares of **reproach**, for eating in public while walking is considered a low-class act of an uncultured person.

4　　The list of cultural differences could be written on a scroll of **parchment** that spans the globe. Traveling can expose people to these alternative ways of viewing the world even if it is through the simple realization that not everyone will or has to necessarily react to situations with the same set of culturally ingrained codes. By frequent exposure to alternative methods of dealing with the world, people can approach differences and conflicts with expansive background knowledge. The man who seems utterly cold and silent at the first meeting might not be overtly rude. Instead, he may culturally be showing respect by listening intently to what is being said. The woman who "crowds" others in the grocery store line, violating their personal space, may simply be following a behavior learned in her home country. Perhaps she hasn't adapted to her new environment yet. Rather than seeing these behaviors as "strange, weird, or rude," the real traveler may be able to find them different yet normal. Thus, frequent travel can help **ameliorate** cultural conflicts through better understanding.

5　　This brings us to what seems to be a fundamental criterion for genuine and educational traveling. Indeed, just because a person logs a hundred thousand miles on a plane or becomes exposed to differences doesn't mean they have "traveled." True traveling involves the suspension—to some degree—of one's own cultural values and expectations. It is precisely because many people who travel abroad fail to do this that so many stereotypes of tourists exist. The "ugly American" is a famed stereotype of the wealthy tourist who expects and demands that everything they encounter be like it is in the U.S. Loud and obnoxious, this stereotypical American tourist is constantly complaining about small sizes, limited English, and "inferior" service. Undoubtedly, Americans are not alone in these stereotypes. The Japanese are supposed to be glued to their cameras to the point of obsession while the British are seen as snobby and condescending. Last but not least, come the Greeks whose constant need to ascertain the superiority of their proud homeland and ancient heritage can be irritating. While these stereotypes *certainly* exaggerate to one degree or another, they also teach an important lesson. Those tourists who **personify** these types of travelers have not only packed their clothes and camera gear with them, but they have also stowed a tight set of cultural values and lenses, expecting that their world should be **replicated** anywhere they go. They are locked, in essence, into seeing the world in only one way and transforming it whenever possible. Such travel merely changes the architecture and the climate; it does not change the way in which these travelers view the world. So, why not save the money, stay at home, and watch a show on the Travel Channel?

Real traveling should open our mind to alternative lifestyles and modes of   6
thought. This doesn't mean that we should entirely abandon our own values or system of doing things when encountering other lands, people, and cultures. It doesn't mean, for instance, that if in one culture horse meat is considered a delicacy we should sit down to a feast of stallions. In Italy, for instance, horse meat is regularly eaten while in California it was made illegal by proposition. Travel to Italy does not entail that we should feast on horses; however, we should not immediately condemn Italians as barbarians for doing so. Besides photo albums and souvenir collections, real traveling can be **conducive** to education if we see it as an opportunity to reevaluate our own cultural preconceptions and understand, if not appreciate the culture of the place of destination.

Wide exposure to many of the world's cultures through travel stimulates   7
our critical faculties. We are more likely to evaluate why we do certain things as well as to ascertain what preconceptions for behavior and demeanor we all have. Likewise, in the next encounter, when someone appears ill-mannered, we might pause a second or two to consider the possible reasons for this before condemning him as one of "those people". Finally, while travel is no **panacea** for the world's ills, understanding through exposure to other cultures might prove to be an educational adventure as well as a way to strengthen bonds among the world's peoples.

Discussing and Writing About The Text

Discussing Issues:

Make a list of your traveling experiences; do they constitute regular traveling or "genuine" traveling according to the authors' criteria? Compare your findings to those of your peers and try to compile a "Guide for Genuine Traveling."

Writing about the Text:

In a well-developed and organized essay, respond to the reading; be sure to support your views with pertinent examples drawn from your own experience and observations, as well as readings.

Topic 1: According to the authors, what are the steps a traveler has to take in order to have an authentic and educational experience? To what extent do you think modern traveling has or accomplishes these educational goals?

Topic 2: Why do you think people travel nowadays? What does traveling have to offer people and how can they get the most out of their experience?

Developing Vocabulary:

The words below may appear as part of your online quizzes. Please refer to the introduction for study strategies for learning vocabulary.

1. hermit
2. congruent
3. modus operandi
4. reproach
5. parchment
6. ameliorate
7. personify
8. replicated
9. conducive
10. panacea

Understanding the Text

Answer the following questions by carefully reviewing the authors' arugments in the short essay.

1. How do most people view traveling?

2. What are the circumstances necessary for educational traveling?

3. In what ways can traveling contribute to people's education?

4. What are stereotypes and what do they prove?

Analyzing Writing

Answer the following questions by carefully reviewing the authors' arugments and writing strategies from the short essay.

1. Examine the use of process analysis in the text and the components of the explained process.

2. Examine the use of definition in the essay. Identify the concepts that are defined and comment on the definitions' effectiveness.

3. Examine how the authors employ refutation in the text. Can you cite the specific sentences or paragraphs?

29 Let's Blame the Teachers

The education system in the United States has been for some time now going downhill, and teachers have been **patently** the ones to blame—if not entirely then partially—for this decline. Thousands of angry articles and emails written by "concerned citizens" express the widespread distress in the system about the **plight** of schools. Like a spotlight, much of the **ire** and fervor focuses on teachers as indicatively encapsulated by an email submission to an Internet discussion board by a citizen, Linda Taylor:

> I believe that most of the blame for the current blight in public education lies with the teacher training institutions. Without a doubt, they turn out poorly educated, untrained teachers. Additionally, I take teacher unions to task for not pressuring the teacher-training colleges to actually teach teachers how to teach. Representing strong, competent teachers would allow each union to bargain from strength, rather than having to bargain from weakness, so one might think that unions would realize the folly of protecting too many teachers who are ineffective, unscholarly, untrained, and some even ignorant.

First of all, this kind of vehement, **vitriolic** attack on teachers does not help solve any of the problems facing schools. It just exacerbates these problems. While there are certainly untrained and ignorant teachers working within the education system, the argument that teachers are not sufficiently trained is not only a drastic oversimplification of the quite complex issues at hand, but it is also patently false, according to the National Education Association (NEA). If anything, as the latter asserts, the accreditation process for teachers has been consistently becoming more difficult and strict, not less so.

Blaming teachers, however, is yet another **red-herring** argument that sidetracks educational discussions from the real factors in the nation's failing school districts. Instead, a host of other factors should be evaluated as significant in the failure to provide students with a quality education. The real issue then is not that teachers are untrained; it is that they don't have the resources to be effective. Consider the average class sizes in today's high schools. In many states across the country, class sizes reach thirty-six students per class, and many teachers typically carry a five-course load. Teachers are dealing with over 180 students throughout the year in addition to various other administrative tasks. It is overwhelming just to calculate the hours it would take to effectively and thoroughly grade 180 three-page essays or 180 problem sets for mathematics. Furthermore, in many of the poorer school districts, teachers face crumbling and **antiquated** facilities—buildings where bathrooms don't work, where classrooms aren't up to code, where there might not even be enough classrooms to go around. Consider that many schools cannot afford to provide a book to every student, so students only have books at their disposal while in class. As a consequence, it becomes quite hard, if possible, to assign any substantial homework if students won't have access to the textbooks at home. Consider also that in addition to mastering the curriculum and formulating effective class sessions, teachers face increasing discipline problems in the class, which take up valuable class time. Evidently, untrained teachers are not the cause of all these problems.

4   Rather, systematic under funding of schools is the single biggest factor in the deterioration of student performance. However, as long as we are doling out blame for the failure of the education system, let's do it equally. Let's blame students too. While teacher/student ratios and school resources certainly contribute to poor performance, at least part of the problem with student performance is students themselves. According to the 2005 Kaiser Family Foundation report on media usage in the U.S., children and teens between the ages of eight and eighteen spend 6.5 hours per day on average with media. What does this mean? It means that these kids watch a lot of TV (3.04 hours per day), listen to music (1.44 hours per day), use the computer (1.02 hours per day), read magazines (.43 minutes a day), go to theatres to watch movies (.25 minutes per day). All these activities leave a **paltry** fifty minutes on average for homework. This time distribution and prioritization of tasks clearly prove that students bear some responsibility for the overall decline. After all, don't they have a duty to participate in their own education? The tendency is to place blame on everything but the students and to treat the latter as passive products that go through the mill of the education system. On the contrary, however, students can and should be proactive participants in their learning. Unfortunately, too often they are more interested in the new video game or film release to pursue knowledge on their own, let alone pay attention in the classroom.

5   The finger should also be wagged at parents for their **abdication** of their educational responsibilities to schools and teachers. Too many parents—and by no means does this refer to all of them—rely entirely on teachers for their chil-

dren's education. This is too much of a burden. Teachers can, at most, provide the basic framework and curriculum to educate students, but it also depends on parents to work with their children to contextualize subjects as best they can and to provide more resources at home for further study. Parents, too, have an obligation for the success of their children's education, and it is too often these days that parents are uninvolved in school. Indeed, the statistics about parental involvement do not lie. According to a national study of parental involvement with homework, (*NLTS*, 2001), responses showed 12% never helped with homework, 12 % helped once per week, and 37% helped once or twice per week. Also in the same study, a conservative estimate by teachers concluded that parents fail to attend parent/teacher conferences 58% of the time.

Lastly, it's time to blame the voters who keep electing representatives who tie school funding to property taxes, thereby creating a class-based school system. These representatives have consistently under-funded school systems across the United States, and then they have the nerve and the **gall** to blame teachers and school districts for being dysfunctional. It's like telling a carpenter to build some shelves but not giving him any wood. Voters do have the power to alter the status quo, but unfortunately the percentage of people voting in elections is even worse than that of parents attending teacher conferences—and even worse for local elections.

Attacks on teachers are **demoralizing**, simplistic, counterproductive, and patently wrong. In fact, the next time statistics come out with low test scores for schools and someone has to be blamed, don't blame the messenger. Teachers have been complaining for some time now that they need more resources, better schools, fewer kids in the classroom, and more parental involvement, but no one seems to listen. The Internet is full of poisonous assertions of teachers' incompetence, and politicians want quick answers and fixes to complex problems. The teacher is always the easy scapegoat, who is too busy grading the 180 papers just turned in to be able to offer up much of a defense. It's time that everyone take a good hard look and dole out the blame where it belongs.

Discussing and Writing About The Text

Discussing Issues:

Do you think you are responsible for your education? Discuss with your peers possible ways to take your education in your "own hands" and make some improvements.

Writing about the Text:

In a well-developed and organized essay, respond to the reading; be sure to support your views with pertinent examples drawn from your own experience and observations, as well as readings.

Topic 1: To what factors do the authors attribute today's education system's decline? To what extent—if at all—do you agree with their arguments?

Topic 2: In a solution paper, suggest ways to improve the current education system in high schools or colleges.

Developing Vocabulary:

The words below may appear as part of your online quizzes. Please refer to the introduction for study strategies for learning vocabulary.

1. **patently**
2. **plight**
3. **ire**
4. **vitriolic**
5. **red herring**
6. **antiquated**
7. **paltry**
8. **abdication**
9. **gall**
10. **demoralizing**

Understanding the Text

Answer the following questions by carefully reviewing the authors' aruguments in the short essay.

1. What is a commonly shared view about teachers today?

2. What is the role of political decisions and voters in the education system?

3. How are students responsible for the current situation in the school system?

4. What is the responsibility of parents in the school system?

Analyzing Writing

Answer the following questions by carefully reviewing the authors' arugments and writing strategies from the short essay.

1. Examine the style and tone used by the authors in the text.

2. Find the focus-theme (topic sentence) of each paragraph, and write it in the margin next to each paragraph. Is each paragraph organized around a specific focus or not?

3. Underline the sentences that include the authors' counterarguments. Are the latter sufficient and effective?

30 The Class System in Schools

We recently completed a number of presentations at various local high schools in Southern California concerning the University of California's (UC) Analytical Writing Placement Examination (AWPE), and the experience was eye-opening if not shocking. In this program, prospective college students take the UC's version of an English placement examination to see in what composition course they would be placed should they be admitted to college and what writing improvements should they make during their junior and senior high school years. These exams are then graded analytically (with full comments in the margins as well as suggestions). In this way, students receive feedback from college instructors who routinely grade these placement exams, and they learn what specifically is required for this kind of essay examination. The **culmination** of this process is an in-class presentation and information session by the UC instructor at the host high school whereby students receive their graded exams and can have the UC instructor address their questions. This High School Outreach program is an integral part of the transitioning process from high-school to college writing.

Our own experience at two of the schools could not have been more different. Located in a well-to-do suburban area, the first school was equipped with modern buildings, **manicured** lawns, and a polite and professional office staff. Walking onto the school grounds, we were stopped by a school yard **proctor** who asked about our business on campus and then informed us that we were required to sign in at the administration office. While signing in, we were welcomed to the school by the vice-principal and were shown to the classroom where the presentation would occur. The instructor herself was dressed professionally in a suit jacket and blouse, and her room was quite "colorful" and inspiring. Indeed, besides the traditional classroom posters with themes of rock climbers and titles like "success," "motivation," or "endurance," the classroom walls also featured numerous "A" level student essays, setting an example for the students to come. Moreover, these essays were all analytically graded, which proved the instructor's painstaking grading method and her dedication to her students and her profession. Last but not least, what made this experience particularly pleasant was the students' personal investment in the improvement of their writing; not only were they well-behaved and attentive, but they were also willing to participate and ask **pertinent** questions, which easily explained their exceptional performance on the graded exams. Overall, we were quite impressed by the school and its staff.

3 The following week we were asked to do some additional presentations and grading of ELWR papers for a different school, which we gladly volunteered for, given our previous experience. However, from the very beginning the signs indicated that this visit was bound to be at least different, if not **disheartening**. The papers themselves could have served as a bad **omen** for the visit, for they were much less developed and burdened with numerous grammar errors; it seemed almost as if the students had only put a minimum amount of effort or care into their production. No more effort was made by anyone to turn the school into a pleasant or inspiring environment. If anything, the buildings of this second school were reminiscent of a prison with its grey walls which were cracked in places and connected by a ten-foot tall, chain-link fence. Despite the appearance of "security," however, it was quite easy for us to pass through the gate and go directly to the designated classroom without having to check in first, for there were no proctors or security officers to be seen anywhere. The classroom then completed the image of neglect: located in a portable, a large trailer-like classroom that was towed into place, with only the colorful, empty-worded "motivation, endurance, and success" posters to display on the tan-grey walls, it all seemed incredibly ironic and pitifully at odds with the school dynamic and the students who represented a different demographic entirely. With the scarce exception of some who were trying to pay attention and learn, most students had hardly any interest in the presentation. Instead, they were too busy doing homework for other classes, correcting their make-up, and sending text messages on their cell phones, behaviors which the instructor did not even bother **reprimanding** them for. Having finished the presentations, we could not stop but wonder about the explanation to the vast gap between these two schools.

4 The answer, of course, is class. Despite some people's protest and the overall illusion of equality, the system of education in the United States is a class-based system. Evidence for this can be easily seen in the disparities in the funding awarded for each student across the country. A 2005 National Education Association (NEA) study indicated that in New York, for instance, school districts received 13,623 dollars per student. During the same period, school districts in Utah received 6,206 dollars per student. Why the huge difference? Well, schools receive money partly from the federal government, partly from the state, and partly from the property taxes in the area. Thus, while most schools get roughly the same government dollars, the actual amount they have to spend per student is really determined by property values and property taxes. The richer the area, the higher the property-tax bills and the more money the local

school gets. Unfortunately, things haven't changed much since the landmark publication of Jonathan Kozol's book, *Savage Inequalities: Children in America's Schools*, in which he investigated some of the severe class inequities in the U.S. educational system way back in 1990.

Parents have not responded to this class inequity by fighting for equal **appro-** 5
priation of funds for schools. They have not banded together to fight for the fair treatment of all students; instead, those parents who are aware of the situation look to the hundreds of websites and other materials that rank and evaluate schools in particular geographical areas, so they can place their child in the best school in the district. Wealthier families have the ability to move into neighborhoods with higher rents and higher home prices, which significantly affects school funding. In fact, one of the most important decisions in buying a new house is not the state of the landscaping; it is the state of the school system in the area. On the other hand, low-income families have no other choice than to remain in the poorer areas and continue contributing to the vicious circle.

To further complicate the picture, the federal government introduced The No 6
Child Left Behind law in January of 2002, which was designed to implement accountability of schools and teachers based on systematized testing. This law ties school-district funding to attendance, test scores, graduation rates, and overall student improvement. A good idea, is it not? Schools that fail to meet even one of these goals must formulate an intervention plan and have two years to do so. If the school does not meet federal guidelines for three years in a row, the state must restructure it in the fourth year. Last year over 11,000 schools in the U. S., most with high minority and low-income populations, failed to make federal guidelines; in other words, the schools have been required to participate in the pole vault when all they have is a pogo stick to do it with.

Americans need to wake up and stop papering over the real issue involving 7
schools: class. Because school funding is tied **disproportionately** to property taxes, students across the country cannot get a fair share. Studies about how students learn, about student demographics, or even about the No Child Left Behind law simply avoid the obvious: a rich school district that receives over twice as much money as its poor neighbor will obviously have the resources to meet the various requirements and deliver high-performance results. The two schools we visited in the same area didn't have a set of students who were incredibly smart and another set who were just plain incompetent. No, the difference was obvious: money. With another 5,000 dollars a year per student, the school in the poor neighborhood could also be repainted, could hire proctors for the yard, could purchase new text books, and could provide the same **sterling** education as the first school. Class politics should be left out of the class.

Discussing and Writing About The Text

Discussing Issues:

Describe and evaluate your high school along the lines of the authors' observations. Compare your description and evaluation to those of your peers and seek the explanation for differences or similarities.

Writing about the Text:

In a well-developed and organized essay, respond to the reading; be sure to support your views with pertinent examples drawn from your own experience and observations, as well as readings.

Topic 1: Why do the authors believe there are certain minor and major discrepancies between schools? To what extent, if at all, do you agree with the authors' explanation?

Topic 2: According to your opinion, what kind of specific measures, decisions, policies, and actions can secure a high level education system and equality among schools?

Developing Vocabulary:

The words below may appear as part of your online quizzes. Please refer to the introduction for study strategies for learning vocabulary.

1. culmination
2. manicured
3. proctor
4. pertinent
5. disheartening
6. omen
7. to reprimand
8. appropriation
9. disproportionately
10. sterling

Understanding the Text

Answer the following questions by carefully reviewing the authors' aruguments in the short essay.

1. What were the characteristics of the two schools the authors visited?

2. How does the funding system affect schools?

3. How does the "No Child Left Behind" guidelines affect schools?

4. What do the authors mean by "the class system in schools"?

Analyzing Writing

Answer the following questions by carefully reviewing the authors' arugments and writing strategies from the short essay.

1. Examine the description of each one of the schools.

2. Find the definitions the authors provide and examine their thoroughness and ef-fectiveness.

3. Examine the use of cause and effect analysis in the essay.

31 The Lesson About Learning

The irony about the educational system in the United States is that while there is a significant investment in research of proper and advanced teaching techniques, there is little—if any—questioning of the overall **premise** for education. Today, teachers are better informed about educational theory than at any time in the past, for teachers across the country must complete strenuous **accreditation** courses that include the history of education, education theory, as well as courses for practical implementation of curriculum objectives. Despite the systemic problems of under funding, bureaucracy, and the occasional inconsistency of training programs, most teachers today are highly trained professionals that have a real understanding about learning **paradigms**. Even so, the basic philosophical backbone to our entire education system, that is rewards and punishment, is rarely touched on, discussed, or changed. In its most basic sense, our education system today operates on a behaviorist model, which means that suitable behaviors are rewarded with good grades and praise, and unsatisfactory behaviors are punished with bad grades and disapproval. Conceptualized by the famous psychologist B. F. Skinner, the behaviorist model argues that people are a collection of behaviors and that these behaviors can be modified according to whatever the person in charge wants. If parents want a child to learn Latin, they could reward the child with a chocolate every time the child learns ten vocabulary words; likewise, if the child fails in the task, they could punish him by taking away TV privileges or making him weed the yard. Every child has seen this behaviorist approach in action in one way or another.

The irony in the current education system is that teachers are taught all about the emotional component of learning; they are taught various techniques to stir the intrinsic motivation of students and to interest them in the process of learning. In fact, the basic format of any lesson plan starts with a teaser (some way of interesting students in the lesson) and seeks along the way to go "beyond" the initial activity. Every teacher hopes that students will become interested in the subject material on their own (i.e. intrinsic motivation). However, even the most skilled or excited teacher is fighting an uphill battle, for the very educational system is **predicated** not on intrinsic motivation, but on extrinsic rewards or punish-

1

2

ment. High school students are rewarded not for following their own learning paths, but for learning the material and performing on some kind of test or paper evaluation. If they fail to learn the specific material required for the course test, they receive a bad grade and are scolded by their parents—the stick and the carrot are in full view. Furthermore, the ultimate reward for learning what they are supposed to is not specifically the "A" or even the social prestige associated with it, but it is the diploma and the good job that follow superior grades in school.

3   Now, proponents of grades—and there are many—argue that grades help "situate and measure" a student's progress in a course, which prepares them in **microcosm** for the real world where people are measured all the time. It is through grades and some kind of ranking system that we understand our place in the world. We understand what excellence is, and we learn to strive through friendly competition with fellow students for a performance above and beyond our normal abilities. Competition for grades, they argue, elevates our learning potential. Furthermore, grades measure a student's progress and ensure the student has mastered (or not) a certain curriculum. A poor grade is likely to motivate students to try harder because they will have recognized their failings.

4   However, plenty of research has shown that grades often have the opposite effect; instead of motivating students intrinsically to learn the material, to master the **curriculum**, and to even learn material beyond what is covered on tests, grades often corrupt the entire process. According to Alfie Kohn, an author of scores of articles and books on the U. S. education system, giving grades definitely reduces the intrinsic motivation for learning something. Students who learn material only to perform on a test often forget the material shortly thereafter. Creativity also goes downhill once students are graded even if they ace the tests. Indeed, one study in 1991 of Japanese students taking a history test showed that if students knew they would be graded, they would pick the easier questions instead of trying to tackle the challenging ones.

5   Overall, the focus on learning in order to perform well on tests and to secure good grades sacrifices other parts of the curriculum and damages the entire process of learning because it alters students' motivation. If students in a history class are to be tested only on dates for World War II, they are unlikely to pursue their interest in Winston Churchill's memoirs because that material won't count. There is no reward for reading Churchill's masterful (but very long) collection on the war and the **intricacies** of governmental decisions. Ironically, grades actually limit a student's desire to learn anything outside the purview of the assignment, which is the exact opposite intent of so-called "education." Schools are not educating students; they are merely training them in test-taking skills. They are not

creating educated students who have a desire to learn above and beyond what they are forced to.

What happens then when the student graduates and the carrot or the stick is no longer rewarding or punishing learning behavior? What happens when students no longer have to study for tests or the extrinsic, external rewards are taken away? What happens when the teacher or anyone else for that matter is not there to reward the learning behavior? Well, plenty of research studies have shown that in all of these cases the learning process slows down significantly, for the motivation has been taken away. Like rats in a maze with no cheese at the end, people's motivation to work and learn on their own decreases without extrinsic pressure or rewards.

6

Of course, this development is perhaps the most lasting **legacy** of the behaviorist approach. It is not that students fail to learn when the stimulus (reward or punishment) is not present. On the contrary, students over the last fifty years have learned very well that they should put effort in not for the process itself, not for the knowledge itself, not for the enjoyment. They have learned that any effort on their part should have an **extrinsic** reward whether that is a grade or a hefty paycheck. This has larger, important social **ramifications** as can be seen in the choices of jobs. Many students who are interested in subjects that do not pay well, such as English or Philosophy, often times end up selecting a career in a different field that may pay but not please. Therefore, this shows that students at least have learned one lesson about learning; it just isn't the lesson that educators intended.

7

Discussing and Writing About The Text

Discussing Issues:

Make a list of the educational approaches you have been exposed to in your career as a student. Next to each approach make a note about its effectiveness or lack thereof. Compare your list to those of your peers and try to determine the best and most effective educational paradigms.

Writing about the Text:

In a well-developed and organized essay, respond to the reading; be sure to support your views with pertinent examples drawn from your own experience and observations, as well as readings.

Topic 1: What are the authors' concerns about the current educational system? To what extent—if at all—do you agree with their concerns?

Topic 2: According to your opinion, how can an educational system survive without a grade basis? What are the alternatives if there are any? To support your opinion, you need to examine relevant and specific examples from a variety of sources.

Developing Vocabulary:

The words below may appear as part of your online quizzes. Please refer to the introduction for study strategies for learning vocabulary.

1. premise
2. accreditation
3. paradigms
4. predicated
5. microcosm
6. curriculum
7. intracacies
8. legacy
9. extrinsic
10. ramifications

Understanding the Text

Answer the following questions by carefully reviewing the authors' aruguments in the short essay.

1. What are the ironies about the current educational system?

2. What are the arguments of the proponents of grades?

3. How does the focus on grades affect students?

4. What are the authors' concerns about the long term effects of such systems?

Analyzing Writing

Answer the following questions by carefully reviewing the authors' arugments and writing strategies from the short essay.

1. Isolate and identify the type of counterarguments used by the authors and examine their effectiveness.

2. Underline at least five transitional devices used by the authors in the text. Then try to replace them with an alternative device without changing the meaning.

3. Examine the use of definition in the essay. Which terms are defined and how? Do you think there are terms that the authors should have also tried to define for the reader?

32 The Canon and the Curriclum

In academic circles, the question of the canon has been a major concern for humanities departments across the country since at least the mid 1980s. While the word may be reminiscent of its homonym brother cannon, its meaning is not that of large artillery pieces bombarding or defending fixed positions. The actual term hails from the Greek word "kanon," meaning rule, and was later used by the early Christian church to mean the **decree** of the church. This meaning has come down to academics as the fixed set of texts that are worth reading, the epitome of which was the Great Books project of the 1950s that purportedly printed the major works of Western literature in fifty-four volumes.

1

The canon has necessarily expanded —and rightfully so—from its strict adoption of Western white authors to include authors such as Maya Angelou, Toni Morisson, Sandra Cisneros, Chinua Achebe, and a host of others. These authors and their texts have enriched the storehouse of experience and knowledge that modern day students and scholars can access. Yet just as these authors are included, others are necessarily excluded, for there is not world or time enough to teach everything available in the schools and universities of the United States. Thus, this **articulation** of what to teach has been the site of major struggle for at least thirty years. Two important questions arise from the new re-articulation of canonical texts: 1) what is to be included in the canon, and 2) who decides what is included. Both of these vexing questions have been in the center of a complex and complicated struggle within academia, and there has been no victor. One of the big statements in this battle was written by Prof. Harold Bloom in 1994, who has drawn a lot of fire for his book *The Western Canon*. At the end of his survey of Western literature, Bloom attacked the ideologically motivated changes in the books that are taught in universities across the U. S. Bloom included a long list of texts he argued should be taught because they are "great works." Of course, this did not appeal to everyone, and his book was soundly **savaged** by many who viewed his attempt to preserve a certain canonical set of books as catering to an **entrenched** power structure. Basically, they said, Bloom wants to keep the books of all the "dead white authors" and maintain the status quo. The voices of minorities, his opponents argued, should be heard loud and clear with the selection of differ-

2

ent texts...and the feud goes on.

3   The importance of the continuing debate over the canon to be taught in universities—as well as high schools—cannot be underestimated, for these choices form the curriculum of material that is to be studied. This is not some isolated battle waged by ancient academics behind the closed doors of university conference rooms. The texts chosen as part of the canon form the educational backbone for students and show in visceral form what is thought to be worth knowing. The choices made are incredibly important, for students will naturally assume that the books they are asked (or forced) to read are highly important and contain what is necessary for their education. Another reason for the importance of this selection process is that the texts contain within them the seeds of viewing the world through a particular lens. This way of viewing the world and of being acculturated is what academics, teachers, and politicians are fighting over; while the specific books do matter to some extent, it is not precisely the particular books that form the battle ground. The debate over which books to include in the canon is predicated on the idea that education is primarily a socializing mechanism in training students to think and believe in a particular way.

4   This may all sound like something too far gone from the experience of the average student, but it isn't. The material that is taught in high schools and universities across the country helps construct how students view the world first in the choices of the books provided and secondly in what the books actually say. This is what is meant by a socializing mechanism. For example, many high school history texts in the U. S. in the early 1970s explained the Vietnam War as a defensive offensive designed to curb the **onslaught** of **menacing** communist forces that threatened to overwhelm the rest of the world. In this way, the U. S. selflessly sacrificed its citizens to give freedom to the Vietnamese and defend democracy. Of course, nowadays, history texts complicate this view by including material about the **atrocities** committed by U. S. soldiers as well as the invasion of nearby Cambodia. Some text books go so far as to show how the extensive bombing of Cambodia that finally ended in 1973 led directly to the establishment of the genocidal regime of the **Khmer Rouge**, a group responsible for the murder of millions of Cambodians. The "truth" can be complicated.

5   The books that are selected for classes across the United States do matter because they do help shape what is learned as well as what material is to be discussed. The choices of the canon have long-term effects, including especially the **acculturation** and socialization of students into particular ways of thinking. Now, this is not to say that books simply brainwash those who read them, but certainly the choice of one text over another does matter. Would everyone agree if high

school English teachers only taught Shakespeare plays? Why not? These are classic texts, and Shakespeare is considered one of the most important playwrights of all time. What values would that advocate by the choice of these plays as well as their content? How about if history courses included books that catered only to the side of the U. S.? Would anyone object?

  Indeed, as America's demographics have changed, the canon has   6 changed—slowly—with it. Increasingly, so-called ethnic literature has been introduced that provides a different view of our culture and the events that have shaped it, and the discussions and arguments about the canon conducted around the conference room tables have made a difference. Important inclusions have been made in the literature and history that is taught, which now encompasses many more voices that had never been heard before. At the same time, however, Harold Bloom's call for the preservation of the Western canon should not be entirely dismissed. In the fervor to include other voices and modify our reading materials based on new demographics, we have to be very careful that the masterworks of previous ages are not thrown into the dustbin. Why not? What connection will we have to our **heritage**, tradition, history, or literature if the curriculum to be read is entirely new? There will be a break with the past, and the students of the future will have no connection to those of us in the present.

Discussing and Writing About The Text

Discussing Issues:

In a group, make a list of all the books you can remember having heard about or having read. Which of these books do you think should be taught in high school or college and why? What should the criteria be for choosing texts to become part of the canon? Who should have that authority and why? Do the texts that are assigned have much of an effect on students and how they learn?

Writing about the Text:

In a well-developed and organized essay, respond to the reading; be sure to support your views with pertinent examples drawn from your own experience and observations, as well as readings.

Topic 1: According to the authors, what are advantages and disadvantages of changes in the canon of authors adopted as curriculum in high schools and colleges across the country? To what extent—if at all—do you think the authors are correct in their analysis?

Topic 2: Take the course syllabus for your class and redesign it by inputting books or articles of your choice. On a separate piece of paper, write at least a paragraph justification for your choice. Be sure to include valid reasons why you want to use the texts, what objectives you have with it, and what you expect students to learn.

Developing Vocabulary:

The words below may appear as part of your online quizzes. Please refer to the introduction for study strategies for learning vocabulary.

1. decree
2. articulation
3. savaged
4. entrenched
5. onslaught
6. menacing
7. atrocities
8. Khmer Rouge
9. acculturation
10. heritage

Understanding the Text

Answer the following questions by carefully reviewing the authors' aruguments in the short essay.

1. Where does the term "the canon" come from? What does it mean today?

2. Why are the authors concerned about the current reevaluation of the canon that is taking place today?

3. What are the advantages of adopting non-traditional authors into the canon?

4. What do the authors believe will happen if the traditional canon is thrown out?

Analyzing Writing

Answer the following questions by carefully reviewing the authors' arugments and writing strategies from the short essay.

1. Find at least five rhetorical questions from the text. Carefully examine the context of their use.

2. Locate three lists the authors use. Can you find alternative ways of conveying that information?

3. Examine how the authors employ extended definition in the text. Locate two examples of this technique.

33 Social Education Breakdown

Last Sunday, I awoke to the rattling of my bedroom windows; I thought initially that the San Andreas Fault had finally given out and that Californians were experiencing the long-predicted mega-earthquake. But the mega-earthquake came with a dull, low throbbing, like the growling of an angry dog. Slowly I **discerned** words within the noise, "Bring me the poison" wailed in a high screech. It was 7:00 AM on Sunday, and my neighbor was blaring what could only be the techno band Prodigy from his car—again. This time, though, I was going to put a stop to it. I got out of bed, went down the stairs, crossed the street, and walked down three houses to the offender, who was busily washing his techno club car. After getting his attention through **harried** waving, he lowered the volume, and I asked calmly whether he might lower the volume for good. He responded, "This is my car and this is my music, and I'll do what I want to when I want to on my property. So, get the hell out of here or I'll make you." I was shocked. Did I have to get into a fight to make him understand that music volume that shakes the windows of a house three doors down is not legitimate community behavior? Did his music tastes have to become mine? Despair at the level of rudeness **overwhelmed** me. Did this man have no social education at all?

Unfortunately, I am not alone in feeling that people—in general—have become ruder and less considerate. A poll conducted in 2002 by Public Agenda, a New York non-profit organization, found that 79% of Americans believe that rude behavior has gotten worse. From swearing in public to inappropriate cell phone use, those polled believe that Americans don't know how to act in public. The neighbor's music is but one example of thousands that can be cited of—what in other words—would be called lack of manners. Now, one may argue that what one person might deem rude another might call regular behavior. Wouldn't a grandmother find more things inappropriate than her teenage grandson? Perhaps it was I who had become an old **curmudgeon** and my neighbor had every right to listen to his music at 7:00 AM. Interestingly, however, the survey showed very little variation across the country in what was thought of as rude behavior—from Tennessee to California, people voted for the same kinds of rude behaviors.

1

2

3 So, if rudeness is on the rise, what causes or sustains it? The obvious answer is that the culture that the grandmother grew up in no longer exists. Society, of course, is constantly changing, so necessarily the values and social standards of interaction also change over time. In the nineteenth century, for instance, children were to be seen and not heard while at the dinner table. They should **promptly** answer questions when asked, but otherwise conversation was for the adults. If children **fidgeted**, talked out of turn, or tried to participate in the conversation, their "rude" behavior would have been punished. Clearly, there have been many changes in what good manners are prescribed.

4 Another factor in the rise of rudeness is the significant changes in family and work environments over the last fifty years. After World War II, women increasingly entered the work force, leaving children with other caretakers or dropping them off at school. The socializing process—the slow social education of children in good manners and proper behavior—had been mostly the **purview** of women in the times when women worked in the house. Stay-at-home mothers simply had more time to ensure their children were trained to behave well both in public and at home. It was, moreover, part of their responsibility and reputation to ensure their children would be well-behaved.

5 And it wasn't just the mother who kept children in line and educated them in proper interaction. Proper manners were also instilled by other members of the community, third parties not directly involved in the rearing of the children. However, community structures and ways of interaction have significantly changed over the last 50 years as well. In the past, it would not be uncommon for any adult member of a community to **reprimand** a swearing or misbehaving child. It was a typical part of the job of the community to enforce codes of conduct. So, if a child were noisy or yelling in a public place, any adult could approach them, stop them, scold them, and then bring them home for further discipline. That level of familiarity would be unthinkable now in a society so **litigious**. If anything, most parents nowadays would be furious at any third party interfering with the parenting.

6 The last main factor is the continued development of individualism. My neighbor's comment that he could do whatever he wanted is symptomatic of the cult of the individual. His comment illustrates that his enjoyment of his music was more important than the comfort of other members of the neighborhood. Individualism, while not negative in and of itself, if taken to an extreme, can slowly erode standards of conduct and feelings of community.

In some ways, I can understand my neighbor's behavior. In his micro-teenage culture, his massive stereo system is a way of establishing status within that community. Among teenagers, for instance, it is more tolerated or normalized to play music at ear-shattering decibel levels. This is not particularly shocking to me. What was, however, troublesome was that his parents were at home. There was not the excuse of the parents being away at work; these parents, however, did not deem to control their child. What's more is that while I had heard other neighbors periodically complain about the music, none of them ever took any action. Would this kind of disturbing, rude behavior have been tolerated in the past? Would not the other members of the community put a stop to behavior that was disturbing to all? This hearkens back to the larger social changes already outlined. If his mother and father would not even step in to control his activities, how could I hope to? There was certainly a shift from a greater investment in participation in community versus the fulfillment of individual desires and wishes. In this case, the pleasure of the individual clearly superseded the peace of other members of the community.

On my weary way back to my house, Prodigy in my head and the only recourse to call the police, I couldn't feel angry at this teenager. I knew he was terribly rude, but I **rued** more his lack of education in considerate and respectful social behavior. How could I be angry at someone who didn't know any better? He had been trained by society to fulfill his individual desires over even considering the rights of others let alone the greater good of the community. His parents have not taught him the ABCs of social education, proving that other community members no longer feel obliged or capable of assisting in social education. My neighbor is just part of the social education breakdown.

Discussing and Writing About The Text

Discussing Issues:

Do you think you are adequately socially educated? What in your behavior would attest to your social education? In a group, try to construct an "Etiquette Guide" for freshmen in your college.

Writing about the Text:

In a well-developed and organized essay, respond to the reading; be sure to support your views with pertinent examples drawn from your own experience and observations, as well as readings.

Topic 1: To what reasons do the authors attribute today's social education breakdown? To what extent—if at all—do you agree with their arguments?

Topic 2: According to your opinion, what reasons, if any, mandate people's social education? What should be the criteria and the goals of such an education?

Developing Vocabulary:

The words below may appear as part of your online quizzes. Please refer to the introduction for study strategies for learning vocabulary.

1.	to discern	2.	harried
3.	overwhelmed	4.	curmudgeon
5.	promptly	6.	fidgeted
7.	purview	8.	to reprimand
9.	litigious	10.	to rue

Understanding the Text

Answer the following questions by carefully reviewing the authors' aruguments in the short essay.

1. What does the author mean by "social education breakdown"?

2. What are the causes of this breakdown?

3. What are the symptoms of this breakdown?

4. What are the counterarguments the author refutes?

Analyzing Writing

Answer the following questions by carefully reviewing the authors' arugments and writing strategies from the short essay.

1. Examine the use of humor and irony in the text.

2. Find the focus-theme of each paragraph, and write it in the margin next to each paragraph. Is each paragraph organized around a specific focus or not?

3. Examine the use of sources in the essay. What kind of sources does the author use (personal examples-anecdotes, facts, authorities, etc)? Do you think they are appropriate and convincing? What additional sources would you use?

34 The Knowledge Club

Education is supposed to open doors, but does it also close them, unintentionally or not? Getting a degree can be an exciting step in a person's career, for the degree often promises entry into a more privileged subset of society with all the opportunities that might unfold. But just as doors open, others may close. This is especially true for first generation college students who may not feel the same kind of connectedness and **rapport** with friends and family from the old neighborhood. Now, this growth apart may happen regardless of whether they want it to or not. Some friends or family members may feel resentful of the success and knowledge enjoyed by the college graduate if they, themselves, did not attend college. While this is by no means the way of things in every case, first generation college students face unique challenges with family members who may not understand or even care about college success.

More pernicious, though, is the *intentional* use of educational background to exclude and **demean** others to establish superiority, and this could happen to anyone. We have all seen this in action when a mixed group of professionals gather and the dance of acronyms, even for people within the same major, flows like a torrent: students with B.I.C.S. must develop C. A. L. P. before they pass the ELWR as part of their progress to attain a BA or BS. Now, among fellow English professionals, this sentence can easily be decoded as saying, "students who speak English fluently also have to develop college-level reading and writing skills, so they can pass the writing requirement before they graduate." Indeed, these acronyms do mean something to those in the professional fields of English or education, and correct **terminology** is critically important for one's work. Fluency in the **lingo** of one's field is a necessary requirement for one's professional status and development as well as for the advancement of the particular field. The use of acronyms also serves expediency and practicality within the specific professional community and its discourse: imagine, for instance, if doctors had to use the whole term of Attention Deficit Hyperactivity Disorder instead of ADHD.

The problem does not lie with people being proficient in the specialized vocabulary of their work. Rather, the problem occurs when knowledge (typically acquired through formal education) is used to exclude not to include. In the above scenario of English professionals, this would be the case if the latter were at a dinner party with people from other fields. What if at the same party scientists from various fields were to talk among themselves by hustling out a dictionary of field-

1

2

3

specific **acronyms**? It seems rather logical that communication among the whole group would become very difficult, if not impossible. If this rhetorical grandstanding appears like an unreasonable approach to dialogue, why does it even occur, especially among people, who, if anything, have had education and training in considering their audience when conveying their ideas? Far too often, people use their specialized knowledge to make those around them into **supplicants**. Every time a specialized term is used and left unexplained, the would-be listeners have the options of either pretending to understand the meaning of the term, hoping to grasp meaning through context, or daring to appear ignorant by asking, "What does this term mean?" This process has the effect of making the one who talks appear in control of the specific knowledge, a quite powerful position. Sometimes this is done by accident, for the speaker is simply enthused about the topic or far too **immersed** in his own professional world. Many times it serves the purpose to self-aggrandize—almost like a peacock spreading its feathers. So why do seemingly normal, decent people exercise the power of knowledge in this way?

4   One answer may lie in the new national economy, which has steadily shifted from a manufacturing economy to a "knowledge economy." Since the 1970s, the U. S. has lost millions of jobs in manufacturing to other countries, and the job market has reinvented itself based on an information or knowledge economy. One of the issues with this trend is that there are few ways or devices of measuring people's actual knowledge. In the manufacturing world, for instance, it is pretty easy. A worker can be hired for a probationary period, asked to assemble some part or perform a mechanical task for which he had been trained. If he can do it, he knows his stuff. If he doesn't, he is fired. In the knowledge-based economy, discerning a person's actual abilities is a bit more difficult.

5   One of the ways, though, is through educational degrees. Indeed, those with BAs, MAs, and Ph.D.s are presumed to know their stuff, but even here there must be gradations. The prestige and difficulty of the particular degree-granting institutions are taken into consideration when evaluating the "worth" of a particular degree. A Harvard graduate is presumed to know more than a graduate from a community college. That's why the *U. S. News and World Report* publishes a yearly guide to the best colleges and degree granting institutions. The *Report* measures everything from student satisfaction to student/teacher ratio to the core level of academics. People, then, can partly base their presumed knowledge on where someone went to school.

6   But supposed ability and knowledge background in one's field cannot simply be measured by the degree one received. A "D" grade point average at Harvard does not equate to an "A" grade point average from a public state school. There is a more interesting way of discerning knowledge "level," which may or may not measure a person's actual knowledge, but it does measure their ability to display the knowledge they do have. If two people in a group have the same degree, often a competition of sorts will break out. This involves a form of mental

arm wrestling whose battlefield is the ability to exchange information and to subordinate others through rhetoric. This sounds pretty fancy, but the concept is easy to understand. Display of knowledge is the new currency in the information economy. In older days, hierarchies and status were maintained through exchanging personal stories and anecdotes where social status could be clearly marked through tales of wealth or marriage. Just try reading a Jane Austin novel to learn this lesson.

Instead, today social relationships, especially among the college educated, often revolve around exchanging information and the performance of the delivery of that information. For example, say you were browsing and happened to read an article about Bovine Growth Hormone. You could present the material like this, "I read an article in *MIT Technology Review* about BGH and its **carcinogenic** effects." The listener who has neither read the article nor is a specialist in the field of growth hormones is almost forced to ask what the *Review* is, what does BGH stand for, and what kind of carcinogenic effects this BGH has. The **rhetorical** presentation of the information puts the speaker clearly in the superior position of knowing and the listener in the inferior position of petitioning for explanations. An alternative statement would then be, "An article in *MIT Technology Review*, a journal that looks at potential technologies, has called attention to the cancer-causing properties of this substance called Bovine Growth Hormone (BGH). This is cause for alarm because this additive has been given to all cows in the U. S." A close look at these two similar statements reveals that the second version de-privileges the "I" by taking the listener into consideration and not forcing him to ask questions. It assumes that the listener would have little or no knowledge of the topic and so seeks to inform instead of intimidate.

In this way, knowledge (i.e. information) about something, even if it is simply about an **esoteric** article one read, is used to enlighten others, not to put them in their place. Unfortunately, the first example is far more common, for it was used to show the superiority of the speaker and the breadth of information at his disposal. This happens all the time, and a person does not necessarily have to hold a certain degree to do this although this certainly helps in solidifying the person's authority as a source of knowledge. The new economy based on knowledge promotes the establishment of a rhetorical hierarchy, and those with the greater skill in making "you" ask the who, the what, and the when have control over the conversation. Next time you are in a conversation, mark how often the interlocutor contextualizes anything, considers the audience, or plays like the sole arbiter of entry into the knowledge club. You'll be surprised not only how important knowledge is, but how one displays it.

7

8

Discussing and Writing About The Text

Discussing Issues:

Do you think that most people try to rhetorically control conversations by turning the subject to something they know everything about? Among your friends who have the same educational background, do you measure status in any way? Is it through the display of knowledge or in some other way? Do you think it is naturally for humans to try to gain more prestige, status, and power in whatever way they can?

Writing about the Text:

In a well-developed and organized essay, respond to the reading; be sure to support your views with pertinent examples drawn from your own experience and observations, as well as readings.

Topic 1: According to the authors, how do many people working in knowledge-based jobs act towards others? Why do they do this? Do you think that people use rhetoric to display knowledge? To what extent—if at all—do you think the authors are correct in their evaluation of rhetorical use among people?

Topic 2: Listen to the way your friends talk among themselves for one full day. Using a compiled "listening" rubric, record instances where particular friends utilize rhetorical control over the conversation and instances where information is contextualized and shared. Then write a paper analyzing your results.

Developing Vocabulary:

The words below may appear as part of your online quizzes. Please refer to the introduction for study strategies for learning vocabulary.

1. rapport
2. demean
3. terminology
4. lingo
5. acronym
6. supplicants
7. immersed
8. carcinogenic
9. rhetorical
10. esoteric

Understanding the Text

Answer the following questions by carefully reviewing the authors' aruguments in the short essay.

1. The title, "The Knowledge Club," only appears in the last paragraph of the essay. What is it?

2. What is the connection of education with the so-called new economy?

3. How did some people act in the past to indicate status or hierarchy?

4. How do some people today indicate status or hierarchy?

Analyzing Writing

Answer the following questions by carefully reviewing the authors' aruguments and writing strategies from the short essay.

1. Notice the first paragraph. How does it connect to the rest of the essay?

2. Do the authors exercise any of the tricks to rhetorically enforce their own status or hierarchy within the text?

3. Find at least five transition devices and analyze how they work and how effective (or not) they are.

CHAPTER
FIVE

Family

35 Are Families Naturally Close?

Movies typically portray American immigrant families as tight-knit communities full of love and camaraderie in their search for the "American Dream." The first generation is very close, meeting on Sundays with members of the community and having large meals where nearly everyone is invited. The father works hard; the mother takes care of the children; the children of family friends play together, get into mischief, and ultimately go share many of life's important moments. But trouble is **lurking** beyond. Soon enough, the children who have no recollection of the "old country" and have only second-hand ideas of the country or original culture through some bits of language and a few **esoteric** food dishes may get jobs in the next county or city, may move off to college, or may simply move out into their own house. Novels and movies—and there are dozens of them—seem to lament the "loss" of close family ties and of home-country traditions. This seems to be the typical depiction of the "American" experience of immigrants in the *Godfather*, *Once Upon a Time in America*, or even *The Joy Luck Club*. The "immigrant" family story is a cycle of intense bonding followed by alienation and loss once the "American" family story begins to unravel.

1

It is common for people of other nations to think of Americans as a people without "family ties or values" who may eagerly sacrifice family on the altar of money and success. Is this true, or is it one more anti-American stereotype? Considering what families look like elsewhere, we may have a more critical glimpse into this issue. True, in many other parts of the world, both industrialized countries and developing ones, people often appear to never abandon the "family cocoon." In foreign countries, it is far more common that children live with their parents and grandparents in the same household for many years beyond adulthood. Occasionally, they may move away for a few years to pursue college studies, but eventually they come back to the "family nest." And it is not only the nuclear family that inhabits this nest. Above and beyond this nucleus of parents and children, often uncles, aunts, cousins, grandmothers, great grandfathers, godfathers, godmothers, and others, whose exact **genealogical** relationship may be too complicated to name, are also part of the same community of the same town. And with the exception of the student years, it is, moreover, rare that someone should move away

2

from the hometown, the state, let alone the country; in many of these communities, for instance, moving to another country and more so to America has been for years **synonymous** with metaphorical "death," for it is feared that the person may never return to the "hometown"; and even while immigrants dream of the "hometown," they eventually grow further and further away from it in the America that "swallowed" them and made them forget.

3   Hollywood doesn't help with this stereotype. On the one hand, films about the immigrant family experience promote a sense of loss from a family community at the same time that numerous other films show how vacant and forced that community can be. Just count the number of films that include "family reunions" where the characters who return to the long-left town are completely *alienated* from relatives who may have known them when they were young. What's more, these reunions seem to bring all the crazies out of the asylums: crazy Aunt Edna who never changes her cloths and always tries to kiss the young boys; the neurotic mother who is practicing Scientology and Yoga; the overbearing grandfather who doubts you've done anything of worth in your life.

4   These images of family—all **warped** in some way or another—fail to tell the true story. The "American" story is neither American, nor is it about the breakdown of family; it is about the economic emancipation of children from their support networks—their families and communities. In the United States and other industrialized countries, children leave their family units because they have the economic and social means to do so. In many parts of the United States, even eighteen-year-olds can afford to move out on their own, secure their own apartment, and purchase their first car. This does not mean that it is easy, but it means that it is possible. The immigrant story featured above that has been retold a thousand times, then, is a story about economic **prosperity**. When the children have enough capital to begin life on their own, they do it, and no family can hold them back from the dream of financial independence.

5   It is a peculiar myth-making that concocts the image of a large, extended family living peacefully together, a giant support network easily co-existing. In fact, it is natural for people to desire their own space and control over their own capital. This same "break down" in family units can be seen in almost every country with rising per capita incomes. When "children" of thirty years can afford their own place, will they stay with their parents?

6   Furthermore, in industrialized societies the **infrastructure** replaces the family support networks. For example, in the "hometown" of immigrant imagination, a son might get a job through an acquaintance of the father's. A daughter might discover a job opportunity through a family friend who comes to dinner on

Sunday. This kind of informal networking is absolutely necessary in places with minimal formal infrastructure. In the United States, on the other hand, the same son could just as easily find a job through an ad posted in the paper or on the Internet. The daughter could electronically enroll herself in college and fill out student loan applications in the same afternoon. While social networks can still assist in upward mobility, they are not absolutely necessary.

One should also not ignore the significance of geography in countries that are physically smaller than the United States. In the relatively confined space of many European countries and towns, for instance, staying "close" is easier, not only metaphorically but also and primarily literally. Finding a job in another town may not turn out to be *detrimental* to the closeness of the family in foreign countries because that town may be very close; a thirty-minute flight, a one-hour drive, or a forty-five minute train ride would not be an insurmountable obstacle to frequent family gatherings and celebrations. Distances in the U.S. are vast, so a job in the next town could easily mean a three-hour drive, which militates against frequent contact.   7

Families are not naturally close. No group of people with such **disparate** personalities would naturally congregate and remain so close for so long unless there were some kind of social need that was being served. Nowadays, economic independence and good civic infrastructure allow for geographic mobility. People move away from their "hometowns" because they can; they pursue jobs elsewhere, or they simply like the climate elsewhere. They are not locked into staying in one place as part of a community. In the past, in communities different than the American one, or especially in immigrant families, family members may not have had a choice to leave; they may have stayed by necessity.   8

Discussing and Writing About The Text

Discussing Issues:

Make a list of families you are familiar with, including your own family; write down the elements that you think connect or separate the members of each family (e.g. character, geography, social circumstances, etc.). Discuss your findings with your peers. How do you think relationships could be improved?

Writing about the Text:

In a well-developed and organized essay, respond to the reading; be sure to support your views with pertinent examples drawn from your own experience and observations, as well as readings.

Topic 1: Why do the authors believe that families are not naturally close? To what extent—if at all—do you agree with this view point?

Topic 2: According to your opinion, what is the ideal family? Examine the components that are necessary in building and sustaining such a family and give reasons for their validity.

Developing Vocabulary:

The words below may appear as part of your online quizzes. Please refer to the introduction for study strategies for learning vocabulary.

1. **lurking** hld
2. **esoteric** obscure
3. **genealogical** study of family descent
4. **synonymous** closely associated with
5. **alienated** isolate
6. **warped** deform
7. **prosperity** state of being prosperous
8. **infrastructure** physical & organizational structures
9. **detrimental** tending to cause harm
10. **disparate** things so different they can't be compared

Understanding the Text

Answer the following questions by carefully reviewing the authors' aruguments in the short essay.

1. How is the American family typically portrayed in the media?

2. How do families often operate in other countries?

3. Why do immigrant families usually have to "stay close together"?

4. What is the role of economy, infrastructure, and geography in family dynamics?

Analyzing Writing

Answer the following questions by carefully reviewing the authors' arugments and writing strategies from the short essay.

1. Where do the authors construct lists and how do these occasions work as a writing strategy?

2. Examine three topic sentences for how they effectively (or not) orient the reader.

3. Examine the use of definition in the essay. What concept do the authors decide to define?

36   "Keeping Close to Home" Revisited

In an essay titled "Keeping Close to Home" by Gloria Watkins, she argues that families can stay together and remain close even if class and education separate them. In her poignant piece, she describes the **travails** she went through as a child born to working-class parents, who simultaneously supported her educational **endeavors** while trying to limit them. This **ambiguity** on her family's behalf nurtured in her a constant confusion about the value of her own higher education aspirations and the values appreciated by her family. Actually, it was only when she left for Stanford University that she was able to recognize the importance of folk tradition, of her father's work ethic, of the closeness of her community. Indeed, she concludes that "open, honest communication" is one of the keys to remaining close to one's family.

Being one of those first generation college students, I looked forward to learning how I could maintain my relationships with family members despite the ever-increasing gap of class and education that divides us. However, Watkins' response, while heartfelt, proves inadequate in helping first generation college students "keep close to home," for it is a drastic oversimplification of actual family dynamics.

Don't get me wrong here; I do applaud Watkins' respect of her father's work ethic and her acknowledgement of the richness of folk traditions, such as story-telling or quilting. This understanding and respect are crucial in maintaining connections to the community in which one grows up. There are very few things more annoying and distasteful than someone who grew up in poor circumstances who returns to that community after college only to brag about accomplishments and **condescend** to old acquaintances and friends.

I personally witnessed this drama play itself out with an acquaintance of mine whose parents were originally from Panama. The daughter of an immigrant angler, she worked very hard in school, became fluent in English, and eventually graduated with her Ph.D. in Neurobiology. She had ardently pursued the "American Dream," and she had achieved it with a great deal of sacrifice and hard work. However, this dream came at the cost of her relationship with her family. Over time, she began to treat her parents with **disdain** as simple peasants who had nothing to offer and whose fundamental ignorance was beyond improvement.

5   This extreme denial of one's past is certainly not healthy for any relation-ship and represents only one end of an extreme. But how healthy is Watkins' ap-proach of acceptance? In her account of familial reconciliation, one needs to notice that it was she who put in all the effort to understand and appreciate the family values and traits. It was she who tried to retain her connection to the com-munity and to not be **ostracized**. Nowhere in her story do we hear about her par-ents or grandparents putting any effort into valuing her for her commitment to and achievement of higher education except for their lukewarm encouragement of what they deemed as plausible educational goals –"an all black community col-lege." In her narrative, the responsibility of retaining the familial bonds entirely fell to her.

6   Besides this one-sided effort to keep close to home, Watkins also appears to have overlooked another significant issue. In the real world, families and com-munities often and perhaps unconsciously resent members that become or wish to become better, richer, or more educated than them. Indeed, upon return to the community, the person who chose a route of extra-community improvement—Stanford versus an all black community college—is often viewed as a traitor and a potential threat to the community's good old ways. Instead of being greeted with "palm fronds," the one to return is often greeted with personal attacks or con-descension. Indeed, the home-comers will often be cautioned that "being smart [does] not make [them] a 'better' or 'superior' person." In fact, my own personal "home-coming" as a Ph.D. has been "welcomed" in a similar way. In a recent po-litical debate with my parents, I compiled a list of facts to counter some of their arguments. I was really shocked to discover that this well-crafted but mostly well-intended debate was received as a "personal attack" upon their personalities, their way of life, and their overall belief system. The debate shifted then from politi-cal issues to a clash between my supposed snotty academic background and their down-to-earth worldview. There was an elision of the actual material and a re-sponse full of ad hominem attacks on my character. And as I kept reading the list of personal condemnations, I could not help but think of Watkins, for her mother's voice clearly echoed in the last line of my mother's email: "having a Ph.D. does not mean 'Put her Down.'"

7   Therefore, when it comes to a family or generational gap in education, the only real way for an educated person—and by this I mean anyone, regardless of degree, who reads and analyzes material beyond a surface level—to "keep close to home" is to keep their mouth shut. Watkins claims that "open, honest commu-nication" is the key to bridging that gap, but I can only doubt the validity of this

Understanding the Text

Answer the following questions by carefully reviewing the authors' aruguments in the short essay.

1.   What are Gloria Watkins' arguments in regards to familial relationships?

2.   Does the author agree or disagree with Watkins and to what extent?

3.   According to the author, what problems do first generation college students encounter in their families?

4.   What are the author's suggestions for overcoming these problems?

Analyzing Writing

Answer the following questions by carefully reviewing the authors' arugments and writing strategies from the short essay.

1. Examine the summary of Watkins' essay "Keeping Close to Home"? Does it have the elements necessary to a summary?

2. Examine the use of irony in the essay. Underline the phrases and words that are used ironically, and evaluate the effectiveness of this tone.

3. Examine the use of sources in the essay. What kind of sources does the author use? Do you think they are appropriate and convincing? What additional sources would you use?

37 The Importance of Being Married

The debate over gay marriage, many believe, is one of the most divisive factors in American society today, and a plethora of essays has been written either **decrying** such marriages as **abominations** or supporting them as the evolution of human relationships and communities. Here follow some of the most pertinent arguments of both sides. On the one side, marriage conservatives feel that 1) marriage is rooted in male/female sexuality and is thus meant to exist between a man and a woman; 2) marriage between a man and a woman is a religious sacrament; 3) marriage serves as a stabilizing institution in society; 4) also for some, most homosexuals cannot handle the responsibilities of marriage. On the other side of the debate, proponents of same sex marriages **vehemently** refute these claims. They argue that for significant portions of the population, same sex sexuality is equally as strong as the heterosexual one. They believe that equality before the law mandates that the state broaden its legislation to include same sex unions while they promote the expansion of the same idea for religious ceremonies. They scorn the argument that homosexuals lack responsibility by pointing out that same sex partnerships can be equally as durable and strong as heterosexual unions. Besides, if homosexuals are considered competent enough to hold posts of responsibility at all levels of society, why would they be less capable within marriage?

1

The problem, however, with this debate is that it is asking the wrong question. Instead of "why should homosexuals marry," one should ask, "why should anyone get married?" What is it that makes marriage such an important or even mandatory institution today? To begin to answer these questions, one should look for the essence of marriage in the origins of its modern **conceptualization**. While people have been "marrying" even before the Romans controlled the world, the formulation of the modern institution of marriage derived from the tradition of Western romantic love in the Middle Ages. In the thirteenth and fourteenth centuries, medieval authors produced an array of what were called "romance" manuscripts that included new notions of romantic love. Indeed, figures such as Chretien de Troye created numerous stories about knights and their damsels who fall in love despite social forces that might be aligned to stop them, and whose **denouement** of these stories is a hoped-for marriage. Undoubtedly, the most famous

2

story of Western romantic love is Shakespeare's *Romeo and Juliet* in which the couple, despite the warring family history, secretly marries and thereafter **consummates** their love. It is mainly through these romances that marriage became figured as the conclusion of romantic love whereby partners choose each other for life. One need only look at modern romantic comedies churned out by Hollywood by the score to find this prevalent notion that love is inextricably connected to marriage. Love is still supposed to bring couples together, and its suitable social culmination is marriage.

3   Despite, however, the literary efforts of poets from the past, marriage for much of its history was not about love at all. Marriage was primarily about economics and alliances. When two people married, their families were combined, and property changed hands. Even in the Middle Ages, despite the literature of the period, marriage was typically arranged by the parents as more of a combination of the resources of the two families than anything remotely relevant to love. So, while many people focus on Romeo and Juliet's undying love for each other, what is so often missed about *Romeo and Juliet* is the underlying premise of the play: the massive traditional social forces of tradition and economics aligned against love. Contributing to this traditional idea of marriage as an economic transaction was also the institution of **dowry**, the ceremonial gift of goods and money along with the bride. Even today, in some countries, dowries still constitute an important part of the ritual of marriage, providing the contractual backbone to the rite.

4   Of course, today and for most of the U.S., marriage has changed quite a bit from its roots as a fundamentally economic institution. Today, a dowry has become an outdated custom or a joke rather than a necessary component of marriage; only few parents arrange the marriages of their sons or daughters; and certainly neither women nor their property is any longer relegated as the legal property of the father or of the husband. Since women have the same rights as men, it is entirely possible for single women to exist outside the structure of marriage; they can be financially independent, and they can have fulfilling careers and access to their own funds. Marriage doesn't even provide a tax break because in many cases couples pay the so-called "marriage penalty" by being charged more taxes than they would be if they filed as individuals. So marriage is no longer the bulwark of economic security that it once was reputed to be.

5   However, one could argue that the significance of marriage as a predominant social institution remains intact. True, besides its economical significance, one other major reason for marriage has been its role in cementing social relationships and providing the only acceptable path towards creating a family. In tighter communities, everyone knows what they are supposed to do, the road they

are supposed to follow, and the social roles they have been assigned; in these societies, marriage is one of the stepping stones into adult life, and the family unit is the primary organizing feature of society. However, any society, including the American one, could be organized on the principal of a **commune** with groups of ten or fifteen people sharing finances, property, and workload duties, but it is not. Instead, the most prevalent institution in our society is the "nuclear" family whose symbol is marriage. Indeed, statistics from the Census Bureau show that 96.7% of Americans will marry at least one time during their lives.

Even the social dimension of marriage might be on the wane. Divorce statistics hover around 50%, and there has been a 40% rise since 1990 in the number of couples who live together but are not married in the U. S. In Europe, this trend is even more pronounced. In a 2006 survey conducted by the German Federal Statistics Office, only 38% of German women and 30% of German men thought marriage was necessary for creating a union. Even having children out of wedlock, one of the primary reasons for marrying, is no longer socially stigmatized but rather legally facilitated and socially more accepted. Across Europe, for instance, one in three children is born to unwed parents, which reflects the six-fold increase in the number of unwed parents since the 1970s; at the same time, most of these births take place in unmarried households by choice.

6

So why would anyone get married nowadays if it is no longer about fusing two families economically, if women have the economic power to live on their own, if no social stigma attaches to having children outside of marriage? The practical significance of marriage as an institution has definitely **waned** and will continue to do so once legislation awards unwedded unions of both heterosexual and homosexual couples and single parent families with the same legal privileges that it awards families of married heterosexuals. Indeed, it is mostly these privileges and perhaps a remainder of the medieval notion of romantic love, as well as religious convictions that still grant the institution of marriage such importance. However, if there were no legal differentiation, couldn't two people "love" each other without the ritual and the paper? So, why should anyone, including same-sex partners, desire to participate in a social institution that is slowly becoming **obsolete**?

7

Discussing and Writing About The Text

Discussing Issues:

Interview people of various ages (grandparents, parents, peers, teenagers) as to what is to them the significance of marriage? Compile a list of the reasons marriage is or is not an important institution according to your interviewees. Discuss your results with those of your peers.

Writing about the Text:

In a well-developed and organized essay, respond to the reading; be sure to support your views with pertinent examples drawn from your own experience and observations, as well as readings.

Topic 1: According to the authors, what is the significance of marriage today? To what extent—if at all—do you agree with their opinion?

Topic 2: Do you think marriage should evolve as an institution and in what way (banned, broadened, etc)? How would this evolution affect people and their various communities? To support your opinion, you need to examine relevant and specific examples from a variety of sources.

Developing Vocabulary:

The words below may appear as part of your online quizzes. Please refer to the introduction for study strategies for learning vocabulary.

1. **decrying** critical ze
2. **abominations** a thing that causes disgust + hatred
3. **vehemently** impetuous violent
4. **conceptualization** process of development
5. **denouement** final outcome of a story
6. **consummates** complete; marriage> have sex
7. **dowry** property & money brought by a bride to her husband on their marriage
8. **a commune** group of people living together
9. **to wane** decline
10. **obsolete** outdated

Understanding the Text

Answer the following questions by carefully reviewing the authors' arugments in the short essay.

1. What should be the focal issue in the marriage debate today?

2. What is the idea of modern marriage, and when was it developed?

3. What have been the main reasons for getting married in the past?

4. What do the authors predict to be the evolution of marriage as an institution?

Analyzing Writing

Answer the following questions by carefully reviewing the authors' aruguments and writing strategies from the short essay.

1. Examine the role and the effectiveness of the first paragraph in the construction of the essay.

2. Examine the use and role of definition in the essay.

3. What kind of sources do the authors use in support of his thesis and arguments? Evaluate the various sources of evidence.

38 The Loss of Childhood

Parents today often **lament** the loss of childhood. Looking at their six-year-olds with fondness, they regret the inevitable swift changes that puberty is soon to bring about. "Children today grow up so fast" is the drum-beat refrain. One would think that perhaps they just exaggerate, for parents always seek to view their offspring as children even into old age. However, a simple visit to the local mall can attest to parents' concerns. Indeed, twelve-year-old girls stroll along looking like twenty-five in their heavy makeup and adult hairdos; teenage boys dressed in the colors of their favorite music band or sports team and with a cigarette in their hands sit leisurely on the mall patio in their desperate effort to look older and "cool"; meanwhile, both children and teenagers manically message or talk to their friends on their cell phones, trying their best to look more adult-like. Intelligently so, the fashion industry has responded to but has also shaped the desires of children to look, act, and be older than they actually are. Indeed, quite often the only thing that differs between kids and adults' fashions is size where kids look like adult miniatures ("Mini-Mes"). Advertising gurus were incredibly smart to **cater to** "tweens," the official term coined in the advertising industry to denote consumers between the ages of 8-12. Furthermore, an even cruder "adult-ization" of children is seen in companies such as Calvin Klein, Abercrombie & Fitch, and numerous other companies that have increasingly used sexualized tweens in revealing clothing and poses to market their wares. And it's not only parents that become aware of this shift; even eleven-year-olds don't consider themselves to be children anymore, as indicated by the Media Awareness Network; this revelation actually prompted toy companies to change the age bracket for their target audience from 0-14 to 0-10.

The pessimistic view of all these changes in childhood has concerned parents in an uproar. Thousands of resources dot the web, and shelf upon shelf fills bookstores with articles and books on how to protect children from growing up too early. Parents across the country are reading books like David Elkind's *The Hurried Child* for analysis and advice about how to preserve the childhood of their children for as long as possible. But what constitutes childhood? What idea is it that parents wish to **safeguard**? According to one of the most influential sociol-

1

2

ogists in the twentieth-century, Philippe Aries, our modern idea of childhood as a time of innocence and near care-free activity is a total social fabrication. In his influential book, *Centuries of Childhood*, Aries argued that childhood as we know it didn't exist before Victorian times in the early nineteenth century. It was then, according to Aries, that Western culture developed the concept of childhood as a distinct period of life that should be **discerned** from both infanthood and adulthood.

3   According to Aries, in the Medieval period and before (600-1485), children were considered adults by the age of seven, which was coincidentally the age of reason as determined by the Catholic Church. At this age, "children" were considered capable of making rational decisions, committing serious sins, apprenticing to a trade, or beginning work in the fields. Moreover, there was no **elongation** of childhood through the school system because there was no school system; instead, children were forced to become productive members of society, shouldering significant responsibilities in various work environments. Ample evidence for this equalization in the Medieval period can be seen in the portrayal of children as young adults, rather than children. Portraits from the period don't feature children in them; they feature small figures with adult faces who have perhaps assumed adult roles in society. Therefore, both in art and in reality, children during the Medieval period carried not only the attire of adulthood but also its responsibilities, as evidenced from archival materials.

4   It was in the Victorian period, 1837-1901, through the literature and perhaps as a reaction to the horrors of child labor and child mortality, as well as a result of the foundation of a nationalized school system in the U.S., that the concept of childhood was created. The literature of the period can certainly testify to this change. Charles Dickens' *Great Expectations* is at least partly famous for his portrayal of the main character, Pip, and his loss of childhood through his exposure to the real world, as famous as *Oliver Twist* is for his travails in an orphanage. Any number of Victorian poems or novels feature pitiful children suffering, their childhoods "ripped" away from them through brutality and mistreatment. It is during this period—and for the upper classes a bit before—that the romanticized vision of childhood sprung into being.

5   So, parents today who fear the loss of childhood for their children may be fighting a losing battle as well as a cultural construct. If childhood is a romanticized invention that **forestalls** adulthood, it is only a **fabricated** cultural idea, which can, therefore, be changed. It means that childhood as we know it—a time with few cares, few responsibilities, and ample time for play—is not a period that one is genetically predisposed to have. It is something one is culturally privileged

to have. Ironically, children today who seem to be growing up so fast may, in fact, be reverting to Medieval concepts of "children" as young adults by the age of seven. The advertising industry has seemingly recognized this before any of us by diversifying its methodology for "tweens" of 8-12 years of age.

What is interesting about the perception that childhood is slipping away is only partially correct. Children seem to be in a hurry to embrace adulthood, but in reality they only assume the air and image of adulthood and not its **concomitant** responsibilities as they were forced to do in the past. If "tweens" and teens, for instance, have the **accoutrements** of adults (clothes, watches, cell phones, computers, cars) and have access to the same things (sex, drinking, driving, spending), perhaps they should also have the responsibilities of adults (house payment, rent, car insurance, utility bills, food planning, food shopping, house maintenance, contraception). The current loss of childhood is not precisely a loss for children, for they are merely adopting the characteristics, consumption habits, and vices of adults without the repercussions and responsibilities that come with adulthood. If "tweens" were forced to pay for their cell phones, they would be far less likely to call all their friends for hours at night, incurring massive bills. If they had to pay a portion of the rent or utilities, they might not be as eager to spend. If they had to work a job for five hours a day in addition to their school, they might realize that adult life has its costs. How soon would the cares of adult life form **creases** of concern on the foreheads of our children? The only thing that might save the culturally constructed idea of childhood as the carefree time of play (and perhaps school)—if it is worth saving—will be the conscious choice by children that adult responsibilities are for the birds. If they see that their newly learned adult behavior will cost them time, money, and the stress of responsibility, they might prefer to go to the tree house out back until mom calls for dinner, leaving adult life to adults.

6

Discussing and Writing About The Text

Discussing Issues:

In a group compare yourself as a 12 year old to the 12 year olds that you see around you nowadays. What similarities or differences do you observe? What is your opinion about the changes that seem to have occurred? What do these changes signify about people's mentality?

Writing about the Text:

In a well-developed and organized essay, respond to the reading; be sure to support your views with pertinent examples drawn from your own experience and observations, as well as readings.

Topic 1: According to the authors, what is the idea of modern childhood and how could it be safeguarded? Do you think that the modern idea of childhood is worth maintaining and why?

Topic 2: According to your opinion, what should be the ideal conceptualization of childhood? To support your opinion, you need to examine relevant and specific examples from a variety of sources.

Developing Vocabulary:

The words below may appear as part of your online quizzes. Please refer to the introduction for study strategies for learning vocabulary.

1.	to lament	2.	cater to
3.	to safeguard	4.	to discern
5.	elongation	6.	to forestall
7.	fabricated (idea)	8.	concomitant
9.	accoutrements	10.	creases

Understanding the Text

Answer the following questions by carefully reviewing the authors' aruguments in the short essay.

1. How is the "loss of childhood" obvious nowadays according to the authors?

2. What is the idea of modern childhood and when was it developed?

3. What was the idea of childhood before the Victorian era?

4. What do the authors think is the problem with today's early "loss of childhood" and what is their proposed solution?

Analyzing Writing

Answer the following questions by carefully reviewing the authors' arugments and writing strategies from the short essay.

1. Examine the positioning of the authors' thesis. Do you find this positioning effective (or not)?

2. Examine terms and words that seem to be fabricated by the authors. What do you think of this technique?

3. What kind of evidence do the authors use to prove his various arguments?

39 Toys, Games, and Childhood

Not long ago, I was invited to a colleague's house for dinner and happened to notice the children's playroom while being given the tour of the house. The playroom was fairly large, perhaps 20' x 20', and had wall-to-wall shelves loaded with toys of all types: Barbies, trucks, Legos, stuffed animals, a Starwars Deathstar, and even a robotic tank. This was not a toy store or a collection of toys for a dozen kids; my colleague has but two children upon whom he has **lavished** so many gifts. When asked why his children needed so many toys, he responded that children who are stimulated with various toys learn better and faster. According to him, children need exposure to many things and toys to help them socialize and develop their imagination.

However, recent research has pointed directly in the opposite direction, which flies in the face of billions of dollars of advertising and commonplace belief. Toy companies, of course, have a **vested interest** in parents believing that toys will in and of themselves stimulate their children, educate them, and teach them social values. Undoubtedly, children do benefit from play, but is it necessarily with a plethora of toys? A research book published in 2005, *Children and Toys in Play and Learning*, indicates that there is no credible evidence that toys are educational at all. Moreover, according to Krister Svensson, the director of The International Toy Research Centre in Stockholm, "Toys don't teach **cognitive** or motor skills—they just encourage children to practice them….Children can learn just as much from repeatedly taking the lid off a shoe box and putting it back on again." Parents have been, at least in part, **duped** into believing toys are so greatly efficacious for childhood development.

This is not to say that toys entirely lack educational value or that they should be banned from the household. One could argue that certain toys such as Legos, puzzles, and board games like Pictionary or Scrabble can help children acquire knowledge or **hone** skills and traits such as their memory, their vocabulary, or construction skills, and they may well be better than that shoe box lid. Krister Svensson could argue that these skills could be acquired with any kind of item—and not necessarily prefabricated toys or with just one doll versus ten different ones. Furthermore and in defense of toys, children learn how to socialize and in-

1

2

3

teract with other people, which again, however, could be considered a result of interactive play rather than of toys per se. Last but not least, through toys children can develop and **internalize** a variety of social values such as helping the weak as with Barbie the Nurse. But parents must always be aware of messages sent by Barbie in Malibu who drives her own red Ferrari and spends her day shopping and relaxing by her pool and Jacuzzi. However, beyond the normal issues about toy choice and their educational value come three additional problems associated with toys.

4   First, just through the **omnipresent** advertising and the sheer number of toys children own at an early age, they are exposed to the social value of *the plethora of goods*. The playroom in my colleague's house had perhaps a hundred toys, most of which lay neglected after little use. This is by no means unrepresentative of toy consumption by other parents. This over-consumption teaches children in a not-so-subtle-way that more is not only better but also possible. It teaches them to seek to satisfy their every desire, to constantly generate new wants, and to believe that resources, at this age "parental" ones, are inexhaustible. Almost everyone is familiar with the image of children whining in supermarkets and stores for a particular toy, even going so far as throwing a tantrum if they don't get what they want. Equally common is the case of children who soon lose interest in their innumerous toys while they constantly crave new ones. So, if one were to agree that toys have an educational value, in this case the inevitable question is what happens when these children reach an age where either the parents can't afford the new "toy"—be it a computer or a car—or the children as young adults have to buy the "toy"? Having been "educated" to the contrary, these adult children will have a hard time realizing that in the real world neither gratification of every desire is possible, nor are sources inexhaustible.

5   Second, parents today can suffer economic hardship by keeping their children up to date with toys. The latest toy, the latest game, the latest doll, all cost money. It is not uncommon for a doll to cost twenty dollars or a new Xbox video game system to cost around 500 dollars—without any games included. These expenses wear on the family budget, and so far parents have been willing to pay the cost. Indeed, Neil Tseng, an economist in the Division of Consumer Expenditures, estimated in the 2003 Consumer Expenditure Survey that Americans in 2003 spent roughly 36 billion dollars on toys alone. This is separate from other parts of the entertainment budget, which for the year 2000 (the latest full data set available) was 203 billion dollars. It is easy then to comprehend the money stress seen in the face of the mother or father who has to refuse their child again and again in the supermarket even at the cost of an embarrassing tantrum.

Third, the most pernicious and distressing factor with the plethora of toys is the reduction of imagination in playtime. The **oxymoron** here is that the more stuff kids have to play with, the less they will need to create the imaginary or even physical spaces for their characters to inhabit. Instead of imagining a spaceport and building parts of it in a muddy sandbox, kids today get out their Darthvader and Bobo-Phet figurines that fight on a pre-made Deathstar. If they are too lazy for this, they can just load up Starwars on their Xbox or Nintendo Playstation videogame platform and play within an entirely pre-made world. This pre-fabrication of imaginary spaces and figures limits imagination and thought to a certain pre-ordained frame of reference which the child is then unlikely to **transcend**. The spaceport they see is the one from the imagination of George Lucas, not their own. The video game they play is not their own imaginary space, but game-designers. Where is their own imaginary landscape peopled with characters of their own making?

6

Ultimately, toys do teach children a great deal about the world they live in, just not the lessons most parents believe the toys teach when they buy them. Children learn about the social values associated with the world just by the type of toy or game allowed into the house. Although my colleague had his children's interest at heart with the selection of so-called educational toys, he was also modeling for his children other values through the number of toys purchased from a seemingly inexhaustible bank account. By providing his children with so many toys, he may be, ironically, limiting their imagination at the same time. Perhaps all his children need is an old shoe box and some parental time spent in an imaginary space of their own construction.

7

Discussing and Writing About The Text

Discussing Issues:

Try to think of your childhood and the role toys had in your upbringing. Make a list of your favorite and least favorite toys and try to examine how they affected you (and your siblings or friends) in your development. Compare and discuss your findings with those of the author and with your peers. At a further level, interview your parents or grandparents to see what kind of toys they had and how those toys affected their development.

Writing about the Text:

In a well-developed and organized essay, respond to the reading; be sure to support your views with pertinent examples drawn from your own experience and observations, as well as readings.

Topic 1: According to the author, what are the dangers involved with a plethora of toys in a child's life? To what extent—if at all—do you agree with this view point?

Topic 2: According to your opinion, how can toys best contribute to children's development? To support your opinion, you need to examine relevant and specific examples from a variety of sources.

Developing Vocabulary:

The words below may appear as part of your online quizzes. Please refer to the introduction for study strategies for learning vocabulary.

1. **to lavish**
2. **vested interest**
3. **cognitive**
4. **to dupe**
5. **to hone**
6. **to internalize**
7. **omnipresent**
8. **plethora**
9. **oxymoron**
10. **to transcend**

Understanding the Text

Answer the following questions by carefully reviewing the authors' aruguments in the short essay.

1. What is (are) the argument(s) of the proponents of toys?

2. What is the author's refutation of each of these arguments and what is his thesis?

3. What are the author's additional worries about toys and their role?

4. What is, according to the author, the most dangerous effect of toys in children's development?

Analyzing Writing

Answer the following questions by carefully reviewing the authors' arugments and writing strategies from the short essay.

1. Where does the author construct lists and how do these occasions work as a writing strategy?

2. Examine three topic sentences for how they effectively (or not) orient the reader.

3. Examine the use of sources in the essay. What kind of sources does the author use (personal examples-anecdotes, statistics, etc)? Do you think they are appropriate and convincing? What additional sources would you use?

40 The Prodigal Son

The well-known parable of the **prodigal** son in the *Bible* has been used for ages as a metaphor for God's love and forgiveness of the sinner who repents. In this short section from Luke 15, the younger son demands his share of inheritance from his father while his father is still living. He then travels to distant lands where he "waste[s] his substance with riotous living." Soon he finds that he has run through his money and his supposed friends have deserted him the one after the other. He is reduced to working as a swineherd, and then, in these base circumstances, he decides to return home to his father's house, having really no other options. In the meantime, the older son has spent the years tending his father's property, working **assiduously** for the profit of the family. However, upon the arrival of the younger son, the father orders the slaughter of a fatted-calf for an **unprecedented** celebration in honor of the prodigal's return. In response to the older son, who complains about this obvious inequality of treatment, the father argues that he, the older son, was always around to enjoy whatever the father had, while his younger son was lost, but is now found. Therefore, they should all rejoice at the younger son's return. 1

In the American culture, and more specifically among Christians, this parable has also come to set the standards for parental love. This is a pervasive idea, and examples of the real-world implementation of this literary **motif** can be found all around us in a variety of forms. The sloppy kid, who for once manages to clean up his bedroom, becomes the hero of the day. The less diligent and studious daughter, who is accepted in college, has her success celebrated by a huge party her parents throw for her. The reckless teenager, who wrecks the parents' car, is given a new car as praise for attending driver's school and not driving under the influence again. The son, who cleans up after years of drug-abuse, attends college, and gets a job, is now praised beyond comparison for "coming back." 2

Undoubtedly, all these prodigal sons and daughters should be assisted in their efforts at recuperation and be forgiven upon their repentance. Surely, their return from the dark paths they have tread should be celebrated, but should it be glorified? A turkey should be slaughtered, but a whole calf? Too often the reformed prodigal child is not only accepted back without any hint of **recrimination**, 3

245

but he also becomes the paragon of virtue for the family. Parents end up bragging about their prodigal children and "how far they've come" and "how accomplished they are now considering...." Therefore, not only are there seemingly no consequences for the years of "riotous living," but also the parents are there to welcome them back with open arms; not only is their past forgotten, but when it is remembered, it is done in praise of their repentance. Examples of this literary motif abound, just look at Shakespeare's Henry IV, where the main character, Prince Hal, even uses his prodigal status as a political weapon: "So when this loose behavior I throw off/...And like bright metal on a sullen ground,/ My reformation, glittering o'er my fault,/ Shall show more goodly, and attract more eyes/ Than that which hat no foil to set it off (I Henry IV, I.3. 205-212). And just as with the parable in Luke, Prince Hal's reformation was celebrated. Indeed, all too often the prodigal's return becomes the epitome of family pride at the expense of the sibling who was always the "good" kid and whose behavior has been taken for granted. For both illustrations clearly echo Luke's verses "that there will be such joy in heaven over one sinner repenting than over ninety-nine persons who have no need of repentance."

4   In shaping the standards of modern parental behavior, this **parable** has become problematic in that it mandates that parents accept all kinds of bad and destructive behavior from their children in the hopes that the latter will "return to the fold." In this system, just like in the Prodigal Son parable, forgiveness is absolute; it doesn't seem to matter much what harm the child has caused or how badly the child has messed up his own life; the more destructive and anti-social the behavior has been, the more rejoicing and celebrating should be done for the reform of the child. According to Luke, parental love for their offspring is supposed to be unconditional if the latter decides to return and repent.

5   But this type of love has two negative effects. The first one is that it damages the would-be prodigal child by creating an expectation for forgiveness if they **repent**. It sends the message that you can always mess up, for if you eventually repent, you will not only be forgiven but also extremely appreciated for your overall course of action. This is not to say actual repentance—beyond the mere face value of apologizing—is always an easy task, especially in cases such as that of the drug-addict son. Nor is this to nullify all the possible societal and parental factors that contribute to the faults of the prodigal sons and daughters of society. However, in rearing a responsible child, parents should teach them that forgiveness comes under conditions; children should be taught that if they "return home," they will be welcomed but not glorified; they will be forgiven, but not without **repercussions**. One of the important acts of parenting is to teach children about re-

sponsibility and the ramifications of bad behavior, and total acceptance negates that.

The second effect is that this glorification of the return of the prodigal son is clearly unfair to the son that was good all along but whose good behavior and hard work had seemed to be taken for granted. There seems to be an implication that the good son could at all times enjoy the father's love just by being around. It seems as if this son did not really put any effort in being good but that his course of righteous action came to him easily and effortlessly. Therefore, this system undervalues and jeopardizes the choices of the children who follow the rules, do well in school, and become civilized members of society. If they see that there are no repercussions for "living riotously," i.e. lying, cheating on exams, stealing from others, and generally following their own desires, why should they ever **curb** what they want to do? If they see that the best of the rewards, such as the "fatted calf," are saved for the ones who repent after their riotous life, why should they even bother with being good? Are good children never tempted? If they realize that there are few consequences to living riotously with a low risk of never being welcomed back to the family, but perhaps it is worth trying…. 6

In conclusion, it seems that there should be a measure in the appraisal of this "return." The proverbial "slaughter of the fatted calf," i.e. praise and rewards for the return of the prodigal child, should not become the **modus operandi** of parental rearing. The prodigal child should not be given the same benefit as the one who was devoted to his parents and successfully integrated into society without causing any problems or pain to anybody. The prodigal children should definitely be welcomed back, knowing, however, that they will face the consequences, and that they will have a debt to pay back not only to themselves but also to their parents and society. 7

Discussing and Writing About The Text

Discussing Issues:

Think of your parents' course of action when it comes to forgiveness and love. Do you think your parents would be more likely to behave like the father in the prodigal son parable? Should there be a difference in the treatment of the prodigal and the good son? Discuss your conclusions with your peers.

Writing about the Text:

In a well-developed and organized essay, respond to the reading; be sure to support your views with pertinent examples drawn from your own experience and observations, as well as readings.

Topic 1: Why do the authors believe the prodigal son parable is problematic? To what extent—if at all—do you agree with their views?

Topic 2: According to your opinion, how should parents treat their children when it comes to forgiveness and punishment? What would be the optimum course of action in these cases?

Developing Vocabulary:

The words below may appear as part of your online quizzes. Please refer to the introduction for study strategies for learning vocabulary.

1.	prodigal	2.	assiduously
3.	unprecedented	4.	motif
5.	recrimination	6.	parable
7.	repent	8.	repercussions
9.	to curb	10.	modus operandi

Understanding the Text

Answer the following questions by carefully reviewing the authors' arugments in the short essay.

1. What is the meaning of the parable of the prodigal son?

2. What are the authors' objections to the teachings of this parable?

3. What are the two negative effects of parental unconditional forgiveness?

4. How do the authors think parents should treat their prodigal children?

Analyzing Writing

Answer the following questions by carefully reviewing the authors' arugments and writing strategies from the short essay.

1. Examine and evaluate the use and placement of the topic sentences in each paragraph.

2. Examine the use of humor and irony in the text? Do you find them effective, ineffective and why?

3. Examine the use of specific examples in the text; how much do the examples help your understanding of the authors' arguments?

41 Unconditional Love or Parental Selfishness?

Imagine that a new baby arrives in the family, and there is near **raucous**, overwhelming rejoicing about the new arrival. Little do you know how things are going to change for you as well even though it wasn't you who had the child in the first place. Soon enough, it becomes impossible to have a conversation around the family dinner table without some kind of interruption. If the baby drools "expressively," everyone has to stop and "oooh!!!" and "aaah!!!" over this **mammalian** display of mouth juice. If the baby mumbles something, though nonsensical, the attempted discussion among the adults comes to a grinding halt and is not to be taken up again, like a poor, abandoned dog; once the baby has been **ogled** by all, the theme of that conversation has long since been forgotten in the wake of the child's utterance. Even the smartest, most logical parents seem to lose track of who they are, what they do, or even how to keep up a conversation with other adults, for their entire world has been tilted to revolve around the child.

However, having a child was their choice, so why should everyone else suffer? Indeed, this torture for the rest of us does not stop at two years when the baby has been potty trained and may know to at least express certain wants. No, the ride is just beginning. Everybody has to be in constant awe about the child's accomplishments—be it their first step or their first monosyllabic utterance. Once the child reaches school age, uncles, aunts, and friends are invited to the obligatory soccer games, baseball games, football games, gymnastic competitions, music recitals, skits, plays, ballet performances, karate classes, and even teacher conferences. It seems like every weekend and many week nights have some required social obligation for the child and the parents and you, who have been summarily summoned though you never signed up for that ride.

Don't get me wrong. Involvement by friends and extended family in a child's life is definitely important and should not be underrated; however, who really wants to see a **troupe** of stumbling six year olds trying to do gymnastics or attempting a sterling performance of *Swan Lake*? Once or twice is fine, but shouldn't there be an end? After all, who is the parent of the child and why should their decision to have children become everybody else's responsibility? Even worse, many parents these days make their friends and fellow family members feel guilty if they don't pay **homage** to their children by attending these events or by buying gifts on every national and Hallmark holiday in addition to all the birthdays that keep coming up. It is almost as if the people you knew were substituted by a Frankensteinian parent who looks like a **simulacrum** of the person you once knew and now has only one topic of conversation and existence: their children.

4   What force of nature overtakes parents? Is this some part of the mythical biological clock that ticks, ticks, ticks, and then, if left long enough, explodes into some kind of parental care-bomb? Is this biology, sociology, or some sort of demonic possession? Well, the answer is certainly the first two, and the jury is out on the possession. There does seem to be a motherly instinct to protect and nurture children, or at least so claim the millions of blogs on the web. There are, after all, heroic stories of mothers who lift cars, engines, or any number of heavy items off their children when an accident has occurred. Who needs the Incredible Hulk? There are stories of super human fighting power that moms can muster if they have to defend their litter. This I can understand, and I'd even like to harness all that energy to combat the current energy crisis. But forcing everyone to attend every **lavish** school theatre production or to lavish these children with gifts for everything from cleaning their rooms to a good grade indicates a sociological issue, not a biological one. So where's the motivation?

5   Well, it finally dawned on me. It is because modern parents are selfish. Yes, I know this may sound like **heresy** echoing down the sacred halls of the freshly cleaned suburban house space. However, let's think about it a bit more. Ask most modern parents what it means to have a child, and they will answer that the child is everything. And this is *exactly* the problem. For these people, having children is like a rite of passage to a new land where they can only wave to their single friends from the shore of parental responsibility. They take this as their new credo, their very own burden to bear. In fact, the new child does absorb all their time or at least ex-free time. The new parents try to balance two full-time jobs, a big mortgage or rent payment, new cars, day-care, and all that jazz. The children almost inevitably become the center of attention in a very crowded life.

6   It is not that these parents don't sacrifice for their children as can be seen by the harried mother who has no private time or the father who gets home from work to be confronted by homework duties. No, there is personal sacrifice, and often this sacrifice leads to problems between the couple as well when desires and wishes are repressed for long periods of time. So, what happens? These parents transfer all their hopes, dreams, and need for self-actualization onto their kids. Their children become the vehicle whereby these parents receive social praise and fulfillment since they won't get it anywhere else. Like **narcissistic** architects, who

see themselves in every corner of the building, these parents too often see their own characteristics and their own social value tied up in their offspring.

Today's parents sacrifice their own lives once their children come along   7
because their lives are unbalanced. There are no outside interests (or time for them) beyond the kids; there is not time for a vacation; they collapse at night after a day of scurrying around because their lives are overloaded. So, to get any kind of personal fulfillment, these parents turn to their kids, and they transfer their needs onto them. It is for these reasons that everyone else (friends and family members) have to pay homage to the altar of their sacrifice, for the parents have no other fulfillment except through their children. Did they have time or money for the long weekend in Mexico that their "single friends" went on? Do they have time to read an interesting book or learn the piano? No, but they make sure their kids do. So, next time you go to the house of a friend or a family member with kids and *all* conversation revolves around the **mewling** entity (or dies off when the kid does something cutesy), think that this total absorption is not the "unconditional love" of new parents as they would like you to believe. Think that the child is one of the only ways to receive any social validation in a far too unbalanced life.

Discussing and Writing About The Text

Discussing Issues:

What has been the position you have held in your parents' life? What are the factors that explain this position? Discuss your thoughts with your peers.

Writing about the Text:

In a well-developed and organized essay, respond to the reading; be sure to support your views with pertinent examples drawn from your own experience and observations, as well as readings.

Topic 1: According to the author, how and why are parents selfish? To what extent—if at all—do you agree with the author's views?

Topic 2: Write a solution paper for parental selfishness and how to avoid it.

Developing Vocabulary:

The words below may appear as part of your online quizzes. Please refer to the introduction for study strategies for learning vocabulary.

1. raucous
2. mammalian
3. ogled
4. troupe
5. homage
6. simulacrum
7. lavish
8. heresy
9. narcissistic
10. mewling

Understanding the Text

Answer the following questions by carefully reviewing the authors' aruguments in the short essay.

1. What things does the author find particularly disturbing about parents?

2. In what ways do people become selfish when they become parents?

3. How much is nature responsible for parental selfishness

4. What are the main reasons for parental selfishness?

Analyzing Writing

Answer the following questions by carefully reviewing the authors' arugments and writing strategies from the short essay.

1. Examine the use of narration in the text and its effectiveness.

2. Find four or more words that are used ironically and examine their effectiveness.

3. Examine how the author employs refutation in the text. Can you cite the specific sentences or paragraphs?

42 The Humanism Movement

Every morning there are lines of cars waiting to pull into the local day care parking lot to drop off toddlers and pre-schoolers before mothers commute to work. The same long line can be seen at 5:30 pm, as these **weary** mothers return from a stress-filled, and everyone knows that the "work day" does not end at 5:30 pm. There is still grocery shopping to be hurried through, dinner to be made, the house to be picked up, laundry to be folded, children to be played with, homework (if any) to be completed, and finally five minutes of peace and quiet before bedtime. One gets tired just listening to this **litany** of chores and responsibilities. But this kind of day is not uncommon for working mothers who try to balance careers with children and family. In fact, a growing number of articles in *Newsweek*, *Time*, and national newspapers have been pointing out how many working mothers are on the verge of nervous breakdowns, sprinting from one task to the next without any downtime.

1

In the growing national debate about motherhood, a number of authors have ironically denounced feminism for giving women a raw deal. To them, they say, feminism has bequeathed to women the responsibilities and stresses of careers and left them with the **onerous** duties and sacrifices of motherhood. One of the most vocal opponents of feminism, Caitlin Flanagan, an author who has written for the *Atlantic Monthly* and *The New Yorker*, recently published a book (*To Hell With All That: Loving and Loathing our Inner Housewife*) **denouncing** feminism and its ideals. Flanagan argues in her writings that women should return to the simpler days (perhaps of the 1950s) where women were housewives and men were the breadwinners. Furthermore, she argues, women should take care of the household, and a major problem in married couples is that they don't couple. Women, therefore, should sleep with their husbands far more often than they do, and, moreover, they should see it as one of their "duties" in the relationship. Furthermore, according to Flanagan, when women work, traditional dinnertimes and time with the children are "lost."

2

Authors like Flanagan have "gotten up the gander" of feminists across the country, who dismiss these arguments as a full-frontal **assault** on the gains women have made in society. Many feminists argue that Flanagan should not be so quick

3

to dismiss the rights and social progress that she, herself, enjoys. Even today, though definite strides have been made, women don't enjoy full parity in wages with men; they don't have the same opportunities for management positions; they don't have the same respect that men often have. Women, in short, still have the short end of the stick. Thus, Flanagan and her **cohort**, feminists argue, are trying to reverse the gains and undermine the struggles women have made by a hundred years. They argue, and rightly so, that women should not be barefoot, pregnant, or subservient to men. Quite the contrary, equality in privileges and duties is still the only way out of the dead-end modern women seem to face when trying to juggle their multi-personalities of career women, mothers, wives, and housekeepers.

4   However, it seems that something drastically important is missing from these discussions: men. The discussions revolve around them as the great, inescapable force within society who seemingly exist as an abstract notion of "paycheck." In both scenarios above, men go to work, work hard, and return home, **foregoing** most of the household duties, stresses, or time with children. While the stereotype of traditional male roles still holds true to some degree, recent research has shown that men have also taken on more and more household duties and parental responsibilities. A 2004 study, "The 'New Man' is in the House," that appeared in the *Journal of Men's Studies*, concluded that younger men (ages 25-35) were heavily involved in both managing the household and taking care of children. In dual-income households, men actually suffer the same stresses their wives do about career, marriage, and children.

5   Therefore, the problem today in families is not precisely the unequal distribution of house duties between the partners. The problem is that there is too much work to do and not enough time. When both parents work full-time jobs, inevitably something along the way is "lost" as Caitlin Flanagan maintains. When parents work 40+ hours per week, they don't have enough time with their children, time with each other, time to maintain their health, or time to nourish relationships with friends. Of course, the economic necessity for two incomes dictates that both women and men work, for survival on one salary is almost impossible for most middle-class households nowadays. Certainly, as Flanagan observes, a reevaluation of our perceived needs and an effort to **curtail** our spending could prove helpful. However, one cannot overlook other important factors such as the modern economy that demands overwork, the modern employer or manager who frowns upon parents as the lazy "clock-watchers" who have to leave work to pick their kids up, or lastly the modern state that "saves" on child-care benefits. The result, then, is that both partners are often stressed, overworked, and **short-fused**. It is the rare man or woman who can truly juggle both career and family without

sacrificing quality in either one. A household with children, for instance, requires the full attention of at least one of the members of the partnership whether it be the mom, the dad, or both of them. Must it be the man who leaves the house for work and the woman who stays home? Must women work in addition to taking care of the house?

The answer to this problem then is not what Flanagan suggests, a return to a time when women were housewives and men were breadwinners. There can be no return to a "Leave It to Beaver" 1950s housewife mystique, for it never truly existed. Neither should we take the other side and simply blame men for still being lazy around the house, for this is a drastic simplification of male roles in families these days. The answer, instead, is a focus on Humanism, not feminism or anti-feminism. We need to reevaluate our human existence, our relationships with others and our children, as well as the role the state should have in supporting its members. If we reevaluate the needs of our human condition, perhaps we'll realize what is really important. It's time for a new Humanism Movement in which we all ask ourselves how we want to live life. The decision should not be to sacrifice one or the other. Instead, we should reevaluate what really makes us happy, and what we need in order to make that happen. However, in this process, the reevaluation of our personal choices cannot be a panacea by itself; instead **synergy** will be necessary between the individual and society. The Humanism movement should then be a process initiated by the individual but expanded to society and its institutions if a substantial change is to occur.

6

Discussing and Writing About The Text

Discussing Issues:

What do you think should be the position of men and women within the household? In a discussion with peers, try to find ways for modern couples to manage a household, a family, and a career without being overwhelmed or exhausted.

Writing about the Text:

In a well-developed and organized essay, respond to the reading; be sure to support your views with pertinent examples drawn from your own experience and observations, as well as readings.

Topic 1: What are the authors' concerns and suggestions about the modern household? To what extent—if at all—do you agree with their suggestions?

Topic 2: According to your opinion, how can people nowadays manage a balance between all the duties of a career, a family, and a household? Are all of those things mutually exclusive? To support your opinion, you need to examine relevant and specific examples from a variety of sources.

Developing Vocabulary:

The words below may appear as part of your online quizzes. Please refer to the introduction for study strategies for learning vocabulary.

1. weary
2. litany
3. onerous
4. denouncing
5. assault
6. cohort
7. foregoing
8. to curtail
9. short-fused
10. synergy

Understanding the Text

Answer the following questions by carefully reviewing the authors' aruguments in the short essay.

1. What are the main issues in the debate between modern feminists and anti-feminists?

2. What is the authors' response to the debate on feminism?

3. What do the authors think is the role of men in the current debate?

4. What are the authors' suggestions in this debate?

Analyzing Writing

Answer the following questions by carefully reviewing the authors' aruguments and writing strategies from the short essay.

1. At which point(s) of the essay do the authors state their thesis (beginning, middle, end)? How effective do you find this positioning?

2. Find the focus-theme of each paragraph and write it in the margin next to each paragraph. Is each paragraph organized around a specific focus or not?

3. Examine the use of sources in the essay. What kind of sources do the authors use (personal examples-anecdotes, facts, authorities, etc)? Do you think they are appropriate and convincing? What additional sources would you use?

CHAPTER
SIX

Identity

43 Whose Space is MySpace?

There is nowadays a presence on the Internet that has been getting a great deal of attention and media coverage. Its name is not Google, Yahoo, or even Microsoft in one of its guises. Its name is MySpace. Originally created in January of 2004 as an Internet location for musicians to trade songs and discuss the music industry, by 2006 MySpace transformed its identity into a site for everyone, namely its now projected ninety-five million members from all over the world and mostly the U.S. One of the secrets of its success is that membership is free. It just requires registering with one's email address and name. This simple enrollment then **warrants** access to numerous groups of various opinions and interests, blogging (web logging) utilities, and the ability to look for new friends and IM (instant message) them. With its free and simplified rules and processes, MySpace has gradually become a very popular **de facto** community center and staging area for millions of people, ranging from elementary school kids to adults.

MySpace is just the tip of the iceberg and the most recent representative of a new social phenomenon of virtual communities. People, it seems, in our world of disconnected real-life social interaction are seeking cyber relationships through online communities that share similar interests. MySpace is the *par excellence* example of the evolution of the 1980s-style message-boards or bulletin-board systems (BBS) that one logged onto to discuss published articles on specific topics. Listservs are also common and serve the same function today via members' shared emails. However, MySpace and its **ilk** have expanded on these notions of a cyber community and mastered one of the secrets: inclusion. Anyone can get an account regardless of whether their interest is punk rock, classical music, or rocket science. They can also post pictures, music, and animation to the blogging site as well as invite friends to join on-line chat rooms. And MySpace is not alone in this new cyber-community center, for other sites have popped up as well: MSNSpaces, Friendster, or LiveJournal just to name a few. Combined, these sites will enjoy a cyber community of over one-hundred million by year's end, many of whom will be children and teens.

As with any community, there seem to be real or perceived dangers lurking just around the corner. Recent reports of sexual predators hunting teens on

1

2

3

MySpace have shocked parents across the country, who, if the National Kaiser Family Foundation 2005 study is correct, had no idea what their kids were doing online. According to the study, entitled *Generation M,* fifty three percent of children ages 8-18 said that their parents had no rules about media usage in the house (including watching TV, surfing the Internet, playing video games). An additional 46% said there were some rules, but only 20% of those said the rules were enforced at all. In summary, parents were shocked because they didn't know what their kids were doing on the Internet. In response to this alert, MySpace implemented some additional security features to protect teens and to **allay** the fear of parents—and possibly to ensure that parents are not involved in the average teens' hour of surfing the internet per day. With these protections in place, parents could peacefully return to their role of **complaisance**.

4   Surely, sexual predation is something to be cautious of, but according to various reports in newspapers, very few cases of actual approaches of teens by anyone labeled "inappropriate" have surfaced. Therefore, this **predation** by possible sexual offenders may not be parents' worst fear about these sites. Instead, parents should be more concerned about other predators in MySpace. Indeed, even if their children are safe from unwanted advances of a sexual nature, they are targeted on a huge scale by advances of another kind: the advertising kind. The children and teens who use MySpace are so important a consumer group that it is no coincidence that Rupert Murdoch's media **conglomerate** paid 580 million dollars for ownership of MySpace in July of 2005; the hope, of course through this acquisition was to more efficiently study and target the child and teen markets precisely. Therefore, while MySpace may allow kids and teenagers a community center on the Internet for blogging and gathering, it constitutes a community-center built and sustained by big business hoping to sell to and create name brand loyalty among these kids. Does this sound like an advertiser's **utopian** dream? Perhaps, it's not utopian any more, for spaces like MySpace are making it a dream come true. According to statistics, MySpace has accounted for 10% of the viewings of all advertisements in 2006 and is likely to increase this percentage in years to come. This is a huge number of ads that are seen by a potential one-hundred-million + group.

5   In a way, it is disingenuous to claim that MySpace (as well as its competitors) is a community center. Imagine a children's community center with every wall plastered with advertisements, all the sports paraphernalia with big logos, music piped into the loudspeaker system with CDs available for purchase, and teens chatting about their personalities with every other word about the latest gadget to be had. Members of MySpace don't spend all their time chatting with

friends or constructing their blogs. They surf the net from one site to the next, clicking on advertisement banners to check out the latest thing. Ads can even be easily placed on their own site, so the professing of the sixteen- year-old and his biography comes with advertisement banners for Amazon.com. The prevalence of advertisements in these sites is simply overwhelming.

Taking this into consideration, MySpace sounds like a **misnomer**. By providing "free" space on the server to children and teens, companies profit from the creation of a cyber world that is fundamentally founded on, dedicated to, and revolving around material goods. MySpace becomes TheirSpace, and there is only an **illusion** of ownership by the participants in these cyber communities. We need not forget that children and teens are in the specific age group whose identity is still being formed and solidified, and they are, therefore, especially vulnerable to unmonitored social influences. If the process of discovery of oneself, which seems to be one of the goals of socializing within these cyber communities, is so significantly influenced and guided by corporations through omnipresent advertising, this may result in an entire generation whose identity formation has been based mainly on consumer products. While this may be beneficial for the corporations, it certainly cannot be for these teens. Teens need socializing beyond cyberspace and beyond the influence of corporate advertisements. If most interactions among teens become anchored in material goods and sales, this will gradually and fundamentally alter the nature of human relationships.

6

Discussing and Writing About The Text

Discussing Issues:

Make a list of all the friends or family members you know who use MySpace. What are their demographics (age groups)? Have you used MySpace? If so, what has your experience been? In your opinion, what are the dangers of MySpace? What are the advantages to the site that the authors may not have discussed?

Writing about the Text:

In a well-developed and organized essay, respond to the reading; be sure to support your views with pertinent examples drawn from your own experience and observations, as well as readings.

Topic 1: According to the authors, what are the dangers posed by Internet sites like MySpace? Do you think they are justified in their concerns?

Topic 2: Design your own business plan to create an Internet site like MySpace. Who could become members? How would you create a secure site? Why would anyone visit your site and not someone else's? How would you address some of the concerns the authors bring up?

Developing Vocabulary:

The words below may appear as part of your online quizzes. Please refer to the introduction for study strategies for learning vocabulary.

1. warrants
2. de facto
3. ilk
4. allay
5. complaisance
6. predation
7. conglomerate
8. utopian
9. misnomer
10. illusion

Understanding the Text

Answer the following questions by carefully reviewing the authors' aruguments in the short essay.

1.   What is MySpace?

2.   Who can belong to MySpace and what does one do there? How does one become a member?

3.   What are the perceived dangers of places like MySpace? What do the authors fear?

4.   Why are the authors concerned about corporate sponsorship or influence in MySpace?

Analyzing Writing

Answer the following questions by carefully reviewing the authors' arugments and writing strategies from the short essay.

1. Examine the use of renaming and extended definition in the text.

2. Find three transition sentences and analyze how they work and how effective they are.

3. Examine how the authors employ refutation in the text. Can you cite the specific paragraphs?

44 Suburban Existence

For a very long time people have recognized that the space around them—whether natural or built—affects how they behave and how they think. Especially when it comes to constructed space, one can trace a certain significance in its most unique as well as in its most common forms. In the 5th century BC, for instance, Pericles of Athens had the Parthenon built to physically illustrate the power of the city state of Athens; Roman emperors engaged in massive projects like the Coliseum or the Baths of Caracalla not only for the benefit of the people, but to also express the power and grandeur of the Roman Empire. In the modern day the built environment continues to consist of a multitude of signs; in a typical classroom, for example, the positioning of student desks in rows facing the teacher's desk clearly **signifies** the emphasis on the teacher's role; in a courtroom, the power of each side in a trial is also evident in the formulation of the space: the district attorney and the defendant are seated at equal levels while the judge is granted the **preeminent** position behind a large **dais**. It is no surprise then that there is a growing body of critical literature investigating the role of the built environment on people.

1

So, if we take as a given that the built environment does affect people in some way, what is the role of the suburbs—the most pervasive organization of housing in the United States— in the lives of their residents? One place to start is with the definition of the "burbs" as they are **satirically** called. Now, no two people quite agree on what suburbia means, but the name itself can provide some clue. From Latin roots, it literally means outside of or beyond the city (sub + urban). There also can be no denying that suburbia is one of the main ways of living in the United States as can be seen in the double-digit growth patterns of places outside of cities. Las Vegas, for instance, is one of the fastest-growing areas in the United States, but it is not its downtown that has been attracting the 6,000-7,000 people moving to the area per month in the years 2005-2006. It is the suburbs. One of the chief reasons people are moving to Las Vegas as well as most other suburban areas is the relatively cheap home prices. Put simply, people can buy far more house and land for their money in a suburban setting. As a result then of the massive **exodus** from cities and the **influx** from country regions, suburbia is growing incessantly. However, these are simply the numbers, which by themselves cannot explicitly in-

2

form us on how suburbia shapes the people and the culture.

3   One major characteristic of the suburbs is that they typically are not considered a source of jobs; this inevitably entails that residents often need to commute to some downtown area to access their workplace. This flow then during normal rush hours creates massive traffic problems for almost all major cities in the United States. In fact, based on the average commuter, a recent survey calculated that in the U.S. there is a combined amount of almost one billion hours wasted on commuting per week. To add to these numbers, 3.4 million people have to endure a ninety-minute, one-way commute to their job or home per day. Now, even if one were to try to enjoy the commute time in their luxurious car listening to their favorite music and sipping on their coffee, on a daily basis this commute would probably be time-consuming if not nerve-wrecking. So, if the suburban resident spends so much time and energy—both mental and environmental— commuting to and from the workplace, why live in the suburbs at all? What is the **impact** or the significance of the residents' interaction with their environment on a daily basis? What community are they really part of?

4   The first motive, of course, for moving to the suburbs, is, as mentioned above, affordability. In most cases, people tolerate the traffic congestion and the wasted commute time because they cannot afford rent or real-estate prices in the city areas they commute to. Quite often city houses or apartments are not only smaller but also much more expensive than those in the suburbs. Put simply, many people are priced out of the market in city areas, so they have to buy further away. This distance from the city has the **corollary** that suburbanites often experience only the house and the work environments, traveling between the two. Most of them commute to the city for work and leave as soon as they are done, returning to the sanctuary of their homes after a weary day spent at the job and in traffic. This structuralism then makes the suburban house the central focus of most off-work activities. It is quite common to refer to suburbs as "bedroom communities", for what they offer is mainly a place for rest and decompression from the routine of the everyday work and commute. However, even on the weekends, the bigger suburban house remains the focal point of one's activities such as mowing of lawns, weeding of yards, cleaning, and other house projects.

5   Now, should suburbanites want to "go out of the house", where should they go? In suburbia there are only few public areas or spaces to go to. Due to the suburbs' main function as bedroom communities, there is little investment or interest in creating places for entertainment or public interaction. After the weekly commute and the house projects, one does not have the time or the energy to "go out." In that way, entertainment is chiefly located within the house, and it's about watch-

ing TV, renting DVDs, and having barbecues in the yard and drinks by the pool. Of course, there are local supermarkets, shopping malls, and restaurants in the area, but the environment is not as varied as in the city. One leaves the house to run errands, to buy groceries, or to go mall shopping, and perhaps catch a movie or dinner at a restaurant. Otherwise, people who live in the suburbs—by necessity—retreat to their house space. By contrast, living spaces in cities are typically less big and less demanding, so people are more likely to have both the energy and the need to "go out"; besides, entertainment can be accessed within minutes of driving or walking to coffee shops, bars, restaurants, shows, and of course public parks. This is why city life appears to be more vibrant and interesting. It is not because there are more people living in the city; quite the contrary, many suburb areas have more residents than the cities they feed. In the city people are more likely to seek entertainment outside their homes, and it is more likely they can find a variety of entertainment stimuli. Therefore, in the city one's home is not one's focal space of existence.

However, one could perhaps see no harm in that. Indeed, what could be so bad about having your home as "your castle"? After all, many people can easily trade the options for entertainment in the city for the **serenity** of the bigger cheaper house in the suburbs. These advantages, however, also come with the loss of one other very important characteristic of city life, which is participation in an authentic public space. In cities, people of all persuasions are more likely to **commingle** in public spaces. In cities like San Francisco or New York, for example, citizens of all races and income levels use the public parks for recreation. The daily life throws people of all viewpoints together, forcing a kind of interaction among people who would otherwise not associate. In the suburbs, on the other hand, residents are typically isolated based on the purchase price of their home, with residents driving home from work to their houses, passing through all the areas in between. Poorer areas are strictly segmented from richer ones based on property prices. By separating the wealthy from the poor, work spaces from home spaces, and living in a community from experiencing the community, the suburbs do not offer residents a complete environment; rather, they isolate them to their home and away from any form of authentic community.   6

Ultimately, there are many modes of living and ways to organize our living patterns. It would be unreasonable to condemn living in the suburbs as some have done, for there are evident advantages in smaller mortgages, bigger houses, less crowding, and closer access to the countryside. Nevertheless, observation of the effects of suburbia on our national consciousness is essential, for the built environment does affect the way we interact with others as well as the way we evolve as a people.   7

Discussing and Writing About The Text

Discussing Issues:

Examine your residential space (in the city or the suburbs, an apartment or a house) and examine its effects on you. Compare your findings to those of your peers and make a table with advantages and disadvantages for each kind of residential area.

Writing about the Text:

In a well-developed and organized essay, respond to the reading; be sure to support your views with pertinent examples drawn from your own experience and observations, as well as readings.

Topic 1: According to the authors, how does suburbia affect its residents? To what extent—if at all—do you agree with their views?

Topic 2: According to you, what would be the optimum organization of residential space? What should be the requirements and what would be their effect on people and human communities? To support your opinion, you need to examine relevant and specific examples from a variety of sources.

Developing Vocabulary:

The words below may appear as part of your online quizzes. Please refer to the introduction for study strategies for learning vocabulary.

1. **to signify**
2. **preeminent**
3. **dais**
4. **satirically**
5. **exodus**
6. **influx**
7. **impact**
8. **corollary**
9. **serenity**
10. **commingle**

Understanding the Text

Answer the following questions by carefully reviewing the authors' arugments in the short essay.

1. What constitutes suburbia in the U.S.?

2. What do the authors believe are the advantages of living in the suburbs?

3. What are according to the authors the disadvantages of living in the suburbs?

4. What seems to be the most alarming effect of suburbia on people's life?

Analyzing Writing

Answer the following questions by carefully reviewing the authors' arugments and writing strategies from the short essay.

1. Examine the role of statistics and numbers. What is their effect on your reading and understanding of the authors' arguments?

2. Examine three topic sentences for how effectively they orient the reader.

3. What strategies do the authors use to orient the reader and clarify his focus? How effective do you find these strategies?

45 Status Symbol Blues

In Shanghai, China, the Xiang Yang Lu flea market stretches for whole city blocks; merchandise of all kinds and descriptions fills vendor stalls that crowd the sidewalks one street after the other. From Chinese art pieces to North Face backpacks and jackets, this flea market is a consumer's dream: you can find everything for almost nothing. You can buy a Rolex for twenty-five dollars, a Samsonite briefcase for twenty dollars, and a Calvin Klein tie for one dollar! With a little patience and an appetite for **bartering**, you can find almost any major-status brand in this Chinese market and pay only a fraction of what you would anywhere else. Of course, all these items are "**knock-offs**" or copies of the actual brand, for evidently a "real" Rolex costs far more than twenty-five dollars. Although there used to be a huge difference in quality and design between knock-offs and real merchandise, this is not the case anymore. In some instances, actually, the same factory in China that produces the "real thing" also produces the "not-so-real" thing on the side for some "additional profit". Furthermore, often times the knock-offs are almost **indiscernible** from the genuine article, and at any rate people do buy them. After all, who could resist a silk Versace shirt for four dollars? Therefore, the question is what makes people buy these name-brand items?

The obvious answer is that status symbols do exactly what they imply: confer status on their owners within an established social hierarchy. So, if someone arrives at a business appointment on time by their infallible Rolex in their CK suit accessorized by a Versace tie, Gucci loafers, and a Samsonite briefcase, this person is likely to at least **elicit** the assumption of success and prestige. If anything, companies, which are fully aware of this effect, spend billions of dollars every year trying to convince consumers of product potential. Brand creation and brand identity are **booming** businesses, and their primary goal is not immediate sales; it is to turn their products into status symbols and to wrap them in an aura of higher status and exclusivity. Overall, companies are highly successful, and examples of status symbols abound. They range from two-hundred dollar Seven Jeans to the DeBeers diamonds to the MOVADO watches. Eventually, however, what really distinguishes a status symbol from very similar generic items is their positioning as status symbols, not necessarily their superior quality or higher cost of produc-

1

2

tion. Thus, one may be able to find even better-quality jeans for fifty versus two-hundred dollars, but, of course, the former would lack the characteristic stitching on the back pockets. But is that "stitching" worth 150 dollars more?

3   Apparently, for people that see this stitching as their way up the social ladder, it is worth the extra buck. The desire for status items comes with a desire to distinguish oneself and look better or be presumed better than average. As Jack Solomon, author of "Masters of Desire: The Culture of American Advertising," has argued, this is one of the prevailing features of U.S. culture. There are two counter currents running in American culture: the desire for **elitism** and superiority versus the desire for populism and equality. Thus, the supposed pursuit or national consciousness of "equality" is often contradicted by a craze for class and status markers. In layman's terms, we may be similar to others around us in every respect, but the purchase of a status-laden product confers additional status and respect. Or perhaps there is no contradiction, for people do want to be equal but to those of higher social power and standing and not to the masses of average Joes.

4   Therefore, the Xiang Yang Lu flea markets of the world seem to be shaking the foundation of status symbols. If the latter are now available to the masses, how can they make their owners feel special or privileged? The real **connoisseurs** will claim they can tell a real Fendi from a fake one with their eyes closed, and they can never get fooled by posers. However, even if a person does not buy counterfeit knock-offs, genuine status items can be found on sale in "outlet" malls all across the United States. The stores in these malls specialize in extremely reduced sale prices on all manner of status items. Perhaps consumers have to hunt for their size and the style they like, but brand-name items can be found for up to 80% below their regular market price. With a little extra effort, almost anyone can afford the "real thing" at a much lower price.

5   It's time for American consumers to wake up to the big trick. If one breaks things down to "real" terms such as cost of production and circulation, brand names cost so much more than their "generic" counterparts because of the status conferred on those who buy these products; eventually, these additional costs are born by companies while they are sustained and recycled by the consumers who want to cash in on the supposed social benefits of these items. Now, however, with the steady debasement of brand names through knock-offs, massive sales, and low-priced alternatives, it makes increasingly less sense to buy the "real thing"; not even the social value of status is guaranteed anymore if you can buy a knock-off for 95% off the retail price. Furthermore, when there is no correlation between actual value (i.e. the labor, design, and production costs of the product) with the status value (the extra charge tacked on to the price to make the product

exclusive), then consumers should be even more skeptical about this "extra" cost, for eventually that is the one thing that will be real on their credit card. Consumers need to reorient themselves in the actual value of things. The steady **debasement** of brand names should force unwitting consumers to reevaluate their criteria for purchases altogether.

Our status-hungry population has used brand names as a major **demarcation** of personal value. This should change. Personal value comes from our relationships with other people in our community, our education, and our characters. Our value as people should not be attached to whether one is outfitted with a new Cadillac Escalade, Armani sunglasses, Hugo Boss suits, Salvatore Rossi shoes, and a ROLEX. Our culture has inverted its value scheme so that people are too often seen for the "bling-bling" they wear, carry, or drive. However, even this plastic value system based on status items is breaking down, and good **riddance** to that. There is hope in the escalation of fakes and the continued building of factory outlet malls. People do want to cash in on the status of products, but maybe along the way when they buy the Calvin Klein tie for one dollar, they will notice that it's just a tie, CK or not.

6

Discussing and Writing About The Text

Discussing Issues:

Make a list of status symbols you own or would like to own and include the price next to each item. Try to analyze what justifies this price and what explains your own motives for purchasing each item. Discuss your findings with your peers in class.

Writing about the Text:

In a well-developed and organized essay, respond to the reading; be sure to support your views with pertinent examples drawn from your own experience and observations, as well as readings.

Topic 1: According to the authors, how do status symbols function and how can consumers escape from the desire to own these items? To what extent—if at all—do you think the authors' suggestion(s) is (are) valid?

Topic 2: Respond to the authors by constructing an argumentative essay from the perspective of a status symbol proponent.

Developing Vocabulary:

The words below may appear as part of your online quizzes. Please refer to the introduction for study strategies for learning vocabulary.

1. **bartering**
2. **knock-offs**
3. **indiscernible**
4. **elicit**
5. **booming**
6. **elitism**
7. **connoisseurs**
8. **debasement**
9. **demarcation**
10. **riddance**

46   The Less Experience the Better?

Ancient Greeks cautioned against old age, for it did not come alone… Indeed, most of the time getting older comes with an array of losses or **degradations**. Yet, it also comes with experience. In many cultures, this gain of experience is used to counter other losses, including that of hair, and is actually the older generation's **consolation** or basis of any argument that starts with the phrase "when you are as old as I am…" Undoubtedly, as we progress through the decades of our lives, we do gain experience, and we do view the world differently. We view life through changed lenses when we are teenagers versus forty-something. While the body slowly loses some of its vitality with age, we claim that we make up for this with wisdom, insight, clarity, and experience about the world. How true this is depends on the person, of course, for not all people in their forties will be wise or experienced. But experience has the potential of teaching many life lessons: how to discern a person's character quickly, how to separate friends from acquaintances, how to refrain from dangerous activities; as we grow older, we also become more certain about what we like and what we don't in terms of people, music, activities, movies, places. Experience molds our lives and slowly changes the way we interact with the world. If it were not for experience and the lessons we learn along life's tricky road, where would we be?   1

Despite the merits of experience, however, the problem with growing older and purportedly wiser is still not simply losing hair. Sometimes this knowledge of or certainty about "what we want" may become dangerously solid. Many of us know people—be they parents, uncles, aunts, or friends—who order the same food regardless of the restaurant they are in. They are the people that will insist on going to the same restaurant after church every Sunday. They are the people who, even if they agreed to try the new Chinese restaurant in the area, they would ask for steak with mashed potatoes and gravy so as not to disturb their **palette** or their expectations. They are the people who if they ever decided to leave the country they would ask for McDonald's in France. They are the ones who always watch the same TV programs, often re-watching reruns. So their cemented wants and beliefs expand from the types of activities or music they enjoy, to the stores they shop in and the stories they tell at family dinners to pretty much everything about   2 their self and their life. In general, they are the people that are resistant to even the possibility of change while everyone else needs to adapt to their solid wants. We call these people "old".

3   However, these people don't have to be physically old to act "old." There are plenty of young "old" people. This can happen to some extent at every stage of life as we advance to the next stage. Indeed, as we grow older and experience more of life, we progressively begin limiting the types of activities we participate in and the type of people we associate with. Even teenagers elect to "hang out" with certain kinds of friends, choosing not to associate with a host of other teens based on specific criteria. This is a natural process; however, we should be on guard against allowing experience to **curtail** new experiences. If our preferences become too hardened, there is little possibility for continued growth through outside stimuli. This is the real danger of experience and—hence—"old" age.

4   In a world of very **rigid** routines and choices, how can there be space for mental and spiritual growth? How can we gain even more experience, if we never allow ourselves to be exposed to anything new? If we entertain the same people, discuss the same stories, listen to the same songs, eat the same food as we always do, there is no possibility within that existence of meeting others with different backgrounds, listening to other perspectives about the world, hearing new musical artists, or expanding our **culinary** palette. Relying too much on our experiences limits our future growth by systematically curtailing what **stimuli** we are exposed to. In this way, our preferences become hardened, and our choices limited. In this case, our supposed experience becomes the impediment for new experiences.

The doubters of this phenomenon may say that experience is valuable, for it allows us to make informed decisions about our environment. After all, what's so bad about getting "old"? What's so bad about knowing what you want? Isn't that the whole point of gaining experience? At least, you can avoid nasty surprises such as the exotic French dish of "escargot," or in plain English "snails." This is undoubtedly true to a certain degree. Yet if we take a **banal** example, the trouble with experience can be clearly seen. Most children appear to be fascinated by nearly everything in their environment, gawking and pointing at even the **quotidian** rounds of ants or butterflies. They chirp with delight at birds flying and reach out to touch all new things. They want to experience their environment through all their senses, even systematically putting bits and pieces of that environment into their mouths. By the time children become adults, they are—if anything—apathetic to the "flying of the butterfly." Through systematic exposure e. experience), we become accustomed to our environment in such a way that the wonder is gradually replaced with apathy disguised as maturity or experience. Where else does the phrase "stop to smell the roses" come from but from a need to experience one's environment in new ways?

Therefore, growing experienced should come with the caution against becoming too jaded for any new experiences. The secret to growing older is to strike a balance between being awed by everything versus being impressed by nothing. It is the ability to know what we like and do not like, but at the same time it is the openness to new activities, people, music, or foods. The moment we say the old idiom, "there is nothing new under the sun," we **succumb** to the trap of experience and our environment will shrink ever so slowly by the routine paths we tread. Perhaps, the elixir of youth should not be sought in anti-wrinkle creams, hair transplants, and magic potions, but instead in our simple willingness to experience new things and be impressed, if not swept off of our feet.

6

Discussing and Writing About The Text

Discussing Issues:

Make a list of "old" or "young" people you know in the way the authors use these terms. Discuss your findings with your peers to come up with a list of suggestions to avoid "old" age.

Writing about the Text:

In a well-developed and organized essay, respond to the reading; be sure to support your views with pertinent examples drawn from your own experience and observations, as well as readings.

Topic 1: According to the authors, what are thc dangers of experience? To what extent, if any, do you share their views about these dangers?

Topic 2: According to your opinion, what should be the goal for gaining experience?

Developing Vocabulary:

The words below may appear as part of your online quizzes. Please refer to the introduction for study strategies for learning vocabulary.

1. degradations
2. consolation
3. palette
4. curtail
5. rigid
6. culinary
7. stimuli
8. banal
9. quotidian
10. to succumb

Understanding the Text

Answer the following questions by carefully reviewing the authors' aruguments in the short essay.

1. According to the authors, what is the real meaning of being "old"?

2. Why do the authors caution against "too much experience"?

3. What are the merits of experience according to the authors?

4. What is the authors' suggestion in regards to experience?

Analyzing Writing

Answer the following questions by carefully reviewing the authors' arugments and writing strategies from the short essay.

1. Where do the authors use alliteration? What is the effect this use has?

2. Examine the use of irony and humor in the essay. How does it affect the authors' arguments?

3. Examine the point(s) of view employed in the essay. How does each one affect the style of the authors' writing?

47 Retirement: Dream or Nightmare?

It seems ironic but quite common that people spend a large portion of their working lives wishing they weren't working. They **abhor** their morning commutes, **mandatory** meetings, afternoon reports, late nights, and the weekends of catching up in the rat race. At points, it seems that work is a never-ending struggle; like the tormented Sisyphus of Greek mythology, people at the workplace feel equally condemned to continuously roll a boulder up a hill only to have it roll down when it's at the top. It's not uncommon, actually, to notice retirement calendars in people's offices on which they surreptitiously mark the number of days until retirement, just like the lines scratched on prison walls by the **incarcerated** in anticipation of their release date. People also feel compelled to plan ahead, often checking on how much money they will have by retirement, a task rendered quite easy with any of the thousands of retirement calculators on the Internet. Retirement is thus looked at as the "golden years" when people can harvest and enjoy the fruits of their labor in some retirement community. Once the financial issues have been worked out, the money saved, the medical insurance researched, people can retire to take those trips to Alaska or China that they talked about for so long but never had the time, the money, or the chance to realize. They can take bike rides along some beach like they show in the pharmaceutical commercials for active seniors. They can—if they have saved enough cash—buy a recreation vehicle (RV) and drive all over the U.S. Indeed, if one is healthy, it all seems ideal.

While younger, many people assume the only issue with retirement is securing enough of a nest egg to healthily cluck over till they die. However, therein lies a second irony, for retirees may loathe retirement as much as they hated work. Some people attribute this to the ever-unsatisfied human nature. Nevertheless, there is more to it than that. A growing number of mental health officials have begun commenting on the personal and mental issues of stopping work to begin a new life. One of the most important aspects of retirement is the feeling of loss of identity. For many people, work defines who they are. They are a police officer, a lawyer, a doctor, an electrician. So what happens when they stop working and they introduce themselves to others and say "I used to be a police officer, a lawyer, a doctor, and electrician…, but now I'm… retired"?

1

2

3   Apart from the word-choice issues for self-definition and the bundle of cash, work undoubtedly carries with it much more meaning in people's lives. For many people, it is work that gives structure to their days by mapping routines, setting boundaries on what can and cannot be done, and by offering a sense of purpose. This is perhaps even more prominent among Americans than citizens of other countries, for statistically the average American works more than forty-five hours a week (much more than citizens in many other places); according to the *New Yorker*, people in France work 28% less than Americans while Germans work 25% less. Americans are highly invested in the jobs they have, and to some degree the increased workload does not allow for development of other interests and support networks outside of work. Under these circumstances, people are what they do, and work becomes their life; in many cases, even their friends are associated with work. So, it's only logical that when the overall structure, the purpose, the boundaries, and the friends are taken away, retirees can feel at a loss, even missing the boring routine that they once used to loathe.

4   To compound this, work often gives a person a sense of social belonging and prestige, the loss of which can duly affect identity as well. This goes above and beyond the importance of work in mere survival. Besides its self-serving purposes, work is also related to the idea of contribution to society. People perceive themselves as **integral** to the community they live in, and it is their job that creates that notion of society's dependence on their job and role. After retirement, however, this idea of necessity transforms itself into that of uselessness and **redundancy**. Retirees can feel that they no longer play an important role and fear others may view them as burdens on society. They experience a loss of social significance and prestige accompanied by a fear of being **superfluous** or even **parasitical** to society.

5   Active and successful professionals who are used to deadlines, projects, achieving career goals find it difficult, according to a January 2006 *Newsweek* article, to adjust to a life where the only expectations are that they get up and take a laxative. The once longed-for state of abundant free time that retirement affords is now viewed with dread. Indeed, there is a certain *terror of freedom* in retirement that many retirees experience and must adjust to. What should be the land of milk and honey turns into a swamp of a great number of choices, an abundance that can be paralyzing. Despite financial resources and free time, a paralysis may set in whereby retirees end up staying at home with too much time on their hands and too many choices available; then the trips to Alaska may not ever happen nor the RV drive around the country. Unless retirees realize that they need to reinvent a purpose in their lives by pursuing a second career, creating vacation plans, or even

simply establishing the goal of weeding the garden, this paralysis may become permanent.

Undeniably, any time of major change or upheaval may have similar, but not the same, effects. Interestingly, even young people face similar issues during periods of transition. Upon graduation from high school or college, the young have to make decisions about how to organize their time, where to live, and what to do. Their time, which had been organized by the routines of school and homework, is now their own and it may seem too much. The difference, however, is that the young have not yet begun their work life and have not yet **cemented** their role in society based on the jobs they decide to pursue. This is definitely not to say that they do not feel pressure during these periods. The pressure, though, is different, for the road lies ahead and not behind. Indeed, during every major transitional period of life, there may be issues of renegotiation of one's identity; however, retirement may be one of the most difficult of these transitions, for many retirees have built their characters and identities on the **edifice** of their work. Without this support, they may be at a loss of what to do, where to go, or how to behave. They have already proven themselves (or not) in their work environment; they have made enough money (theoretically) in order to retire; and they have a long past behind them and a shorter future in front of them. Once a dream, retirement upon achievement often ends up being a nightmare, for renegotiating an identity that took thirty or more years to form can be a **daunting** task.

6

Discussing and Writing About The Text

Discussing Issues:

Draw a line down the center of a blank piece of paper. Label column one problems with transitions for teens and column two problems for retirees. Make a list of all the issues that you can think of, drawing from your own experience and/or from the experience of family or friends who have retired. Discuss whether the same issues come up in both columns and how each group typically deals with them.

Writing about the Text:

In a well-developed and organized essay, respond to the reading; be sure to support your views with pertinent examples drawn from your own experience and observations, as well as readings.

Topic 1: According to the authors, why might retirees have a harder time transitioning to their new life than they at first think? Why is the transition for retirees worse, according to the authors, than for other groups? To what extent—if at all—do you think the authors are correct about this assertion?

Topic 2: Interview a family member or family friend who has retired. Ask them about possible advantages or disadvantages of retiring. Write a paper from a first person perspective using their voice as the authorial voice.

Developing Vocabulary:

The words below may appear as part of your online quizzes. Please refer to the introduction for study strategies for learning vocabulary.

1.	abhor	2.	mandatory
3.	incarcerated	4.	integral
5.	redundancy	6.	superfluous
7.	parasitical	8.	cemented
9.	ediface	10.	daunting

Understanding the Text

Answer the following questions by carefully reviewing the authors' aruguments in the short essay.

1.   Why do the authors believe that retirement might not be the golden years after all?

2.   What are some the issues that retirees, specifically, have to deal with?

3.   Why do the authors believe that renegotiation of identity can be difficult?

4.   Why is it more difficult for retirees in time of transition than teenagers in time of transition?

Analyzing Writing

Answer the following questions by carefully reviewing the authors' arugments and writing strategies from the short essay.

1. Examine the use of lists in the essay. Where and how are they used?

2. Find at least three idioms (sayings) and analyze their use.

3. Examine the use of metaphors and similes in the text.

48 Speaking Your Mind or Minding Your Speech

In all the **hype** leading up to the 2006 Winter Olympics, a number of news magazines ran cover story profiles on one of the most successful skiers and controversial professional athletes of our time: Bode Miller. Besides his amazing track record of wins at nearly every level of competition, Miller has also put in some of the fastest times in downhill history. Along with this stellar on-the-slope record comes Miller's self-proclaimed belief that he should speak his mind, which has had people in the sports world wishing he would just mind his speech and get on with skiing. In one interview with the national media right before the Olympics, Miller stated, "if it wasn't such a cluster f—- for me to pull out now, I'd definitely consider it…. Look, a lot of the people involved with the U.S. Ski Team—the people that I'm representing—are unbelievable a—holes. Rich, cocky, wicked, conceited, super-right-wing Republicans" (*Newsweek*, January 2006). As expected, Bode's comments fueled an uproar, with some **detractors** asking for his withdrawal from the ski team. However, according to his agent and others in the American public, this is just par for the course; besides, some argued that it "takes guts" to speak your mind and "tell it like it is".

1

In some ways, Miller is simply one of the (currently) best-known representatives (for the sports world at least) of the American value of speaking your mind—in some cases, regardless of the social or career costs. He is certainly not the first pop icon to do so. There have been a long line of American icons that have told the "gritty truth" even though it might bother others. Figures like John Wayne and Clint Eastwood, for instance, capitalized on this value of "a man has to speak his mind" in many of their western films with rough and tough characters who "told it like it is." More recently, Tom Cruise took this idea of speaking your mind to heart when he told Matt Lauer of the *Today* show (national television) that he thought psychiatry was a **pseudo** science, psychiatric prescription drugs were dangerous, and that Lauer did not know the flawed history of psychology as Cruise did—all of this while interrupting and over-talking Lauer. Once more, this created media uproar not only for Cruise's controversial views but also for his aggressive interview with Lauer.

2

3   Now, speaking your mind is certainly not limited to celebrities. We see this in nearly every walk of life. The problem, however, is not that people are speaking their minds about their beliefs, their wishes, their desires. If anything, debates about problems of public or personal interest should be **advocated** and supported. Yet many times people speak their mind without minding their speech. Students in a debate about homosexual marriage, for instance, might blurt out that they think "those gays are going to hell." They have the right to believe what they want, but in a civil discourse, especially in a classroom where others might be offended, they need to present their ideas in a different form. They might, for instance, start out their comment with the definition of marriage and its support within biblical circles. They might mention societal values and the role marriage plays in their development. However, they cannot use the idea of speaking their minds in order to insult a group of people in an **ad hominem** attack. In this scenario, the student's comment privileges their own belief system and their right to utter hurtful things above the **harmonious** co-existence among members of a diverse social group-in this case the class. Furthermore, how would the "packaging" of their comments convince anyone in the class in their belief against homosexual marriage? How would Cruise's accusation that psychiatry is a "pseudo-science" actually make someone believe that? How would Miller's objections—framed the way he made them—to the type of rich Republican supporters actually change anything? Or are we to assume that such utterances aim at insulting rather than convincing others?

4   In their defense, people that speak their mind even in an offensive manner invoke their freedom of speech. Actually, speaking your mind is too often equated with the right to free speech, but **erroneously** so. Indeed, there should be a differentiation between the ability or right to speak your mind via the First Amendment and the restraint not to do so. Certainly, the right to free speech was included in the Bill of Rights in order to allow for and instigate constructive civil debate, not to limit it. Its overall purpose was to ensure that the government could not exclude the views of its citizens in determining the laws of the land. Even so, free speech was not meant to be absolute. A person, for instance, cannot shout fire in a crowded theatre. They cannot distribute literature defaming another race unless they have a specific legal objective. They cannot threaten to kill someone in verbal or written forms. Supporters of absolute free speech doubt the constitutionality of any limitations on the freedom of speech. Despite this ongoing debate, what could be considered as the ultimate criterion for allowing or disallowing speech is the motive of the speaker: more specifically, should speech be protected for the sake of speech or for the sake of constructive dialogue? When Miller calls his rich

supporters a bunch of "a—holes", is he practicing the free speech envisioned in the Bill of Rights? Is he trying to extend the debate about **sponsorship** practices of the U.S. Olympic team, or is he merely trading in insults?

Speaking your mind should not allow a person to say anything they please.   5 Instead, speaking your mind should also entail minding your speech. Indeed, the Founding Fathers and later the Supreme Court imposed limitations on free speech, for they wished to place free speech in the service of constructive dialogue towards a meaningful democracy. Free speech was, therefore, conceived as a means to an end not an end in itself. Likewise, there should be certain social limitations on speech that place it in the service of constructive dialogue and effective communication among people. Speech should be packaged in an appropriate way with a consideration of the audience. This does not mean that one should never say anything that disturbs or disagrees with another person; nor should one always tailor one's speech to avoid hurting even the most sensitive **interlocutors**. On the contrary, people should be encouraged to speak their mind in a way that is **conducive** to a healthy and productive dialogue.

When speaking one's mind turns to speech just for the sake of speech;   6 when this mindless speech becomes idealized by celebrities and other famous people; when, even more dangerously, the symptoms of this speech spread into the field of political debate and are adopted by our elected representatives, then we move inexorably toward an uncivil society where groups spew out attack rhetoric not designed for any kind of debate. This can be seen with California legislator Mark Leno's speech to pro-gay marriage residents of San Francisco about a gay marriage bill. According to Leno, Christians blocking the bill are "loud, they're obnoxious, they're disgusting, and they should get out of San Francisco" (*San Francisco Chronicle*, March 2006). Clearly, this kind of speech, especially from a public elected official, leads to an uncivil society where speaking your mind gives a license to insult anyone and everyone in words not conducive to civilized debate.

Discussing and Writing About The Text

Discussing Issues:

Discuss with your peers the examples offered by the authors as well as similar ones you may be aware of. Do you think that this "speaking your mind" in these cases should be the ultimate value or should it be restrained?

Writing about the Text:

In a well-developed and organized essay, respond to the reading; be sure to support your views with pertinent examples drawn from your own experience and observations, as well as readings.

Topic 1: What is, according to the authors, the value of the "speaking your mind" principle? Do you agree with the limitations the author deems appropriate for this principle?

Topic 2: According to your opinion, should freedom of speech be limited or not? If so, what kind of limitations would be appropriate; if not, what would be possible dangers from imposing limitations on this freedom? To support your opinion, you need to examine relevant and specific examples from a variety of sources.

Developing Vocabulary:

The words below may appear as part of your online quizzes. Please refer to the introduction for study strategies for learning vocabulary.

1. hype
2. detractors
3. pseudo
4. to advocate
5. ad hominem
6. harmonious
7. erroneously
8. sponsorship
9. interlocutors
10. conducive

Understanding the Text

Answer the following questions by carefully reviewing the authors' aruguments in the short essay.

1. What does the value of speaking your mind entail?

2. What is the difference between speaking your mind and minding your speech?

3. What was the intention of the Founding Fathers in establishing freedom of speech?

4. What should be the criterion for what is acceptable speech?

Analyzing Writing

Answer the following questions by carefully reviewing the authors' arugments and writing strategies from the short essay.

1. Examine the types and role of counterarguments in this essay.

2. Examine the role of questions as a rhetorical device. Do the authors answer those questions or are they open to the reader's interpretation?

3. Examine the use of fragments and repetitive sentence structure in the last paragraph of the essay. What is the effect of these strategies in the conclusion of the essay?

49 The Myth of the Individual

The United States of America presents one of the most heavily invested cultures on the planet in the value of the individual. Apart from being a great option for a bumper sticker, the "Be Yourself" message is **omnipresent** and **omnipotent** in the American culture. A plethora of euphemisms and proverbs encapsulate this myth such as "charting your own path, not following the crowd, making your own way, leading the sheep, or taking the road less traveled." Individuality is the value *par excellence* in our society that nearly everyone ascribes to.

1

The indoctrination to this value starts early on with parents who take pride in "what a real character" little Johnny is for **adamantly** denying to do his homework and "having a mind of his own" unlike all those other little kids who don't know any better but to follow the crowd. Yet far beyond proud parents and their offspring, this value is widespread in all levels of societal life with the advertising industry thriving on its exploitation. Indeed, it is neither a wonder nor a "mis-investment" that this industry expends so many of its resources in convincing people that purchasing a certain product "will set them apart from the masses". However, this pitch is particularly paradoxical because what these companies really want is sales a "massive" scale, not an "individual" one. Obviously, one of the main problems with this value is that it is so **all-encompassing** that most people cannot realize its mythological nature. Most people do not even see it for what it really is: a myth.

2

It is interesting, for instance, to observe how so many people wear the same jeans out of personal and individual choice, out of a need to be "THEMSELVES"; how so many teenagers spend 120 dollars or more on designer jeans for their own personal comfort; how to resist the coastal summer heat, so many youths dress in "beachwear" of shorts, Hawaiian prints, flip flops and "out of bed" hairstyles while a simple Gandhi-like loincloth would be far more practical, let alone "individual". Simply put, most people dress suspiciously alike for all their choices to be individual. Hence, the teenager who claims that having his pants tucked below his underwear is "HIS" personal style would have the other hundreds of similarly dressed or undressed teenagers as well as several billions of advertising dollars blatantly refute "HIS" statement. The number of "individuals" who follow

3

the same fashion trends declaring "THEIR" individuality is in the millions, and they are all sheepishly herded by the fashion industry.

4   This may sound cynical, but the days of "Be like Mike" (Michael Jordan) advertising have come and gone. Instead, nowadays Kobe Bryant says "Drink Sprite not because I say so, but because you like it." Indeed, advertisements are currently much more sophisticated, appealing to that seemingly **intrinsic** American value of individuality. Taking this whole marketing a step further, Reebok has its main webpage feature the message "i am what i am". Again, the non capitalized "i" reveres an individual will strong enough to break the rules, in this case the grammatical ones; Reebok strongly supports this unyielding individuality especially through products such as RBK Custom, as in a customized shoe just for…"YOU". Well, in 2004 Reebok sold 3.7 billion dollars worth of "individualized" merchandise.

5   Even the Army jumped on the individualism bandwagon with its series of commercials advertising "Be All You Can Be." Introduced in 1981, their ad-series motto is still remembered and still used. Everyone has been exposed to one form or another of these ads over the last twenty-five years, which have all pretty much had the same thematic motif: the few soldiers who perform technical duties, fly around, **rappel** from ropes connected to hovering helicopters, and stalk enemies in three-foot-tall grass. "Be All You Can Be": the message is that the Army can fulfill "your" desire for improvement, assist in "your" career aspirations, provide money for the college of "your" choice, and help with the pursuit of "your" personal goals. Once more, the irony is that the Army is not about the individual at all. Rather, the entire framework of basic training is designed to "break" the individual and mold the trainee into part of a team. Their spoken messages appeal to a sense of individuality while their unspoken substance forces submission to a group. After all, the army is about organizing large groups of men into a single fighting force.

6   Besides the advertising world, the myth of individuality is also reinforced and reproduced by the numerous success models that are **trotted** out onto media screens and print pages. The list of individual success stories (and sometimes failures) is endless, hailing from every walk of life. At one point or another, Michael Jordan, Tiger Woods, J. Paul Getty, Bill Gates, Steve Wozniak, Albert Einstein, 50 Cent, Martha Stewart, Franklin Roosevelt have all become epitomes of this myth. According to the myth, these are all individuals who defied norms and strove for what they believed in despite all the obstacles in their way; therefore, they have become the **paragons** that all should look to **emulate** in some way or another. Certainly, there is nothing wrong with a culture that pays tribute to successful peo-

ple for their accomplishments; however, for us commoners that wish to imitate the great, there are certain dangers in the often one-sided presentation of these stories as the sole result of individual genius and absolute defiance of norms. What is often missing from these stories of individual accomplishment is the "whole" story of all the hard work, sacrifice, and dependence on others. Students, for instance, often say that Albert Einstein didn't do well in high school math, yet he proved to be a genius. Little Johnny then, who never does his math homework, could be hiding an "Einstein" in him; little Johnny may be too clever an individual to do what everyone else does… homework. However, these students or parents have grown up with only half the real story. Indeed, Einstein may not have received good scores in math, but that didn't mean that he never studied math. Instead, he read the combined six-volume-collected works of all scientific articles that were ever published in physics to be adequately prepared to publish anything in the field.

Furthermore, the myth of absolute individuality is especially dangerous to children and young adults, who are taught that all is possible if they follow their own road. The real world, however, requires at least minimal adherence to certain norms, and this is true in many respects. Try going to a job interview dressed like Snoop Dog and telling the manager behind the mahogany desk, "hey man, nice crib." It is unlikely that the interview would last longer than two minutes. People, especially children, who learn and believe the individuality myth, will have a hard shock when they eventually realize that communities in this society require obedience to a certain norm of appearance and behavior. Deviation from that norm, though possible and often necessary, is most likely to be frowned upon. At the same time, people should realize what is mythology and what is reality: many of our cultural icons as well as most of our advertising industry are focused on praising individuality even while they **surreptitiously** create mass markets of these individual consumers. In the end, the latter should realize that this is a myth that can and does have real effects on having these individuals duped along with everyone else.

7

Discussing and Writing About The Text

Discussing Issues:

Make a list of what you consider your own personal behavior and try to trace your actions or thoughts to what has influenced or inspired them. Are they entirely your own invention or not?

Writing about the Text:

In a well-developed and organized essay, respond to the reading; be sure to support your views with pertinent examples drawn from your own experience and observations, as well as readings.

Topic 1: According to the authors, what is the evidence attesting to the mythical dimension of individualism? To what extent—if at all—do you agree with the authors' concerns about this myth?

Topic 2: Find an ad or commercial that seems to appeal to the "myth of the individual." Analyze, evaluate, and comment on the strategies, techniques, and messages it employs to achieve its goals.

Developing Vocabulary:

The words below may appear as part of your online quizzes. Please refer to the introduction for study strategies for learning vocabulary.

1.	omnipresent	2.	omnipotent
3.	adamantly	4.	all-encompassing
5.	intrinsic	6.	rappel
7.	trotted	8.	paragons
9.	emulate	10.	surreptitiously

Understanding the Text

Answer the following questions by carefully reviewing the authors' aruguments in the short essay.

1. Why do the authors think the concept of individualism is a myth?

2. How does advertising exploit the myth of the individual?

3. Why does the army present a paradox in its messages to the individual?

4. What are the dangers the myth of the individual present?

Analyzing Writing

Answer the following questions by carefully reviewing the authors' arugments and writing strategies from the short essay.

1.   Examine the use of intentional fragments in the text.

2.   Examine the role of irony in the text.

3.   Examine the type of sources and the effectiveness in supporting the authors' arguments.

50 The Blame Game

In one of the most famous psychology experiments in the 20th century, Dr. Stanley Milgram of Yale University tested people's levels of obedience to authority. Concerned by the highly publicized 1960 trial of the high-ranking, Nazi official, Adolf Eichmann, who was partly responsible for the genocide of Jews in World War II, Dr. Milgram began researching the different responses average people had to orders that might conflict with their personal morality. In this experiment, men between the ages of twenty to fifty were randomly recruited as participants from ads in local newspapers and given 4.50 dollars (equivalent to twenty dollars in 2006) for one hour's worth of work. Separated into pairs, the random participant was paired with another man and assigned the role of "teacher" in order to test out how pain can be used as an **inducement** to people's learning. The other participant in the study, the "learner," was an actor and a member of Milgram's staff who was placed behind a glass window in a separate room. The "teacher-participant" was then given an electric shocking device, and a scientist in the testing room required him to ask the "learner" a series of questions and then shock the "learner" when a wrong answer was given. Of course, no shocks were actually given when the "actor-learner" purposefully gave the wrong answer to some of the questions, but the "teacher" did not know that. After a series of **voltage** increases, the "actor-learner" began banging on the window in pain and complaining about a heart condition. Even so and despite objections by the "teachers," scientists suggested and then required that the "teachers" continue the shock treatment. Upon "teachers'" refusal to continue the experiment, the scientist would say that if anything went wrong, he, the scientist, would take full responsibility. With this reassurance, in 65% of the cases the "teacher-participants" shocked the "learners" all the way up to the 450 volt level, a potentially lethal shock. Overall, no participant stopped before the 300 volt level. 1

While the study overtly measured the level of obedience to authority, it also tested another very interesting factor: the need for the participants to **cede culpability** for possible blame to the scientists. The experiment showed a peculiar dynamic between accepting responsibility for one's own actions and the need to blame others for those actions. The "teachers" were reluctant to administer the 2 higher voltage not only because they felt bad about shocking the "learners" but also because they feared getting into trouble for harming them; they conceded to continuing the shock treatment only when the scientist/authority figure agreed to take responsibility for any problem even if that were the death of the learner. Though quite interesting, the results of the study should not be shocking to anyone. Indeed, today, numerous scientists around the world are studying culpable-control psychology, or in other words, the two-edge sword of the psychology of blame and responsibility. On the forefront of this research, Dr. Mark Alicke of Ohio University argues that the human impulse to blame can even be traced back to the evolutionary need to **avert** harm. People do not, in essence, want to suffer the consequences for actions even if they are directly responsible for them. Therefore, it's much more convenient, even morally easier to blame someone else.

3   The culture of blame is all around us in many forms, and we do not need an electric shock experiment to see it. The athlete who comes in second place blames the first place finisher for cheating or blames his own mediocre performance on a bad night's sleep. The student who receives a "C" on an essay blames the teacher for not explaining the assignment thoroughly even though the student had ditched class on the day the teacher gave thorough instructions pertaining to the assignment. The child who breaks a lamp in the house while playing with the dog says "the dog did it". The man who fails in his business blames his bankruptcy on the "system," or the "government," or on everything else but his business **acumen**. The list goes on and on. Obviously, research is only backing up what people already know from experience: blame is a powerful way to preserve the psyche and **shirk** our own responsibility for our actions. Indeed, according to a famous research study (*The Brunel Study*), authored by Dr. Neville Stanton and Dr. Guy Walker, drivers in Britain with only basic-driving training were far more likely to blame accidents on the bad road or on factors other than their driving skill. People seem to psychologically need to blame someone for their failures or misdeeds. Certainly there are cases where somebody else is to blame, but those cases are fewer and often farther between than most people would choose to admit.

4   The psychology of blame is also prevalent and sometimes **pernicious** within the legal system. Many defendants, even if they committed the crime, feel that they are actually not guilty or less guilty because they had no effective control over their actions. In these cases, they argue, there are **mitigating** circumstances that avert their own personal responsibility for their behavior. In Pennsylvania, a man sexually assaulted a cerebral-palsy patient in the hospital and then sued the hospital for not providing a "safe environment" for patients. The Menendez brothers, a case widely publicized, murdered their parents and then

blamed the killings on reputed sexual molestation by the victims. A man sued a tattoo parlor for misspelling a word in his tattoo that he himself gave them. Even minor crimes seem to require blame. The child who shoplifts tennis shoes from a store claims he was forced to steal because all the other kids have that brand and he faces teasing if he doesn't have them.

Certainly, one can argue that in all of the above cases and many others, there are many factors that may have contributed at one point or another to the execution of a certain act. For instance, the lawsuit brought by an obese man against the fast food industry would appear initially as frivolous. The man clearly made the decision to constantly eat Big Macs and buckets of fries. However, his lack of willpower should not be entirely blamed on him, for scientists have claimed that fast food can be as physically addictive as heroin. Indeed, Eric Schlosser's *Fast Food Nation* lends weight to this discussion with his investigation of the addictive chemical properties of food.

However, in most cases individuals do have and should be ready to take responsibility for their acts. The sometimes **farcical** attempts to avoid responsibility and to blame other people for one's actions have the detrimental effect of minimizing an analysis of genuine mitigating factors. What does this mean? It means that the focus for blame (or its avoidance) should nearly always and primarily be on the individual and that individuals should take the blame for their own actions. Eventually it is the murderer who pulls the trigger and kills his victim. It is he who is guilty, not the manufacturer of the gun that supposedly "put the gun" in the murderer's hand. The habit of blaming everyone and everything has the tendency to make us all cynical to the times when someone or something else really is to blame.

Dr. Milgram's experiment showed two things about human nature. First, in many cases people are like sheep, and they obey authority figures with little resistance, despite the impact on other people. Second, one of the key factors of this blind obedience is the deferral of responsibility to those in positions of authority. As Prof. Alicke has argued, the psychology of the culpability is strong, and it may even be hard wired into our genetic system. Now, the question is who is to blame for that?

Discussing and Writing About The Text

Discussing Issues:

To what extent do you think a culture of blame exists? Is it more prevalent at certain age groups or do we "grow out of it?" Do you think "mitigating" factors of blame should be taken into consideration when holding someone responsible? For example, a roommate steals from you, and you are about to press charges. However, you soon learn that he had been beaten as a child and forced to steal to pay for his food. Is this a mitigating factor?

Writing about the Text:

In a well-developed and organized essay, respond to the reading; be sure to support your views with pertinent examples drawn from your own experience and observations, as well as readings.

Topic 1: According to the authors, is the psychology of blame and what are the dangers associated with it? Do you think the authors are correct in their concern about culpability?

Topic 2: Do you think if Dr. Milgram's experiment about obedience and blame were performed today that it would have the same results? Do you think others have both a desire to obey someone in authority and to shunt blame onto them?

Developing Vocabulary:

The words below may appear as part of your online quizzes. Please refer to the introduction for study strategies for learning vocabulary.

1. inducement
2. voltage
3. cede
4. culpability
5. avert
6. acumen
7. shirk
8. pernicious
9. mitigating
10. farcical

Understanding the Text

Answer the following questions by carefully reviewing the authors' aruguments in the short essay.

1. What was Dr. Milgram researching in his study and why?

2. What is meant by the idea of culpability?

3. The authors allude to a "culture of blame." What do they mean?

4. How might the "culture of blame" have a detrimental effect on so-called genuine mitigating factors in a person's behavior?

Analyzing Writing

Answer the following questions by carefully reviewing the authors' arugments and writing strategies from the short essay.

1.   Examine the use of summary of Dr. Milgram's study. How is it done? Are there any techniques you can discern in this part of the text?

2.   How do the authors employ both short and long examples? Examine the context.

3.   Examine the use of sources in the text in terms of relevance, development, and connection to the authors' points.

CHAPTER
SEVEN

Culture

51 Toys Are Us

In the pursuit of decoding a culture, toys can serve as a particularly interesting indicator of cultural beliefs and norms. Though they may seem like innocuous trifles given to children to brighten their day or liven up a Christmas, toys are increasingly reflective of the values a particular culture holds dear and aspires to train or even indoctrinate its younger generation with. In times past, it was more difficult to "read" the cultural meaning of a toy, for many toys were often home-made. Indeed, children might have cobbled together bits and pieces of detritus to create a doll or a wagon, therefore, making it difficult to **ascertain** a shared-cultural value from such an individual toy. However, **in retrospect**, many of the best-selling toys of the twentieth century can be interpreted as signs of the era of their popularity. For instance, in the 1950s Mr. Potato Head was loved by parents and children alike. Mr. Potato Head was the first toy to be marketed over national television and was originally conceived of as a toy to accompany breakfast cereal. Soon enough, however, it became the family's favorite for its educational orientation. On the other hand, in the 1960s G.I.Joe became America's favorite toy, a not-so-surprising evolution in the American psyche, considering the ongoing Vietnam War and the emphasis on the armed conflict of the period.

Toys, however, do not only reflect cultural values, but they also reinforce them, with the prolific Barbie being one of the best examples of this dual role. Many people may not realize the impact Barbie has had on culture since its introduction at the American International Toy Fair in New York in 1959. Since then, over five hundred million Barbies have been sold, and over 95% of American girls have had at least one Barbie in their lives. Key to Barbie's success was the extensive market research the Mattel Corporation did on suburban children to consciously create and promote Barbie as a trendy role-model for the particular audience: the innocent children of today, the promising consumers of tomorrow. It's for this reason that Barbie has always kept up with the latest trends and fashions. For Barbie, nothing is left to chance nor happens by accident. Indeed, when it comes to her wardrobe, for instance, Barbie is no **slouch**; one hundred new outfits are produced for Barbie every year by its maker, the Mattel Corporation (History Channel. *History of Toys and Games*). Nowadays, she even has clothes fashioned by world-famous designers like Yves Saint Laurent, Christian Dior, Valentino, Perry Ellis, and Oscar de la Renta. Through these miniature, signature outfits, little girls are molded into the aspiring young consumers of the real-size apparel and lifestyle Barbie promotes. For besides working as a fashion icon, Barbie has also enjoyed the trappings of a lavish way of life with accessories ranging from a Corvette to a Jacuzzi to a home in Malibu,

1

2

California. Barbie or her mate, Ken, must effortlessly reel in at least 200,000 dollars a year to keep up with their lifestyle!

3   The Mattel Corporation's hard work is not to be ignored in Barbie's phenomenal success; these people were **triumphant** in capturing the cultural essence of the 1950s and reinforcing it even further. This becomes even more obvious when Barbie is compared to other "best-selling" dolls from the past such as Raggedy Ann dolls, so popular from 1910 to 1920. Indeed, were one to hold a doll-beauty contest today, Raggedy Ann would be at a handicap just by her name's pronouncement. In such dire contrast to Barbie's chic style and fashion obsession, Raggedy Ann certainly didn't come with a hundred different high-style outfits, her own Model T, or a palace worthy of a Rockefeller. Raggedy Ann looked more like the doll that a little girl could have put together with her mom from rags found in a sewing box. Tough times, plain dolls. Good times, fancy dolls. Indeed, as a post-war doll, Barbie signaled the increased disposable income people had available from the 1950s onward as well as the focus on an evolving role for women. Even now, Barbie can tell a lot about what little girls deem and should deem valuable. The Barbie website, for instance, is a portal into the American girl's cultural world. In a background of absolute pink, Barbie's website urges every little girl to "Think Pink." Once it loads, Barbie welcomes the same little girl to a colorful room, complete with Barbie's flat screen TV, computer, IPod, cell phone, and shopping bags from her last expedition to the mall. Wearing a red dress and a happy face, Barbie, like a modern Siren, lures innocent passers-by with her song: "You can be who you wanna be! Be-Are-Be-I-Be (Barbie)!" Of course, to "Be a Barbie Girl" requires logging into an array of links on her website and longing for a myriad of "fashion-fever" looks and styles as well as products ranging from sunglasses to magic castles. If you want to be a true believer, this site gives you the opportunity to participate in Barbie chat-rooms where you can communicate with other Barbie-followers and catch up on the latest trends and accessories. All this culminates then with a mutual "educational" experience for all participants: little girls learn from Barbie about values, and Barbie learns from little girls about their needs (to be satiated later on with a new outfit: "Satisfaction Guaranteed!").

4   But Barbie may not be listening too closely, a sure sign of her middle age and her class orientation. Barbie is closing in on fifty years of age, and she is currently engaged in the fight of her life with a new breed of upstart dolls called the Bratz. Born in 2001, the Bratz dolls promise to be Barbie's **formidable** opponent or worst nightmare. Although they feature a shorter and bustier physique than Barbie, perhaps in response to all the complaints about Barbie's "unrealistic" measurements, the Bratz claim to be fashionable, trendy, and hip, but in their own way. With their pouty lips, their waist-long hair of all dyes, their always exposed and ready-to-be-pierced belly-button, and their huge, exotic, and permanently made-up eyes, these girls look determined to bring an end to the **reign** of the good-old blonde-blue-eyed, middle-class, **prissy** Barbie. These girls are all-day hip and all-time ready for clubbing with their girlfriends or for dancing to the next hip-hop hit. Needless to say of-course that, like Barbie, they too come fully accessorized with their own fashion universe, celebrity-obsession, and pink fever, only in a

more multi-cultural and sexualized version. However, they seem, for the time being at least, to be solely focused on personal fashion in their aspiration to become celebrities. Unlike Barbie, who stands in her room of thousands of dollars worth of merchandise and lit by the sparkle of her diamond ring, the Bratz dolls don't need any room, at least not yet. They stand on their own in their shimmering outfits, ready for what the night may bring. However, they do come with a "real" fake diamond ring that girls can actually wear. While Barbie needs all the accoutrements of an upper-middle-class lifestyle to be complete, the Bratz dolls need nothing but their own fashionable personas strutting across the playground.

Barbies and the Bratz are some of the best-known toys on the market, but they are definitely not alone in mirroring and inventing cultural values. It might appear as an oxymoron that the Mattel Corporation, creator of Barbie, is also behind a totally different set of values **espoused** by their line of American Girl dolls. However, business is business whether it comes with revealing cleavage or ankle-long skirts. In response to parents' decrying of Barbie's shallowness, the American Girls emerged to teach little Americans some real values. American Girls look nothing like super-model, perfect-sized adults or club hip-hop dancers striving for an invitation to MTV's Cribs or a chance to star on American Idol. Instead, these dolls look like little girls, who may not have breasts yet, but who are still willing to serve America as role-models in inspiring little girls to "stand tall, reach high, and dream big" (www.theamerican girl.com). American girls can be found amidst a world of accessories such as clothes and bath sets—business is business after all. Nevertheless, their world includes commodities like...books (who would have ever guessed?); indeed, even the dolls have books, as opposed to the Bratz dolls who read fashion magazines or Barbie who is too **preoccupied** with her stuff to read—although at some point she can become a nurse or doctor by purchasing the Barbie medicine bag. American Dolls' interests may have their roots in their literary background, for the original line of American Dolls came from historical figures or characters in famous books, who were made into dolls.

5

It becomes clear then that there is nothing "innocent" about the age of innocence when it comes to toys. When mass-produced and mass-marketed, toys serve both as signs of the culture that creates them as well as inspirations for the culture which is under creation. In many ways, toys help children form a nexus of interpretive commodification; in other words, they teach children what things to value, how to behave, and what to deem normal or abnormal. When buying toys, parents and adults in general are not just buying an inanimate object, but a whole set of cultural values packaged with that object. Toys represent different standards, cultural values, and ideals, valued or rejected by the public. Scary or not, this becomes obvious when one realizes that Bratz outsells her American Girl competition by ten to one; apparently, the latter's standards don't seem nearly as valued as those of the Bratz. Indeed, who wants a **bookworm**-doll when there's clubbing to be done?

6

Discussing and Writing About The Text

Discussing Issues:

In groups try to invent a 21st century toy and explain to your peers its cultural significance, its business prospects, or any other aspects you may deem appropriate. After each group's presentation, the class, as well as the instructor, will be asked to vote for the best toy idea and presentation.

Writing about the Text:

In a well-developed and organized essay, respond to the reading; be sure to support your views with pertinent examples drawn from your own experience and observations, as well as readings.

Topic 1: According to the authors, what are the lessons to be learned from toys? To what extent—if at all—do you agree with this view point?

Topic 2: Analyze the most popular toys for boys in the last one hundred years in terms of their role and contributions to the American (or other) culture.

Developing Vocabulary:

The words below may appear as part of your online quizzes. Please refer to the introduction for study strategies for learning vocabulary.

1.	to ascertain	2.	in retrospect
3.	slouch	4.	triumphant
5.	formidable	6.	reign
7.	prissy	8.	espoused
9.	preoccupied	10.	bookworm

Understanding the Text

Answer the following questions by carefully reviewing the authors' aruguments in the short essay.

1. What is the role of toys in culture and its study?

2. How does Barbie shape the American identity?

3. In what ways are the Bratz dolls similar to or different from Barbie?

4. What is the American-Girl doll and what are her goals and aspirations?

Analyzing Writing

Answer the following questions by carefully reviewing the authors' arugments and writing strategies from the short essay.

1. Discuss the use of humor and irony in the text.
text.

2. Examine three topic sentences in their effectiveness to orient the reader.

3. Examine the use and effectiveness of classification and comparison/contrast in the

52 The Empty Orchestra

Most everyone has had or is likely to have a Karaoke "experience" at some point in their lives, for Karaoke has become almost omnipresent "fun." All one need do is listen to the soft—almost always out of tune—crooning or the vocal screeching issuing from bar doors, hotel lobbies, or even wedding receptions. Karaoke, in case you have not been initiated yet, takes popular songs, elides the voice track while retaining the instrumental track, provides the lyrics to the song on a video screen for the performer to follow, and allows amateur singers to have their "five minutes of fame" in front of an audience of family, friends, or even strangers. Often times, a fair amount of alcohol is required to loosen up **inhibitions** before amateur singers can face—in song—their fellow men. After all, Karaoke can be a fairly daunting social interaction when one is asked, **cajoled**, or generally forced to sing when accompanying a group, for it is far more than singing in the shower or performing with a hairbrush as a microphone. It's a phenomenon with interesting cultural implications.

1

One could start with the basic inquiry of what makes Karaoke so popular. Indeed, ethnomusicologists, ethnologists, cultural anthropologists as well as the guy off the street have all asked this same question since Karaoke exploded into the public consciousness in 1972. Despite the simplicity of the question, however, the possible explanations for Karaoke's phenomenal success and its **ubiquitous** presence are as numerous as the cultures that enjoy Karaoke. Though it started as a distinctly Japanese entertainment, Karaoke—which in Japanese means "empty orchestra"—has been disseminated to nearly every country on earth. To this extensive popularity the accompanying technology has contributed in a major way. Since their first appearance in the olden days when housing a speaker system, microphone, enough cassette tapes to host a party and having almost the size of a refrigerator, Karaoke machines have certainly come a long way. Today, Karaoke has become far more accessible through inexpensive cell phones or cheap software programs that host virtual Karaoke with songs downloadable from the Internet on-demand. And let us not discount Karaoke Podcasts or Playstation music making games!

2

3   The evolving technology, however, was probably only a contributing factor to Karaoke's expansive adoption. Taking a closer look at this phenomenon, one can observe that Karaoke has come a long way thanks to the deeper social needs it satisfies. Indeed, Karaoke can no longer be described as an entertainment outlet, idiosyncratic only to a few Japanese businessmen working too hard for their own good. Karaoke represents a far more fundamental need for humans to be active and creative, instead of passive and **abject**. Certainly, the Japanese businessmen who first started the Karaoke **craze** may provide a few clues as to its success. Indeed, for the Japanese as well as any people feeling bound by fairly strict rules of behavior or fenced-in by constricting workplace norms, Karaoke has provided an outlet of expression as well as a way to be active and creative. Karaoke has permitted a culturally approved and safe mode of expression that requires and encourages direct activity of the participants.

4   The term "empty orchestra" can definitely provide more clues for the interpretation of Karaoke than just a mere literal translation. It can serve as the best representation of people's need for active, creative expression in juxtaposition to passive behavior. In the case of this "empty" or orphaned orchestra, the participant is not to stay outside and listen, but is instead required to actively contribute to the orchestra's performance. This requirement then is indicative of Karaoke's significance in enhancing human creativity. Interestingly, Karaoke developed during the same period as many forms of what one could call passive entertainment. Right when Karaoke escaped the confines of Japan and truly found an international, receptive audience in the late 1970s and early 1980s, television, movies, and videogames were just beginning to capture large blocks of the viewing public. It was during this time that the first movie blockbuster, the 1975 movie <u>Jaws</u> by Stephen Spielberg, was made, and the masses flocked to movie theatres to see it. Likewise, cable television exploded onto the airwaves in the early 1980s with MTV, CNN, ESPN, and a host of other channels catering to specific audiences. Today, of course, the entertainment possibilities seem immense; it's possible to view streaming video, listen to radio casts through the Internet, watch movies on IMAX screens or IPod ones, and play video games on the multitude of the Xbox, GameCube, or Playstation platforms. The problem is that these activities all require passive audiences. The TV or movie watcher does exactly that…watches. All the scenes, the lines, the characters, and the plot have already been imagined and created by somebody else. What is left for the viewer to do but literally and metaphorically "sit back" and enjoy?

5   Television or movie viewers, music listeners, or game players all experience a passive form of entertainment that requires very little—if any— activity,

creativity, or overall initiative on their part. Passive entertainment, of course, does not mean that the viewers, listeners, or players are entirely brain-dead. Viewers may reflect on a TV program or movie after watching it; listeners may sing along with a song or artist; video-game players may have to **decipher** a riddle or solve a **conundrum**. However, these are still fundamentally passive forms of entertainment in which someone else creates and provides the material that is all too often simply absorbed with little thought or reflection.

Karaoke is but one example of the human need for creative activity that engages more of our senses and brain power than mere watching or listening as passive **receptacles** of other peoples' content. Karaoke hearkens back to the older traditions of story-telling and performance inherent in many cultures now lost or fading. Examples of this active, creative tradition from cultures around the world abound. In the Scottish tradition of their national poet, Robert Burns, many Scottish families host dinners (the annual Burn's Supper) in which the guests are responsible for providing the entertainment. Each guest is expected to tell a story, sing a song, or otherwise perform for the rest of the supper guests. There is no TV, movie, or band that allows participants to turn into mere spectators. Indeed, most cultures around the world have a tradition of story-telling or performance of one kind or another. Such activity is certainly not limited to words or song; it might also be exemplified by dance, as is the case with the thousands of participants in Brazil's Carnival who create **pageantry** through parade floats and interactive dance; such activity and creativity might come through cooking interesting, new, and challenging dishes; it might come through painting or drawing; it may come from making origami figures from paper-mache.

The ever-increasing forms of passive entertainment that are now available throughout the world—in the form of TV, recorded music, video games, even fast-food—inhibit and subjugate people's desire for activity and creativity in exchange for passivity and emptiness. We have just to look at recent TV shows such as American Idol or some of the newer video games in which participants dance on electronic pads to certain songs to see that there is a hunger for creative self-expression that is not being sated through popular forms of passive entertainment. It is human nature that propels us toward performance, activity, and creativity and not towards passivity and abject acceptance of our surroundings. This is the **elemental** mark of humanity that differentiates us from other primates; it is deeply connected to the need to not only view our environment, but also to alter it through interaction.

6

7

Discussing and Writing About The Text

Discussing Issues:

Make a list of the main forms of entertainment you have used since you were a child. Based on the authors' analysis, try to categorize them into passive, active, mixed, or other entertainment. Then compare your findings to those of your peers.

Interview your parents or grandparents for the ways of entertainment that were popular when they were your age. Then compare these forms of entertainment to those of your generation.

Writing about the Text:

In a well-developed and organized essay, respond to the reading; be sure to support your views with pertinent examples drawn from your own experience and observations, as well as readings.

Topic 1: According to the authors, in what ways is Karaoke representative of human nature? To what extent, if at all, do you agree with their claim about the passivity within many forms of modern entertainment?

Topic 2: Try to build a comparison/contrast among different forms of entertainment enjoyed by people of two or more different cultures. In your comparison/contrast, you need to describe but also analyze each form of entertainment in terms of elements such as its origins, its social role and contribution, its interpretation, etc.

Developing Vocabulary:

The words below may appear as part of your online quizzes. Please refer to the introduction for study strategies for learning vocabulary.

1. inhibition
2. to cajole
3. ubiquitous
4. abject
5. craze
6. to decipher
7. conundrum
8. receptacle
9. pageantry
10. elemental

Understanding the Text

Answer the following questions by carefully reviewing the authors' aruguments in the short essay.

1. What does Karaoke entail in terms of technology and as an activity?

2. What is the history of Karaoke and how did it become so popular?

3. What are the literal and metaphorical meanings of Karaoke?

4. What is the relationship between Karaoke and other modern or traditional forms of entertainment?

Analyzing Writing

Answer the following questions by carefully reviewing the authors' arugments and writing strategies from the short essay.

1. Examine the use of definition in the text. When and how is it used to help the reader's understanding?

2. Examine three sentences the authors use as transitions in their effectiveness connect different ideas.

3. Examine the use of example in the essay. What kind of examples do the authors use and to what effect?

53 More Graphic Violence, Please!

The clarion call for censorship and reform has become commonplace for avid critics of television and movie violence, who demand that violence be strictly regulated or limited under the increasing weight of evidence of its negative effects on viewers. While the jury is still out on a definitive correlation between violence on the air and violence on the street, there is substantial evidence as well as a long list of advocates for a decrease in the amount of depicted violence. Although due to the common margin of error in human reporting, no one can say with 100% certainty that violence **begets** violence, but it is *nearly certain* that violence fosters more aggressive behavior. The 2003 study in the journal *Developmental Psychology* by scientists at the University of Michigan, for instance, clearly showed that children who watched more violent TV programs were far more aggressive as adults than those who didn't. In this study men who were high consumers of TV-violence as children were far more likely to shove, push, or violently grab a spouse; shockingly, these men were three times as likely to have been convicted of violent crimes than other men (*Developmental Psychology*, 2003, Vol 39).

The list of evidence is mounting. Even the well-known conservative and cautious group of scientists and educators at The United Nations Educational, Scientific, and Cultural Organization (UNESCO) published an exhaustive review of the effect of various media on people. In the conclusion of their book-length study, they confirmed that "under certain circumstances, television can negatively influence attitudes in some areas, including those which may affect society" (*Regulation, Awareness, Empowerment*, 2006, 23).

Under the pressure of such mounting evidence of the correlation between media violence and real-life aggressive behavior, groups like the American Academy of Pediatrics, America's preeminent group of pediatricians, have been **issuing** publications like the 2007 book *Pulling the Plug on TV Violence*, which advocates strong parental action in limiting children's exposure to violence on TV. Due to demands from parental groups and various organizations, manufacturers were forced to introduce the so-called V-chip in 1999 in all televisions 13 inches or greater. This chip has allowed parents to restrict TV content based on a complicated set of codes, thereby controlling what their children have access to. Even

1

2

3

with this control mechanism at their disposal, however, these groups want violent content **eradicated** from the air. Such controversial policy aspirations are bound to bring up the issue of censorship, the limitation of free speech, and the ire of artists and producers across the country, something no one wants. Indeed, censorship can be particularly damaging to democracy, and possibly detrimental to business.

4   It becomes obvious then that even if media violence goes away, the debate on media violence is not going to, so something should be done. There can be no denying the accumulated weight of scientific evidence and just plain commonsense. This social problem, however, will not be solved through V-chips, review boards, congressional oversight, or censorship. Interestingly, the solution may lie within what initially appears as a daring oxymoron. Instead of less violence on TV, there should be more graphic violence, for the negative effects of media violence may **stem** not from the amount of violence but from its portrayal. *So, the more blood, guts, and gore, the better.*

5   Most media violence critics —from parents to pediatricians to TV producers—focus almost entirely on the quantity of the violence portrayed, ignoring its quality. Media violence is, for the most part, easy, clean, and often glorified. In violent altercations on TV or in the movies, few heroes get seriously hurt even if they fall from twenty feet or take a bullet in the leg. They may grit their teeth, they may yowl for a while, but they certainly keep on fighting. Even worse, violence is often glorified as the hero/protagonist steps into a bar (as Steven Seagal or Arnold Schwarzenegger so often do in their films) and proceeds to spectacularly break arms, legs, noses, teeth, pool tables, and bar stools. In most movies, these scenes are directed to appear appealing, **invigorating**, and stimulating, so it's no wonder that younger viewers especially are impressed. However, after the exciting music and raucous are over, no one sees the aftermath of the "bar-fight" scene, for the cameras have already followed the hero to the next scene and the next fight. No one is there to see what happens to all the "thugs" who have been beaten to a pulp. Yes, they might deserve it because they are "evil," but the film never shows how a shattered knee-cap will require multiple operations, traction, pain medication, and **rehabilitation**. Thug or not, a person with such an injury is likely to never again jog or even walk straight without a grimace.

6   Were this aftermath to be shown, perhaps the appeal of violence would diminish. In this proposal, children should not be inured from media violence either; instead, violence should be made so unappealing and **unpalatable** that they would not want to watch it. As with adult content, there needs to be a reformation in children's programming so that if violent acts are shown, they are shown with

their unflattering effects. An animation character that is kicked in the head five or six times should have a broken jaw, a lot of pain, and six weeks of eating soup through a mesh of wire. This is what ought to be shown.

What is needed is not less violence or increased censorship but *increased graphic violence*. Violence should be shown for all its grit, gore, and gall. Viewers should see the whole picture of a violent act to realize just how horrific and revolting violence really is. One model for this might be Quentin Tarantino's *Reservoir Dogs*, often hailed by critics as a terribly violent film. Make no mistake. This is a very disturbing film partly because for the entire duration of the film one of the main characters played by Tim Roth lies on the floor slowly dying of a gunshot to the abdomen. Through his suffering, the audience has an opportunity to see what it must mean to take a bullet: the **hemorrhaging** body, the **excruciating** pain, the heavy breathing, and the pre-mortal agony. Compared to any other "action" film with Schwarzenegger, Seagal, Van Damm, Pitt, Norton, the body count in *Reservoir Dogs* is quite low. However, that one body makes all the difference in the imprint this movie leaves with viewers.

Violence should be shown, but for how terrible and grim it really is. Viewers should not only see the actions of the perpetrators, but they should also see the suffering of victims, whether the latter be heroes or villains. War films especially should imitate movies like *Saving Private Ryan*, in which the opening fifteen minutes is supposedly the most realistic war sequence ever made. In this recreation of the invasion of D-Day, bullets fly and death rains from all sides. Men lie on the bloody beach with guts all shot out and medics who can do little to save them. In more recent years, films like *Letters from Iwo Jima*, *Stalingrad*, and *Enemy at the Gates* have also attempted to show the true face of violence with the aspiration of realism and deterrence.

It seems, therefore, ironic—if not hypocritical— that news channels will suffer significant fines by the Federal Communications Commission (FCC) if they broadcast "violent content" from ongoing wars such as the one in Iraq or Afghanistan. Indeed, news channels are currently prohibited from showing mutilated or blown-up bodies of soldiers or civilians; instead, they can merely mention the count of bodies and injuries, without putting a face to the number and statistics. Perhaps, however, more **graphic** images of war will make citizens reconsider their voting patterns or their ease of entering war. Images of bloody troops, bombed-out villages, mutilated kids, and bereaved widows on the news will bring war home and make it more tangible in its horrors.

7

8

9

Discussing and Writing About The Text

Discussing Issues:

In groups compare/contrast news broadcasts or movies on the same event (e.g. D-Day) and focus on their depiction of violence.

Writing about the Text:

In a well-developed and organized essay, respond to the reading; be sure to support your views with pertinent examples drawn from your own experience and observations, as well as readings.

Topic 1: What is the authors' suggestion in regards to media violence? To what extent—if at all—you think their suggestion could be plausible and effective?

Topic 2: Find some of the regulations the Federal Communications Commission (FCC) imposes for violent TV content. Evaluate these regulations as solutions to the problem of TV violence.

Developing Vocabulary:

The words below may appear as part of your online quizzes. Please refer to the introduction for study strategies for learning vocabulary.

1.	to beget	2.	to issue
3.	to eradicate	4.	to stem (from)
5.	invigorating	6.	rehabilation
7.	unpalatable	8.	hemorrhaging
9.	excruciating	10.	graphic

Understanding the Text

Answer the following questions by carefully reviewing the authors' aruguments in the short essay.

1.   What are some of the arguments and evidence of the critics of media violence?

2.   What are the proposals and issues concerning the reduction of media violence?

3.   What do the authors believe could counter the damaging effects of media violence?

4.   What is the evidence the authors use to support their suggestions?

Analyzing Writing

Answer the following questions by carefully reviewing the authors' arugments and writing strategies from the short essay.

1. Find various transitional devices used in the text and examine their role and effectiveness.

2. Examine the type and quality of counterarguments offered by the authors.

3. Examine the use of sources in the essay. What kind of sources do the authors use (personal examples-anecdotes, statistics, etc)? Do you think they are appropriate and convincing? What additional sources would you use?

54 The Happy Meter

It should come as no surprise that the United States has turned happiness into big business. One has only to think of Disneyland, Hollywood, or Coney Island to know happiness **incarnate**. Yet contrary to common assumptions, happiness is not measured by the prevalence of or attendance at entertainment hotspots like Las Vegas casinos, the consumption of favorite foods, or visiting amusement parks, despite the claim that Disneyland is the "happiest place on earth." No, sociologists and economists don't measure happiness by decibel of laughter in a community or obesity rates among children; they employ a whole, somewhat **opaque**, methodology that seeks to quantify happiness across the United States, and their studies seem to signify an interesting and important shift in modern day concepts of happiness.

1

Certainly since the industrial revolution, if not before, happiness was generally connected to a country's Gross Domestic Product (GDP), the measurement of personal consumption, investment, and government spending. As early as the 1930s, economists such as John Maynard Keynes directly connected increased consumption of goods and products with a person's general wealth, health, well-being, and…happiness. In this system, the better the economy is doing, the more income individuals have, and thus the happier they are likely to be. Born in the heart of the depression, this ideology made a great deal of sense. Indeed, for the millions of Americans daily striving for the basic needs of shelter and food, happiness at the time was synonymous to a bowl of soup, a hot stove, and a roof over their head.

2

The Great Depression is over, yet this method of connecting happiness to economic "progress" has persisted, in many ways intact, until the present day. Nevertheless, a revolution in the way we assess happiness is currently underway. **Stemming** from an overall dissatisfaction with the "old way" of doing things, this new approach to measuring happiness may very well alter significant aspects of our lives such as our professional choices, our social interactions, or our identities. In the last ten years, scientists and economists have expressed grave doubts as to the **efficacy** of straight correlations between the GDP and happiness. Indeed, statistical data conclusively indicate that people do not feel happier now in comparison to 1970 even though the GDP has basically doubled during this period. Even more

3

so, the GDP from 2000 to the present, seemingly the best in world history, has not **budged** the so-called happiness level (*Economist*, Dec 23rd, 2006). It is no wonder then that scientists have shifted toward formulas more complex than the plain GDP in their effort to evaluate happiness.

4   In pursuit of a more accurate "happy-meter," a number of new methods have emerged. Leading the way and devised by Canadian scientists, the Gross Domestic Well-Being Index accounts not only for economic **output**, but also health, welfare, and environmental factors. Similarly, other indexes such as the 1995 Genuine Progress Index (GPI) include economic data and additional variables such as human well-being and environmental impact. The most generic of these new indexes appears to be the GNH, Gross National Happiness Index, for it is based on survey responses to nonspecific questions like "how happy are you these days—very happy, happy, not too happy?" Though frivolous such an index may seem, happiness is now serious business especially considering the existence of a *Journal of Happiness Studies* which was founded in March, 2001 to solicit submissions from scientists from all over the world.

5   All of these indexes seem to be pointing to the same assumption: that the **Holy Grail** of happiness-studies relies on identifying the variables that constitute and contribute to happiness. This task becomes even more challenging when looking at data from outside the U.S. or other developed countries. Fine, the GDP cannot solely determine happiness, but should it be excluded from these indexes? How can scientists explain the 2003 survey according to which people in Nigeria, Mexico, Venezuela, El Salvador, and Puerto Rico had the highest happiness index in the world (*BBC News*, Oct 2nd, 2003)? How is it that in the same survey, the U.S. came in 16th place, behind many so-called "poor" countries? The answer to this conundrum may, therefore, lie more in human psychology and culture than in economics.

6   One important factor that those invested in the happiness discipline need to study is the role of culture, for it seems that happiness—in many ways—is culturally conditioned. Considering the tremendous cultural variety in the world, devising a single set of variables to encapsulate happiness for all must be out of the question. Indeed, the social justification of any culture is inextricably related to the pursuit of happiness: teaching its participants what happiness is and how to attain it. Why were notions of happiness so different in the **Great Depression** versus today? Why do many children in the U.S. equate Christmas presents to happiness? Why do parents become happy when their children draw pictures they dedicate to mom and dad when the pictures are, objectively, of very poor quality? The answer lies in the dissimilarities of cultural systems. While individual tastes

and experiences certainly inform ideas of happiness, it is the cultural systems to which people belong that create the framework for deciding what happiness is.

The second factor to determining happiness is even more primary to our make-up as human beings, for human beings are psychologically pre-disposed to unhappiness. This is not to say that we are all born "on the wrong side of the bed" or have a genetic pre-disposition to be sullen and dissatisfied. However, the very moment when happiness becomes an **ephemeral**, transitive, and always threatened state of being occurs at the moment of…consciousness. It is precisely at this moment when infants realize that the world is not an extension of themselves, but rather that things and people exist outside of them, that they feel a "lack." This may sound like insane pop psychology, but there is a whole discipline of psychoanalysis which maintains that people constantly feel desire for what they don't have; once they achieve their desire, the lack is briefly fulfilled until the next desire creates a lack.

When, for instance, do people feel happy? Usually happiness comes from the response to a "lack." People tend to become happy when they feel a "lack," a "need" for something—whether it is a loved animal, friends, food, a job, a completed education degree, power, or anything else for that matter is satisfied. People in the great depression lacked food, a warm hearth, and a roof over their heads, so for them happiness came when these conditions were fulfilled. This idea may seem simple or even simplistic, but it may well explain why the happiness index hasn't gone up for people in the U. S. in the last forty years. Our ever-expanding, consumer-driven society has simply created more "lacks" which most people cannot satiate even though they are much better off economically than in previous decades. We must only notice the behavior of children at Christmas to understand why. They seem supremely happy to receive their toys, but they quickly become inured to the happiness the toy provides. How often do children (and adults) simply want more once one desire has been satisfied? Interestingly, this also explains why people in certain poor countries, according to the polls, feel happier than those in richer countries. Those residents are burdened by fewer "lacks," and the ones they do have are more readily satisfied for a greater length of time.

Until determining and comprehending these various factors that affect and shape our happiness levels, the happiness-industry will continue to flourish in all its forms, from Disneyland to science. In the meantime, it is certain that our economical system will keep instilling "lacks" and "desires" into people, for this system undoubtedly colludes with what some consider basic human psychology. Of course, instead of worrying about devising a "happy-meter," some take refuge in the teachings of Buddha: **Nirvana**, complete happiness, with no needs or lacks.

7

8

Discussing and Writing About The Text

Discussing Issues:

Try to construct your own "happy-meter" and then compare it to those of other students. Discuss differences and similarities and the possible causes for them.

Writing about the Text:

In a well-developed and organized essay, respond to the reading; be sure to support your views with pertinent examples drawn from your own experience and observations, as well as readings.

Topic 1: According to the authors, how has happiness been measured and what are two important factors in its measurement? To what extent, if at all, do you agree with their views?

Topic 2: Compare/Contrast your views about and criteria for happiness to those of an older member of your family. Try to analyze and explain the possible differences and similarities.

Developing Vocabulary:

The words below may appear as part of your online quizzes. Please refer to the introduction for study strategies for learning vocabulary.

1. incarnate	2. opaque
3. grave	4. efficacy
5. to budge	6. output
7. the Holy Grail	8. the Great Depression
9. ephemeral	10. Nirvana

Understanding the Text

Answer the following questions by carefully reviewing the authors' arugments in the short essay.

1. How was happiness measured in the beginning of the 20th century and why?

2. What do more recent studies suggest about happiness and its indicators?

3. What do the authors suggest should be a primary factor in determining happiness variables?

4. How does basic human psychology affect happiness?

Analyzing Writing

Answer the following questions by carefully reviewing the authors' arugments and writing strategies from the short essay.

1. Isolate and identify the type of sources used by the authors, and examine their effectiveness.

2. Underline five different transitional devices and examine their effectiveness.

3. Examine the role and effectiveness of the various rhetorical techniques used by the authors.

55 "If It Ain't Broke, Don't Fix It"

It is common for many Europeans to criticize the U.S., especially since the invasion and occupation of Iraq have shown no progress. Many sit in small companies of four or five in smoke-filled coffee-shops, nursing cappuccinos or stronger drinks while discussing the flaws in American politics and culture. The U.S., they say, is devoid of values or any quality for that matter. "Just look at what they eat…McDonalds, Wendy's, Pizza Hut. What is their national food, arterial sclerosis?" "Just look at the movies they watch; how can they even compare to what 'we' see in Cannes, Venice, London, or Berlin?" The films and overall culture, they say, tell the story of an empire, very much like the Roman Empire, that has become corrupt and stagnant, whose citizens are dramatically uneducated and uncivilized, and whose **prominence** in the world is owed only to military power. To them, Americans and America might embody one of the greatest threats to world security. Their distrust goes to the point where millions of citizens of "friendly" countries such as Germany believe that the U. S. itself was behind the September 11th attacks in order to justify invading Iraq (*National Public Radio*, October 2003).

1

Of course, not all Europeans think this way, but enough have formed this simplistic notion of the United States as a homogenous, violent creature that lumbers through the world, bent on violence by military force and cultural domination through the spread of Hollywood films and McDonalds. Of course, the U.S. is an incredibly diverse country with a multitude of regional, racial, ethnic, and cultural variations; contrary to simplistic belief, neither the military nor Hollywood represents every American, nor do they epitomize the American experience. While these critics around the world focus on the surface of things, they fail to delve into the deeper, problematic issue that explains many of the social ills and much of the international behavior of the U.S.: America's passion for quick fixes. This characteristic can be seen in nearly every aspect of American culture and informs who we are and how we operate domestically and abroad.

2

One of the best ways to understand American culture is through the idiom, "if it ain't broke, don't fix it," a reference to government official Bert Lance who is credited with coining the phrase in a 1977 interview. This ideology, indeed, can be seen in nearly every aspect of American life, from education to international politics. Take, for example, a student's progress in English. Most university systems across the United States administer an English placement examination, which seeks to identify students whose English reading and writing competence is not at

3

a "C" level or above. Students are "failing" these exams in droves. In fact, The University of California fails more than 50% of students who take this exam, requiring them to complete developmental writing courses. Instead of identifying the core issues that cause this dramatic failure rate (overcrowded classrooms in the K-12 system, insufficient writing assignments, little comprehensive grammar instruction, lack of coherent English as a Second Language programs), the UC system is forced to deal with the effects of the problem by creating programs after the problems have occurred. In the meantime, students suffer mental **anguish** because of often perceiving themselves as "failures".

4   This same ideology can be seen in law enforcement. "Suddenly," someone becomes aware that the crime rate has skyrocketed, and this is a real problem for the citizens of the community. Instead of analyzing why the crime rate has gone up so much, the politicians address the symptom of the problem by adding more police and greater prison capacity. Little thought is given to the complex causes of these problems. Little is done to increase wages or create jobs in severely depressed areas, the places where criminals are **incubated** until ripe. Little attention is given to the prison educational system in training convicts to be functional members of society after their release; and 95% of inmates are eventually released. Instead, the emphasis is on punishment and doing hard time in an incredibly violent atmosphere. What is supposed to happen when these convicts are released without an education, without training, and without a real ability to function in the world? No wonder **recidivism** rates have topped 67% according to a 2006 study by the Commission on Safety and Abuse in America's Prisons.

5   One doesn't have to look far for examples of this quick-fix mentality. Just examine hurricane Katrina and its effect on New Orleans. Report after report that indicated the levies holding back the Mississippi might not be strong enough for an intense hurricane was shelved. The federal government denied funding to strengthen the **levies**, even after various agencies argued that a mere 18 inches added to the levies would have prevented much of the flooding of New Orleans. Such a program, proposed in 1998, would have cost fourteen-billion dollars (*NY Times*, Sept 2nd, 2005); after hurricane Katrina, estimates speculate the clean-up cost for New Orleans and its surroundings to exceed 150 billion dollars. The list goes on and on. The huge wild fires in California that burned over 400,000 acres and cost almost one billion dollars could have been lessened to a great degree through removal of dead trees, underbrush, and better management of land resources. It was only after this catastrophe occurred, despite numerous proposals for preventative care, that the Healthy Forest Restoration Act was signed into law on December 3rd, 2003. This was little consolation to the owners of the over 5,000 structures (houses, businesses, etc.) that were destroyed by the fires.

6   Americans and American culture seem to operate by responding to crises, not by preventing them. This can be seen by the 83% of Americans who gave to charity in 2006 (*Chronicle of **Philanthropy***, December 29, 2006). Americans of

all kinds gave money to education, to religious organizations, to relief efforts for hurricane Katrina. But even this is indicative of how Americans—both in the private sector and in government—respond to problems. In American culture there is little energy or effort spent on investigating foreseeable and identifiable problems. Instead, most energy and effort are spent on addressing symptoms of problems, many times by responding to emergency situations. This quick-fix modus operandi merely addresses the most pressing problem for a time; it does not address the underlying causes of the problem.

One reason for the quick-fix methodology to solving problems may well lie in the educational approach still widely employed throughout the United States in thousands of schools. John Dewey's (1859-1952) progressive approach to student learning valued the student's experience and participation in the learning process more than the traditional approach of instruction where teachers lectured, providing students with "all they needed" to know about a subject. The result of this educational paradigm, to a large extent, can be seen in how many—certainly not all—Americans interact with their environments and react to new stimuli. They learn through hands-on, empirical experience, experimentation, and examples. Take, for instance, the concept of global warming with all the data already collected. The **undisputable** warming of the earth based on scientific studies did not register with most Americans until they saw or heard about Al Gore's movie, *An Inconvenient Truth*, which contained examples of what a one to two degree increase in the earth's temperature would actually mean: flooding of most of Florida, parts of Manhattan under water, millions of fleeing refugees, and a multitude of other "**tangible**" catastrophes. Beyond, however, this emphasis on empirical data, which are scientifically sound, this educational paradigm acculturates Americans into a focus on the "solution" of a problem rather than its "prevention." Americans develop the mentality of the "problem-solver" which undoubtedly comes with benefits but also with a **glitch**. This mentality creates an unwillingness to solve problems for good in order to prevent future ones. "If it ain't broke, don't fix it." This mentality gives Americans the oftentimes **arrogant** confidence that they can solve any problem if and when a problem arises. "It's ok…for now. If there is a problem, we'll fix it."

Through this education system and the overall culture, Americans are programmed to look at examples and rely on experience in order to form opinions and then react with decisiveness and determination. Because of this, Americans very often respond to problems after they occur by applying—what at the time—seems a good solution. However, with a bit more background, forethought, and planning, there might not have been an emergency to respond to at all.

7

8

Discussing and Writing About The Text

Discussing Issues:

In a group think of a problem that you would like to solve and outline the steps toward solving it. Then compare your approach with what the authors describe as a quick-fix approach. (The instructor could assign the same problem to all groups and then compare/contrast the various approaches to its solution.)

Writing about the Text:

In a well-developed and organized essay, respond to the reading; be sure to support your views with pertinent examples drawn from your own experience and observations, as well as readings.

Topic 1: According to the authors, what are the causes and effects of the quick-fix mentality in the U.S.? To what extent, if at all, do you agree with their ideas?

Topic 2: According to your opinion, what should be the ideal educational paradigm when it comes to problem solving? To support your opinion, you need to examine relevant and specific examples from a variety of sources.

Developing Vocabulary:

The words below may appear as part of your online quizzes. Please refer to the introduction for study strategies for learning vocabulary.

1. prominence
2. anguish
3. to incubate
4. recidivism
5. levies
6. philanthropy
7. undisputable
8. tangible
9. glitch
10. arrogant

Understanding the Text

Answer the following questions by carefully reviewing the authors' aruguments in the short essay.

1. What are some of the common criticisms of the U.S.?

2. Why do the authors find these common criticisms superficial?

3. What is the mentality of quick fixes, its causes, and its effects on the American people?

4. What do the authors suggest for fixing the quick-fix mentality of Americans?

Analyzing Writing

Answer the following questions by carefully reviewing the authors' aruguments and writing strategies from the short essay.

1. Examine the use and effectiveness of informal speech in the text.

2. Find five different transitional devices that the authors use and try to replace them without changing the meaning.

3. Examine the relevance and effectiveness of the sources of evidence used by the authors in support of their arguments.

56 Shedding Light on Culture

It would not be an exaggeration to suppose that the definitions of culture may equate to the number of cultures themselves, each one insisting on particular elements of the term "culture." To some, culture is represented by a certain set of manners or behavior that people of the same country or community abide by. Indeed, it is not that difficult to identify in a crowd those who comport themselves like Americans, Germans, Chinese, Mexicans, or other nationalities without even hearing them speak. Their similar body language, facial expressions, sense of personal space, or a multitude of other subtle indicators may give them away, setting them apart from members of other cultural groups. Other definitions of culture focus on the shared language and the idiomatic expressions afforded by a particular mode of communication. Indeed, it is not uncommon for learners of a second language to stumble over the obstacle of precise expression, not for lack of a good dictionary but simply because the second culture and therefore the language lack an idea particular to their native culture and language. Still, others find culture primarily within the sculpted walls of symphonic halls or the arranged spaces of museums where superlative collections illustrate and represent the best a culture has to offer.

1

Culture is all of these things at once, but such plurality in a definition leaves only a sense of confusion, the sense that culture can be anything and everything. In this vein, it is helpful to understand first what culture is not. Culture has nothing to do with one's place of birth or the nationality typed into a passport. That is mere chance in the lottery of life. A person born in Germany who immigrates to New York at the age of three might carry a German passport, but the cultural upbringing will be American, specifically New York American. An American **expatriate** who has lived abroad for most of his life will be a citizen of the United States, but he will most likely be a cultural citizen of some other place entirely. Likewise, just as nationality or citizenship has little to do with cultural affinity, race is often misidentified with culture. A Chinese woman might be genetically

2

Asian, but if she were raised in South Africa she might very well speak Afrikaans, Dutch, or any of the half-dozen local African languages and **comport** herself as a native of those cultures although at first sight she would probably be considered a "foreigner."

3   So, how can one make sense of this Tower of Babel, this chaos of definitions? A suitable framework for this discussion might be to identify two major components of culture. The first could be called the *externalized culture*. As the term implies, the external consists of all those things about a culture than can be empirically identified through the senses. It can include elements that range from buildings or other spaces to clothes, hair styles, foods, body language, or anything observed to be common to a certain group of people. These cultural artifacts and human behaviors are only **manifestations** of the culture, its mere symptoms. It is these observable elements, the cultural artifacts or behavioral manifestations that tourists most often come to know and acknowledge as particular to a certain culture. A tourist to Germany, for instance, might visit Munich during Oktoberfest and assume that most Germans drink too much beer, eat Bratwurst, have cuckoo clocks in their houses, and own a pair of lederhosen (leather pants). However, cultures are far more complex than tourists are likely to appreciate, for most tourists—even those who read about the history of the country, the geography, the places of interest—very often observe only the external elements, the symptoms of the culture. After all, it is these limited observations that often lead to the formation of stereotypes; what these observations lack is the understanding of the non-obvious, internal elements of culture.

4   Deeper analysis of culture suggests that a whole other level of complexity exists. Underlying all the observable, empirical, physical elements of external culture is the *internalized culture* which causes and molds the external. Elements of the internal can be found in the communal knowledge, language, typical life patterns, common historical experience, and worldview of a group of people within a community. This is not to say that cultures can produce carbon-copy **clones**, for there will always be individual variations in how and what people learn, how they speak, and how they perceive the world around them. However, it is this combined internalized culture that **melds** together into what informs the way individuals of a particular culture are *likely* to behave and what they are *likely* to believe in.

It seems, therefore, necessary that a person live in the cultural space of a   5
particular community, learn and speak the common language, and experience the
patterns of life within that group in order to internalize a culture. It also seems natural that cultural misunderstandings should occur when people come together and
there is a disjunction among people and the expectations they hold due to their internalized culture. For instance, in China it is commonplace for audience members at a music recital to talk, tell jokes, and generally create a boisterous
atmosphere while the musician is playing. If American musicians were performing there, they might think the Chinese audience was incredibly rude and **uncouth**
when in reality the audience was trying to "honor" the performance in their own
way. Likewise, American guests would be considered rude by Chinese hosts if
they didn't eat to their absolute capacity at the dinner provided for them.

In pursuit then of an authentic cultural experience, one should look for   6
both the external and the internal elements of a culture. Cultural **authenticity** is
far more than the meaning assumed by museum curators who judge whether works
of art are **forgeries** or not. It deals with the origins, attributions, commitments,
beliefs, and "genuineness" of people and things within a cultural system. Considering this, four levels of cultural authenticity can be discerned in the way various groups of people experience culture:

Category One (Indigenous): these are residents of a community who par-   7
ticipate in both external and internal culture. They live in an area that has
been shaped by the cultural values of its residents, and they themselves
are fully integrated into that community, having adopted its belief systems
and world view.

Category Two (First Generation Immigrants): these are residents of a   8
community who have imported an internalized culture, but they lack in
the new community most of the external elements that constituted their
culture. They themselves are typically not fully integrated into the new
community, having retained internalized cultural values from their point of
origin and often seeking to reproduce the external **artifacts** through customs, cuisine, and traditions or even through building their own "towns"

such as China Town, Little Tokyo, Astoria, and others.

9   ***Category Three (Second Generation Immigrants):*** these are members of a community whose elders have a different internalized culture. They themselves typically have a limited experience of external cultural elements through cuisine, traditional dances, and visits to the old country, but they lack the wide spectrum of internalized cultural values of their parents or any shared memory of the "old country," the "old culture," the "old ways." Being born and **bred** usually within a duality or a multitude of cultures, they often find themselves confused and trapped in a system of two languages, two cultures—often antithetical to each other—and two worlds.

10   ***Category Four (Tourists):*** these are visitors of a community who typically experience only external culture through observation of its external elements. Tourists visit a place, observe its architecture, the people, style of dress, and a host of other empirical items, but they usually do not have access to its internalized culture but only through background knowledge.

11   The concept of authenticity, useful for judging a person's position within a culture, can also provide a framework for reducing cultural conflicts due to misunderstandings. Take, for example, a Chinese man from Beijing who has lived in the city all his life. He has experienced both the external and internal elements of Chinese culture within that city, is known in the community, and is aware of how everything operates. If the same man moved to Kansas City, he might soon become frustrated because nothing works the way he expects, from purchasing groceries at the supermarket to hosting a dinner party. A further level of conflict might arise if he has children in Kansas City. This second generation born in the United States will have only knowledge of China through the memories of their father while they have all the external and internal cultural influences of U. S. culture. Their "authenticity" in Chinese culture will be lessened. The grandchildren of this immigrant from Beijing might have become so acculturated in the U.S. that when they visit relatives in Beijing, they are effectively tourists who marvel at the city, the crowds, the people, and the food. They might even be disturbed by how

people behave so differently from their own cultural expectations of proper manners.

Cultural conflicts can arise when one or more of these categories come
into contact because the expectations of both external and internal culture will be
different for people. The key for more fluid interactions with both people and
places is to first recognize the cultural authenticity and second to decode what
cultural expectations each group is likely to have. Thus, indigenous residents
might be upset with immigrants when expectations for certain types of behavior
are not met, but if both groups are aware of these issues, misunderstandings can
be avoided.

12

Discussing and Writing About The Text

Discussing Issues:

Think of your own personal or family culture in terms of both its external and its internal elements. Make a list of these elements and discuss it with your peers to discover differences and similarities as well as possible sources for cultural misunderstandings.

Writing about the Text:

In a well-developed and organized essay, respond to the reading; be sure to support your views with pertinent examples drawn from your own experience and observations, as well as readings.

Topic 1: According to the authors, what constitutes cultural authenticity? How valid and/or accurate do you consider the authors' classification of different levels of authenticity?

Topic 2: According to your opinion, how can cultural conflicts be avoided in a society that has people of all levels of cultural authenticity?

Developing Vocabulary:

The words below may appear as part of your online quizzes. Please refer to the introduction for study strategies for learning vocabulary.

1. **expatriate**
2. **to comport**
3. **manifestation**
4. **clones**
5. **to meld**
6. **uncouth**
7. **forgery**
8. **authenticity**
9. **artifact**
10. **bred**

Understanding the Text

Answer the following questions by carefully reviewing the authors' aruguments in the short essay.

1. What is the focus of the various definitions of culture?

2. What do the authors mean by *externalized* and *internalized* culture?

3. What are often the reasons for misunderstandings and clashes among cultures?

4. What is cultural authenticity and what are its four levels?

Analyzing Writing

Answer the following questions by carefully reviewing the authors' arugments and writing strategies from the short essay.

1. Examine the use and effectiveness of classification in the text.

2. Examine the role of definition in the text.

3. Find the focus-theme of each paragraph, and write it in the margin next to each paragraph. Is each paragraph organized around a specific focus or not?

57 Why do Clichés Rub Teachers the Wrong Way?

Clichés seem to be as welcome as a skunk at a lawn party when it comes to English papers, for English teachers don't seem to be able to stomach the use of one **cliché** in a paper, let alone one drop in a bucket. It burns them up, chaps their hide, gets their goad up, works them into a lather, makes their blood boil. But why do clichés get teachers so bent out of shape, especially when they are as easy to use as shooting fish in a barrel? Every student knows that using clichés in a paper represents either a last ditch effort to spice it up or an invitation to push up the daisies. Unfortunately, students many times receive a thorough tongue lashing by teachers who blow a gasket when students take the easy way out by hoping against hope that their point will be made in the nick of time. Teachers complain time and again that clichés have a long row to hoe if they are to actually **impart** in one fell swoop the real substance of a message. Otherwise, they claim that clichés are **devoid** of meaning and should be thrown out when push comes to shove.

"Specific description, description, description" instructors remark time and again in the margins of papers, infuriating students to no end till they climb the walls. For teachers, accurate and specific writing about life has nothing to do with Forest Gump's adage that "life is like a box of chocolates. You never know what you gonna get." Instead, students need to learn that no one knows what "shooting for the moon" really means or what level of impatience "spinning one's wheels" indicates. For example, a student, who is sharp as a tack, needed to write a paper on increasing minimum wage for a hard-nosed, college instructor who makes no bones about failing student papers that lack specificity, detailed analysis, and clear organization. Therefore, the student tried to avoid clichés like the plague. Despite chewing the fat with the instructor during office hours to plan the essay, the student still felt thick as a brick when she sat down to write the paper in the eleventh hour. So, to describe the real plight of minimum wage workers, who don't have a glimmer of hope, she wrote how these workers were "not born with a silver spoon in their mouths, so they couldn't bring home the bacon." Well, without betting your bottom dollar, this elicited a severe response from the instructor who wrote, "Writing a paper isn't like rocket science. This is college where you have to sink or swim, and right now this paper has gone belly up. You are in a do-or-die situation for your revision. In two shakes

1

2

of a lamb's tail, you should revise this essay because I'm not getting any younger."

3   In the above scenario, the unfortunate student **slinked** away from this encounter with her instructor like a dog with its tail between its legs. While the teacher's heart was in the right place by wishing against all hope that the student's work would improve, such negative reinforcement typically leaves students fit to be hog-tied or ready to fight like cats and dogs with the instructor. Students often see no light at the end of the tunnel when they write papers, so they grasp at straws by using clichés. This bad habit isn't all its cracked up to be, but students know that their writing needs time to improve; after all, Rome wasn't built in a day.

4   Clichés, unfortunately, have received a bad wrap. While it is true that they are as common as the fish in the sea, they have not received their just desserts, for, in many ways, clichés represent important aspects of culture. As old as dirt and long in the tooth, clichés have an admirable history that helps cultural anthropologists understand how language develops and what is important to its speakers. Thus, clichés are worth their weight in gold, for they help such scientists clearly analyze culture like a knife through hot butter. In this way, students who frequently use clichés are not "dumber than a box of rocks," as one cliché goes, for they participate in a cultural phenomenon that is as old as sin. Clichés are part and parcel of a long cultural tradition that makes a language more **vibrant** where a rainy day is not simply wet but "is raining pitchforks."

5   So, English teachers should wait a New York minute before condemning clichés as useless cultural artifacts. Furthermore, teachers ought to realize that students who use clichés might very well, dollars to doughnuts, be attempting to provide meaningful description for their papers without specifically knowing how. Now, that's better than a sharp stick in the eye. However, students may be simply jumping from the frying pan into the fire! Despite their metaphorical or cultural value, clichés may **ultimately** do more harm than good: they may affect how students think, making them a few sandwiches short of a picnic. How are students in harm's way? Well, far beyond a bad grade on a paper that drives both students and instructors up the wall, clichés may cause students to think very superficially and unrealistically about life. Take, for example, the cliché, "it's not the size of the dog in the fight; it's the size of the fight in the dog." While this is admirably hopeful, it flies like a pig in real-life. Even literally, a small Chihuahua doesn't have a snowball's chance in hell of **overpowering** a bulldog. Yet, this cliché gives people an unrealistic worldview to pin their hopes to. So, while a person may have a heart the size of Texas, their real-world ability may not add up to a hill of beans. Both the Chihuahua and this person might as well wish upon a star at that point.

While hope springs eternal, clichés too often teach the wrong lessons that students gobble up like there is no tomorrow. In another vein, take, for example, the popular sentiment found in many romance comedies, "love conquers all." This often becomes the excuse for improbable couples to get together like nobody's business. Because romance is in the air, the practical side of life—that includes paying bills, getting jobs, and living every day life—is thrown out like a baby with the bathwater. In this, the wheel is turning, but the hamster is dead. Unfortunately, life is really not like a bowl of cherries, and there is typically no easy way to cash out your chips from a complicated relationship. It is for this reason that one sees teenagers no older than a baby's bottom who want to tie the knot at their earliest convenience. It is not so much that love is blind and allows the couple to overlook their partner's **inadequacies**; it's that the cliché teaches them not to see any of the potential real-life problems they could face as if they were an ostrich with its head in the sand. Marriage is certainly not about lugging around the old ball and chain, but it does have a lot to do with putting one's nose to the grindstone, which requires the right kind of mate in the relationship. Popular culture with movies, TV, and the Internet make mature relationships seem like child's play when really it takes two people with compatible characters to tango.

6

Another common cliché found in many movies is "time heals all wounds." Most discussions of any real substance are dropped like a hot potato and quickly **dismissed**. A significant loss in life, a terrible event, a crushing personal blow is dealt with on a superficial level: "every rose has its thorn," "all's well that ends well," "life is the pits," or "you need a new lease on life." In such films, the flood of tears lasts for about thirty seconds before all the characters realize that the sun will come out tomorrow. Real life, however, is not the land of milk and honey where everyone eats his peaches and cream; a person who is **traumatized** in life is swimming in deep water, and grief cannot simply be nipped in the bud so easily, for keeping one's fingers crossed doesn't heal deep wounds or allow a person to recover. Instead, a person may have to cry a river in front of a therapist before the semblance of normal life can return.

7

The axe to be ground here is not that clichés are devoid of specific meaning, liven up papers, or are culturally as good as gold. The real issue is how clichés, especially the ones found a dime a dozen in movies today, cause people to react superficially, illogically, and unsystematically to real life events. It's time that people, especially younger students, turn over a new leaf to discover that life is far more complicated than what can be encapsulated in a superficial cliché. Advising somebody who didn't get accepted to graduate school to "make lemonade when life gives you lemons" or that "it's a dog-eat-dog world" will neither necessarily nor in any concrete way help this person make the right decision. Next time, do not take solace in the motto "nothing wagered, nothing gained."

8

Discussing and Writing About The Text

Discussing Issues:

Contradictory Clichés: In groups choose several clichés either from the text or other sources and try to define their meaning and determine which real-life situations they could apply to. Compare your findings and then try to examine whether the same real-life situation could be handled with a cliché of the opposite meaning.

Writing about the Text:

In a well-developed and organized essay, respond to the reading; be sure to support your views with pertinent examples drawn from your own experience and observations, as well as readings.

Topic 1: According to the authors, what are the positive and negative aspects of clichés? To what extent—if at all—do you agree with the author's views?

Topic 2: Try to rewrite the essay by avoiding all the clichés used. Then compare the two essays in terms of content, style, tone, effectiveness.

Developing Vocabulary:

The words below may appear as part of your online quizzes. Please refer to the introduction for study strategies for learning vocabulary.

1. cliché
2. to impart
3. devoid (of)
4. to slink
5. vibrant
6. ultimately
7. to overpower
8. inadequacy
9. to dismiss
10. to traumatize

Understanding the Text

Answer the following questions by carefully reviewing the authors' aruguments in the short essay.

1. What is the common reaction of English instructors to clichés?

2. What is the role of clichés in culture?

3. How do clichés affect the average person in a negative way?

4. Which clichés do the authors use to support their thesis?

Analyzing Writing

Answer the following questions by carefully reviewing the authors' arugments and writing strategies from the short essay.

1. Examine the use of clichés in the text and their effectiveness.

2. Find five different clichés in the text and try to determine their literal and metaphorical meaning.

3. Examine how the authors employ refutation in the text. Can you cite the specific sentence(s) or paragraph(s)?

58 The Pursuit of 'Happyness'

The movie *The Pursuit of Happyness*, set in 1981 bustling San Francisco, garnered Will Smith the Oscar in 2007 and was viewed, by many critics, as the performance of his career. In the movie, Smith portrays a **downtrodden** salesman, Chris Gardner, whose wife leaves him after years of financial struggle, hinging on Gardner's inability to sell some expensive bone-density scanners. Left with very little money, the very real threat of eviction, and mostly the care of his five-year-old son, Gardner realizes that the "real" money lies in selling stocks. However, without any formal education and with a very spotty resume, Gardner's chances of landing a prized six-month internship at Dean Witter, a high profile brokerage company, are quite slim. Despite the likelihood of failure, Gardner finds clever ways to **ingratiate** himself with a contact at Dean Witter, even loitering outside the manager's office until he is afforded an opportunity to interview for the internship. Through Herculean efforts Gardner lands the internship only to find that the company won't pay a single dime for the entire six months; and as if free labor were not enough, twenty more interns vie for this same one job; only one of these interns—the person with the most stock sales— who will be hired by the company on a permanent basis. Though faced with the dire possibility of being homeless and sacrificing six months of intensive work for nothing, Gardner decides to risk it all and take his chances. In the meantime, of course, he struggles to take care of his son. Indeed, unlike the other interns who work twelve to fourteen hours a day, Gardner can "only" work a **scant** eight hours; he then has to pick up his son from daycare and literally run to the homeless shelter before all the beds are taken by other homeless people. To make up for the "missed" time, he has to study under the dim to non-existent light of a defunct lamp. All the while Gardner has to keep strong for his son and keep smiling for his bosses.

1

The majority of the film chronicles the desperate circumstances Gardner endures and overcomes to eventually complete the internship and prevail over his nineteen competitors. Based on a true story, the movie ends with footage of the real-life Chris Gardner, now a multi-millionaire and pillar of the finance community, glorifying the power of one man's drive for success and "happyness." Undoubtedly, Gardner did deserve the success he so struggled for. However, after watching the movie, one should wonder about those other nineteen interns in the brokerage firm. Were

2

these people so less deserving? Did they not work well into the night, every night of those six months? Did they not serve the company at the best of their capacity? Were they so **reprobate** that they should be dismissed as failures, despite having labored so intensively for six months and for nothing? According to the movie, almost all the interns secured contracts for hundreds of thousands of dollars—1981 dollars—for Dean Witter, yet in the midst of the glory awarded to Gardner, both the company and the film so easily dismissed them, their efforts, as well as their probable frustration and disappointment.

3   The movie leaves its viewers with the feel-good story of a man who faces extreme adversity and through force of iron will overcomes. It comfortably fits into the underlying assumptions of fierce capitalism as stated by one of its best spokesmen, the robber baron **tycoon,** Andrew Carnegie: "the law [of competition] may be sometimes hard for the individual, it is best for the race because it ensures the survival of the fittest in every department." In this Darwinian philosophy, Chris Gardner showed the strongest drive, the best intellect, as well as the ability to secure **lucrative** contracts for his employers. The other nineteen interns, while hard working and reasonably successful, were not able to equal Gardner's exploits. In this system, competition, therefore, raises everyone's motivation while forcing all competitors to rise to the challenge or be **vanquished**. Sounds good for the future of the species, right?

4   Wrong. This type of rapacious, hyper-competitive capitalism eventually promotes a "dog eat dog, leader of the pack" mentality where "the winner takes it all" and nothing is left for the "loser." While this type of business model may produce high sales figures for a while, it is eventually unsustainable and destructive to itself and to the people participating, for if the only thing that is valued at the end of the day is the "bottom line" in sales figures, then employees will do *anything* to surpass their competition. "Anything" may range from forgoing time with family and friends and sacrificing personal health to breaking the law, making unethical decisions, misleading customers, or sabotaging other employees. In this system, the workplace becomes a battleground where colleagues are viewed as adversaries and teamwork is a concept promoted in corporate boardrooms but **derided** by the water cooler as quaint and antiquated.

5   This fierce individualism is not limited, of course, to the brokerage house, nor is Dean Witter particularly guilty of creating a group of overly competitive, aggressive, alpha personalities bent on sales at any cost. The cult of the individual is glorified in nearly every aspect of American culture where people rise above their circumstances through great efforts on their part to eventually become wildly successful. Though the job may change, the story remains the same populist rags-to-riches narrative. In sports, a young athlete practices harder than anyone else to make it off the street by dis-

playing near supernatural physical powers; in music, a rap artist down to the last dime manages to break through with a mega-hit; in education, a high school student **defies** the odds of a poorly run school to get into Harvard. The list is endless as individuals are made heroes for overcoming incredibly challenging circumstances.

However, what is the lesson for thousands of athletes who never make it to the NBA, the rap artists who never get the album deal, the high school students who are rejected from Harvard, or the nineteen interns fired by Dean Witter? Should they just "try harder"? The most disturbing aspect of the movie, *The Pursuit of Happyness*, is that most critics only discuss it as an "inspirational story" of a man who conquers despite major adversity. Nowhere is there any substantive discussion of the flawed social system that leaves Gardner without a home and without any real job prospects. Nowhere is it mentioned how unfair Dean Witter is to the other nineteen interns who work like slaves for six months only to be cast out with nothing to show for their effort. Nowhere do we learn how through wealth or connections some people have enormous advantages against those who merely work very hard. Instead, the message of the film, as with so many other stories of the same type, asserts that "you can do whatever you want if you just try hard enough." Apparently, those who fail have only themselves to blame; they did not try hard enough, and someone was simply more motivated, more skilled, and more diligent than they were. However, the systemic problems of unequal and unfair conditions are simply elided and glossed over by focusing on the one successful individual in a forest of "failure." 6

It may be too much to ask from mainstream moviemakers not to oversimplify life's complexities. Besides, where would one find national identity, if not in the nation's cultural mythologies? However, it may not be too much to ask from critical viewers who like questioning such oversimplifications. Perhaps those viewers would have been more satisfied with a movie that would not focus entirely on Chris Gardner's success but would spare a few camera shots on those nineteen highly motivated employees who for six months played the company's "game" to be only dismissed before the next group of free interns was about to arrive. Oh, and how do we know there were no other Chris Gardners among those nineteen interns? Just because they did not make it in a system of fundamental social and economic injustice? 7

The Pursuit of Happyness was a successful movie, but unfortunately it cannot guarantee success for anyone, not even the future Chris Gardners, for it misses one very important point of real life. By focusing so much on the few amazing individuals who eventually "make it" despite their misfortunes, people become **sidetracked** from core social and institutional problems. Individuals like Chris Gardner should be highly praised but not at the expense of those who strive but "fail" in a system that is designed to create failure. 8

Discussing and Writing About The Text

Discussing Issues:

Try to interview one or more people from your family or community whom you consider successful and then try to determine what was key to their success. Present your findings to your peers and try to come up with a list of factors that may influence a person's success in life. Be sure to include a definition of "success."

Writing about the Text:

In a well-developed and organized essay, respond to the reading; be sure to support your views with pertinent examples drawn from your own experience and observations, as well as readings.

Topic 1: What are the authors' concerns about the movie *The Pursuit of Happyness*? To what extent—if at all—do you agree with these concerns?

Topic 2: How should personal success be defined and what does a person need to become successful given the existing system and circumstances? To support your opinion, you need to examine relevant and specific examples from a variety of sources.

Developing Vocabulary:

The words below may appear as part of your online quizzes. Please refer to the introduction for study strategies for learning vocabulary.

1. downtrodden
2. to ingratiate
3. scant
4. reprobate
5. tycoon
6. lucrative
7. to vanquish
8. derided
9. to defy
10. to sidetrack

Understanding the Text

Answer the following questions by carefully reviewing the authors' aruguments in the short essay.

1. What is the story in the movie *The Pursuit of Happyness*?

2. What is the message the movie tried to send to viewers?

3. Why do the authors object to the main message of the movie?

4. What are the issues that the authors identify in the movie?

Analyzing Writing

Answer the following questions by carefully reviewing the authors' arugments and writing strategies from the short essay.

1.   Isolate the counterarguments used by the authors and examine their effectiveness in the authors' reasoning process.

2.   Find the topic sentences or main themes of each paragraph in the essay. Then try to examine how focused each paragraph is.

3.   Examine the use and effectiveness of the various rhetorical techniques used in the essay.

59 The High Cost of College Education

Much of the stress of attending college has traditionally been focused on the effort required to gain admission to a favorite would-be *alma mater*. Students would mostly worry about securing a high GPA, graduating summa cum laude, garnering good letters of recommendation, and, of course, succeeding on the dreaded SATs. Increasingly, however, the challenge of college is not only about the **exertion** requisite to enter the Ivory Tower; it is how to pay the rent once they get there! Indeed, it is no great revelation that it has become progressively more difficult for students to pay the rising costs of college as tuition and fees have vastly **outpaced** income or inflation. According to The College Board's *Trends in College Pricing 2006* report, college costs for four-year public institutions have skyrocketed 54% from 1996-2006, with students paying an average of $17,200 per year for tuition, fees, books, and minimal housing expenses. As for private, non-profit universities, the National Center for Education Statistics 2006 (NCES) report on *Student Financing of Undergraduate Education 2003-2004* places their average costs at a **staggering** $28,300 per year.

Not surprisingly, the same period of time also shows a corresponding rise in loans assumed by students. In 1996, the government student loan organization (FFELP) distributed 19.7 billion dollars in loans; in 2006, they distributed over fifty-five billion dollars in loans (NCES). These figures do not include the burgeoning industry of privatized student bank loans, which distributed 10.6 billion dollars in 2003-2004 and only 1.3 billion in 1995-1996. These figures also far outweigh the 21% increase in student enrollment that occurred during the same period. According to the Project on Student Debt, an industry watch-dog group, average debt levels for graduating seniors more than doubled from $8,000 to $17,250 (a 116% rise) from 1996-2006 for public institutions. However, it is not simply the amount of money being borrowed; it is also the number of students doing the borrowing. The American Council on Education (ACE) records that from 1993-2004 the number of student loans doubled from 4.8 to 10.8 million. Of course, one should keep in mind that these numbers do not refer to law school, medical school, or business school which are even more expensive; Graduates from such public university systems matriculate with an average of $63,500 in student loan debt (ACE)

3   For most students, these additional costs are not borne by a generous Uncle Sam or paid for by pan-handling cheap t-shirts on Hollywood Blvd. Clearly, students (and their parents) suffer the consequences of a systematic lack of tax-payer support and funding of our university systems. Because of this, the *majority* of students (over 60%) graduate with substantial debt, which can be particularly **onerous** for them just starting out in their chosen profession. Lower income students are even more at a disadvantage for having "borrowed at levels that suggest a substantial share... may experience difficulty in repayment" (*Federal Student Loan Debt: 1993 to 2004*). Furthermore, even hefty student loans don't cover all the costs incurred during college. According to a study by the State PIRG's Higher Education Project, 75% of full-time students have jobs, and nearly half of them (46%) work more than twenty-five hours a week. So, if students devote more than half the work week earning a paycheck to pay tuition, how much time can they spend studying? Unavoidably and in addition to stress about money, students suffer increased anxiety due to severe limitations on time for school which can **dramatically** affect school performance, academic growth, and possible future job prospects. This seems like a **vicious circle**, and it is one students are well familiar with.

4   The most far-reaching impact of the growing mounds of student loan debt has yet to be felt, but it promises to alter the social bonds that hold our society together. No, this is not the threat that students will simply **boycott** college, for a college education is still considered a venue for future success. However, according to a 2007 survey conducted by the UCLA Higher Education Research Institute:

> Financial considerations, including future earnings, have become a much stronger motivation for all students attending college over the last 35 years. In particular, first-generation students are more likely to report 'being well off financially' as a very important or essential personal goal (81 percent vs. 73 percent) (*Executive Summary*).

This means that the vast majority of students consider their college major in direct correlation to the likelihood of high monetary earnings when selecting their careers. The choice of their vocation, in many ways, is not primarily tied to their ability, desire, or interest in a particular major; it rests squarely on how much money they can earn once they graduate.

5   The effects of this evolving **scenario** can already be seen with students flocking to majors and career paths that promise them significant financial returns even if their interests lie elsewhere. Although some may rush to explain this kind of decision-making process as evidence of greed or absent idealism in modern so-

ciety, it is entirely understandable and merely pragmatic, especially since students (and their parents) are footing more and more of the bill for college. Can one really blame students for this preoccupation with money when over 66% of graduates find it difficult to repay student loans (PEW Charitable Trust, 2006)? Take, for example, a student who graduates from a public university with thirty-thousand dollars of debt (a very reasonable estimate); with current rates and a ten-year repayment plan, the monthly payment would approach four-hundred dollars per month, and our graduate would need an approximate yearly income of $44,000 to just make the minimum payment. How likely is it, then, that students burdened with such loans will choose the career path of, say, a social worker, teacher, pastor, councilor, or police officer when those service career paths have very little to promise in terms of monetary return? How likely is it that this graduate will join the Peace Corp for two years to help out children in Africa? The student repayment plan would probably stall if not entirely banish such noble aspirations.

There are those who argue that the university system nowadays more accurately reflects the marketplace as undesirable majors with little income potential are "weeded out." Furthermore, they say, students *should pay* for their education because not only will they try harder, earn better grades, and value their education more, but they will also make better career decisions that will enable them to succeed in an increasingly competitive world. The danger, however, in allowing the marketplace to decide "value" by saddling students with enormous debt is that it erodes one of the core principles of a liberal arts education: service to the public. Not only are students having to work while attending school, they are now being forced to choose between careers that service the public and those that service the minimum student loan payment. In this new system, service-oriented jobs that don't secure six figure salaries must compete with business-oriented jobs with healthy **remuneration** packages. Furthermore, students who might have taken time to become well-rounded individuals and discover "a meaningful philosophy of life," by traveling abroad, taking courses in other majors, or donating time to a charity will have to postpone or once and for all forget about these plans and focus on making money. The goal of university systems across the U. S. had been to enable full participation in Democracy by a culturally diverse population because it was assumed that having broadly educated citizens was in the best interest of Democracy. Now, however, exposure to diverse ideas, following one's interests, and providing service for the public good must take a back seat to the **pragmatism** of debt.

6

Discussing and Writing About The Text

Discussing Issues:

In groups, try to compare the current cost for a degree in your college and compare it to the cost five to ten years ago. Select two or more other educational institutions to run the same comparison. Discuss your findings with your peers.

Writing about the Text:

In a well-developed and organized essay, respond to the reading; be sure to support your views with pertinent examples drawn from your own experience and observations, as well as readings.

Topic 1: According to the authors, in what ways does the cost of college tuition alter the individual and society? To what extent, if any, do you find their arguments convincing?

Topic 2: Do you think higher education should be free, or should college-like any other service-be paid for by those who benefit from it?

Developing Vocabulary:

The words below may appear as part of your online quizzes. Please refer to the introduction for study strategies for learning vocabulary.

1. exertion
2. to outpace
3. staggering
4. onerous
5. dramatically
6. vicious circle
7. to boycott
8. scenario
9. remuneration
10. pragmatism

Understanding the Text

Answer the following questions by carefully reviewing the authors' aruguments in the short essay.

1.   In what ways have students' concerns about college education changed in recent years?

2.   What do the statistical data indicate about the current situation with student loans?

3.   How do college expenses affect one's academic performance?

4.   How do college expenses affect personal and professional choices and society as a whole?

Analyzing Writing

Answer the following questions by carefully reviewing the authors' arugments and writing strategies from the short essay.

1. Examine the role of statistical data in the essay as well as their relevance.

2. Examine the integration of sources in the essay and their effectiveness.

3. Examine the use of cause and effect in the authors' arguments.

CHAPTER EIGHT

Science & Technology

60 Climate Change Culprits

There is no longer a shred of doubt. The climate is changing all over the globe due to global warming caused by increased greenhouse gases. Although scientists have been discussing the issue for years, there is now near unanimous **consensus** that the earth is warming at an alarming rate, and this temperature change is being caused by **emissions** of carbon dioxide (CO_2) into the environment. It doesn't require a person with a Ph.D. to determine that something unique and startling is occurring. It can be seen in the freakishly hot temperatures of which twenty of the twenty-one hottest years on record have occurred in the last twenty-five years according to Al Gore's book and similarly titled movie *An Inconvenient Truth*. It can be seen in the bizarre weather patterns, resulting in far more frequent and powerful storms such as hurricane Katrina that demolished New Orleans. It can be seen in the vast **fluctuations** in weather—even during winter—where the temperature might be hot one week and freezing the next. California avocado growers, citrus growers, and wine producers know all about this due to a prolonged cold snap in 2007 that froze and destroyed billions of dollars worth of crops. Climate change is not a forecast; it is already here.

But it isn't a surprise. Scientists have known about the mechanism for global warming for some time, for its normal function is exactly what makes the earth a hospitable environment for life. It works like this: the earth naturally has CO_2 in the atmosphere from natural forest fires, decomposition of plants into methane, even from cow manure. This blanket of gases, most of which occur naturally, operates as an insulator from the sun's fierce rays. These gases both deflect some of the sun's energy as well as trap some of it inside the atmosphere, forming an insulating layer between the earth's surface and space. Without this insulation, earth would be at zero degrees and nearly lifeless. However, with the massive build-up of CO_2 in the atmosphere due primarily to humans burning fossil fuels, this insulating layer has become so thick that it retains too much heat. It would be similar to having a heavy quilt on your bed during a summer heat wave. Because heat is trapped in the atmosphere, the polar icecaps, glaciers in Canada, and huge sections of Greenland have begun to melt at an alarming rate.

4   It may seem like a great idea to reduce the amount of ice on the planet; after all, who needs all that ice? Climatologists answer that there is a direct correlation to the amount of fresh water in the sea to increased sea temperatures, more frequent and ferocious storms, and to rising sea levels. According to a 2005 MIT study, major storms in the Atlantic Ocean have increased in **ferocity** and intensity by 50% since 1970. In 2004, the record for the most tornadoes in the U.S. was broken. In Africa, water resources are being depleted at an astonishing scale as the desert relentlessly advances. The amount of heat in the atmosphere, the amount of ice on the poles, the amount of freshwater in the oceans, and the temperature of the oceans, are all closely related.

4   The only debate among scientists now is how serious climate change will be and how much it will affect the environment and our current ways of life. Predictions to this vary because: 1) the melting of ice is occurring at a much faster rate than previously thought, making "nightmarish" scenarios distinctly possible; 2) scientists don't know whether we have passed the so-called tipping point, the point in which humans have done so much damage to the environment that global warming cannot be stopped. What is clear, however, is that global warming and climate change may alter sea level by twenty feet in the next one-hundred years, possibly affecting hundreds of millions of people and costing billions of dollars.

5   Until recently, there have been two responses to scientists reporting on climate change. The first was to deny climate change by **muzzling** federal scientists and discrediting independent reports as inconclusive. This was done through President Bush and his hand-picked director of the Environmental Protection Agency (EPA), who redacted and edited from EPA reports any mention from federal scientists about climate change (*Washington Post*, April 6, 2006). This was further perpetrated by Phillip Cooney, American Petroleum Institute lobbyist who was hired as chief of staff of the White House Environment Office under President George Bush. Of course, the White House was not alone in their climate change denying. Republican Senator James Inhofe, Chairman of the Senate's Environment & Public Works Committee, characterized global warming as "the greatest hoax perpetrated on the American people." To prove his claim, he cited Michael Crichton's fictional novel *State of Fear*.

6   The second reaction, far more common among those in power, has been the recognition that global warming affects climate change, accompanied by the consternation that curbing emissions will damage the economy too much. These naysayers have so far refused to take significant action to **stabilize**, let alone reduce greenhouse gases, especially CO_2. The argument here is that our current economy relies extensively on coal-powered power plants and that people are ad-

dicted to cheap oil. Decreasing emissions will cost too much. This argument, of course, completely elides how all the clean and environment-friendly technology already exists and can help to dramatically reduce our carbon emissions; nor does this argument mention how new "green" industries could sprout up if the government so chose to subsidize them or provide tax incentives.

Ironically, what is often missing from the discussion of global warming   7
and climate change is the average person's contribution to it. Too many Americans tend to think of global warming, if they consider it at all, as the problem created by big industries that burn coal, **belch** enormous amounts of CO_2 into the environment, and greedily consume megawatt after megawatt of energy. The truth is that *consumers in the U.S. are collectively responsible for more than half of the CO_2 emissions per year* (Energy Information Administration Report, 2007). This estimate includes all the energy used to heat our houses, care for our yards, clean our water, and power our cars. The average American citizen, despite the best of intentions, is increasingly responsible for a large share of global warming.

What we need in the United States is a moral revolution. People need to   8
treat climate change as a moral decision, not one based only on a cost/benefit analysis. Because of our individual decisions to consume far more energy than we should, suck up gallon after gallon of gas, and vote for politicians who refuse to pass comprehensive reform, we become co-conspirators in a massive crime against the other **denizens** of the earth. Who would willingly go out and shoot polar bears? Who would participate in the genocide of penguins in Antarctica? Who would order the destruction of millions of acres of rainforest? Who would condone the extinction of a thousand bird species who can't survive the changing climate? The average American would think such destruction is immoral and **reprehensible**, but we unwittingly help commit these crimes. The same American who may give money to save the penguins may buy a sport utility vehicle (SUV) to commute to work; the same American may have a huge pool which requires hundreds of dollars of electricity per month to power; the same American may vote against taxes to research alternative fuels. These choices DO affect the environment, and they are moral choices.

The answer to climate change and global warming may well lie in our-   9
selves and in our sense of personal morality. Once people finally decide to take responsibility for their actions—to see that their consumption decisions have effects—perhaps we'll move from simply wondering whether global warming is happening to personal ways of preventing it from becoming worse than it already is. Who is the **culprit** for climate change? We all are.

Discussing and Writing About The Text

Discussing Issues:

How responsible do you consider yourself and your family for this climate change? Make a list of your CO_2 contributions and then visit www.climatecrisis.org to examine your personal or family CO_2 footprint. Compare/Contrast to other students' footprints and discuss possible ways to reduce your contribution to the climate change.

Writing about the Text:

In a well-developed and organized essay, respond to the reading; be sure to support your views with pertinent examples drawn from your own experience and observations, as well as readings.

Topic 1: Whom do the authors blame for the current climate change and what do they suggest people do? To what extent—if at all—do you agree with their arguments and suggestions?

Topic 2: Analyze your community or neighborhood's contribution to the climate change problem. Try to propose and support certain solutions that would help improve the situation. Then, try to contact the people in charge of your community to present your ideas to them.

Developing Vocabulary:

The words below may appear as part of your online quizzes. Please refer to the introduction for study strategies for learning vocabulary.

1. consensus
2. emission
3. fluctuation
4. ferocity
5. to muzzle
6. to stabilize
7. to belch
8. denizen
9. reprehensible
10. culprit

Understanding the Text

Answer the following questions by carefully reviewing the authors' arugments in the short essay.

1. Which phenomena prove the ongoing occurrence of climate change?

2. What are the causes and scientific explanations of climate change?

3. Who are the culprits for climate change?

4. What are the authors' suggestions to combat climate change?

Analyzing Writing

Answer the following questions by carefully reviewing the authors' arugments and writing strategies from the short essay.

1. Discuss the use and validity of the evidence used in the essay.

2. Examine the use of the writing technique of definition in the essay.

3. Examine and discuss the effectiveness of three different rhetorical techniques used in the essay.

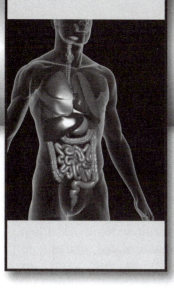

61 Harvesting Organs from the Living

A thousand thoughts race through your head as you walk down the brightly-lit streets of downtown Los Angeles, euphoric after viewing the award-winning ensemble perform *The Lion King*, its 30th **consecutive** season. You think of the expensive costumes, the extreme heat in December due to global warming, the coming year, 2020, and the challenges it will bring. You don't think anything of the three men in suits walking nearby until you feel the sharp jab in the neck as if a violent dentist missed his mark. The last thing you remember—before waking up in a local hospital having lost a kidney, an eye, your left lung, and part of your large intestine—is a utility truck filled with a stainless steel table and a rack of scalpels.

1

While this nightmarish, **futuristic** (2020) scenario of abduction and organ theft is reminiscent of William Gibson's cyberpunk world or director Ridley Scott's movie *Blade Runner* in which technology, violence, and corporations rule the streets, dramas and movies today have already envisioned a time when the surgical theft of organs might be a big business—and let there be no mistake, functioning organs are big business. Currently, according to the Battelle Institute at the Seattle Research Center, transplant costs are high: 148,000 dollars for the average heart, 51,000 dollars for a kidney, 235,000 dollars for a liver, 210,000 dollars for a lung. This is a great deal of money and represents all the costs of procuring and "installing" the new organs. Unfortunately, the current system only operates based on the donation principle. Those unlucky enough to die due to accident or crime can have their organs **harvested** if they have signed an organ-donor card. In other cases, living "Good Samaritans" can choose to donate organs to aid a close personal friend or family member. Combined, these two types of organ retrieval account for the 26,500 dollar-average transplant operations that occur every year in the United States, according to the U. S. Organ Transplant Network. Indeed, more than 26,000 transplant operations may sound significant, but there are an estimated 86,000 people on the waiting list who **morbidly** hope for someone of their blood type to die, so they obtain this person's organs—and the list keeps growing every year. Finding more donors is a huge problem, and various foundations have had only limited success in reaching out to potential donors.

2

3   Thus, while procuring organs through murder or sale may seem **ghoulish**, outlandish, or fictional, it is already happening all over the world. In 2006, according to the *South China Post*, Chinese prisoners were executed and their organs harvested to be sold on the black market. In one case, an older Japanese businessman, Kenichiro Hokamura, paid over 400,000 dollars for his new kidney that was taken directly from an executed prisoner. In defense of his actions, he argued that there are only ten kidney transplants conducted in Japan every year, so he was likely to die if he did not receive a new one; he couldn't just hope for an unknown, potential donor. As shocking as this might seem, it is not an isolated incident, according to Nancy Scheper-Hughes, Professor of Medical Anthropology at the University of California, Berkeley. According to her findings, the illegal trade in human organs is strong, **robust**, and has been going on for many years now. She should know. She heads a team of scientists who attempt to track the international (illegal) trade in organs. And this trade is on the rise despite the passage of the National Organ Transplant Act in 1984 in the U.S., which outlawed the sale of organs. Organs can be found on the black market all over the world for bargain prices.

4   The solution to this problem should not be found in the theft and later black-market sale of stolen organs. This criminalization of organ transplants makes the process far more dangerous for every participant. A black-marketer is unlikely to run all the necessary tests, screening procedures, or to pay the willing donors what they deserve. Organ recipients face time in jail or, worse, organs that have not been suitably screened. Instead, the solution lies in willing, knowing, and consenting adults who choose to "donate" their organs for money. At first, this may sound suspiciously like Jonathan Swift's satiric "A Modest Proposal" in which he **facetiously** and ironically advocates that the Irish sell their "excess" children for food. This could not be further from the truth. In this organ-sale scenario, current class and working patterns are simply taken to their logical ends—without the baggage of pseudo-ethical dilemmas. Why should a poor man—or any man for that matter—be prevented from selling a kidney, an eye, a lung, or even his heart for money?

5   Some people object to the ethical "shadiness" of selling one's organs. They claim that the only real way to have a transplant bank is to increase donor awareness. More importantly, they maintain that buying organs primarily from the poor is a supreme form of **cannibalism**. But who is having these ethical dilemmas? What these ethicists don't realize is that they can afford such high moral standards and can differentiate between selling and donating organs, but these ethical quagmires do not help the poor man who can barely survive on the scraps from the rich nor do they help the man who desperately needs an organ.

People already sell their bodies for money, and this is no allusion to the world's oldest profession, prostitution. Nowadays, prospective parents legally hire surrogate mothers who carry children to term for them and then relinquish them for money. The **surrogate** mother in question merely sells her "labor" for the best price. In a more quotidian vein, people sell the use of their bodies every-day for eight hours. Iron workers risk chronic back pain because of repeatedly lift-ing heavy loads; it is rare to find a tile-layer whose knees haven't degenerated by the age of forty-five. Even administrative assistants and staff members face Carpal Tunnel Syndrome because of stress on tendons due to repetitive typing. Most workers risk mental and physical health for an hourly wage, and this is even more prevalent in poorer countries where there is no Occupational Safety and Health Administration (OSHA) to protect them from hazardous work environments.

What is the difference in working ourselves to the bone and making a con-scious decision about our own bodies? A poor man in India should have the right to sell an extra kidney or lung for 20,000 dollars, an amount of money that would completely sustain him and his family for at least five years. For millions of peo-ple on earth, the last thing they have to sell is their bodies themselves. Who are we to deny them the opportunity to make some money with the last commodity they have? Who are we to say that a person can donate an organ out of altruism, but the same person cannot sell the organ for money?   6

The organ-sale debate is part of a larger social issue that is currently being discussed in the courts of law: the rights a person has over his or her own body and life. This debate can be seen in the statutes against assisted suicide; it can be seen in the tenets against self-mutilation; it can be seen in the **fervor** over abortion and the right of a woman to control her own body. Ultimately, organ sales should be taken off the black market and put into the commodities market as trade goods like everything else. We should put aside our pseudo-ethical dilemmas; otherwise, kidnapping for organs may become the next trend in crime.   7

Discussing and Writing About The Text

Discussing Issues:

Form two debate groups based on your positions and views on assisted-suicide. Each group is to argue their case at the Supreme Court, which consists in this case of nine neutral students. Try to construct your arguments carefully and support them with valid evidence.

Writing about the Text:

In a well-developed and organized essay, respond to the reading; be sure to support your views with pertinent examples drawn from your own experience and observations, as well as readings.

Topic 1: According to the authors, why should selling organs be legal? To what extent—if at all—do you think the authors' suggestions will be beneficial?

Topic 2: Imagine you or a person you care about is suffering from a severe heart disease and is going to die in a year from now unless a donor is found for a heart transplant. In a well-developed paper, describe the steps you would take to find a solution to this life-threatening situation.

Developing Vocabulary:

The words below may appear as part of your online quizzes. Please refer to the introduction for study strategies for learning vocabulary.

1. consecutive
2. futuristic
3. to harvest
4. morbidly
5. ghoulish
6. robust
7. facetiously
8. cannibalism
9. surrogate
10. fervor

Understanding the Text

Answer the following questions by carefully reviewing the authors' aruguments in the short essay.

1. What is the current situation in regards to organ transplants?

2. What is the authors' thesis on organ trade?

3. What are the main arguments of critics who oppose organ trade?

4. What are the main arguments of the authors on organ trade?

Analyzing Writing

Answer the following questions by carefully reviewing the authors' arugments and writing strategies from the short essay.

1. Find and evaluate rhetorical devices that the authors use in the text.

2. Examine the role and effectiveness of anecdotes in the text.

3. Examine the type of sources used in the text and evaluate their validity and effectiveness.

62 The Morality Device

The question of morality—mainly in its trespass—is often a staple in the news. A politician may be accused of **embezzling** money or breaking his marital vows in an illicit affair with a co-worker. A police officer may be the focus of an investigation for accepting bribes. A priest may be faced with condemnation for molesting little children. Your average Joe may have just entered a school and gunned down three instructors and five students. The list of lapses is continuous as is the call by prominent people or institutions for a return to the moral universe of the past. Like modern allegories of improper behavior, these incidents send us didactic messages on *how not to behave*. They become the tales of wrongdoing whose inevitable denouement is punishment of the guilty and a mandate for return to a "moral universe," until the next lapse that is.

1

For some, the "moral universe" is clear and orderly, where moral rules are objective and must simply be adhered to. According to certain moral philosophers, humans have an innate sense of morality, an interior voice that whispers to our conscience and helps us distinguish between right and wrong. It is this voice that stops a child from shoplifting in a store or stealing a friend's cell phone. It is this nagging voice that prevents us from doing whatever we want whenever we want. It is this very conflict within a person, the *psychomachia*, which forms the basis of humanity for many religions. In other words, people inherently know what is right; doing the right thing or doing the wrong thing is only a matter of choice, for people also have free-will given by God. In contrast to these beliefs of innate and universal human morality stands moral relativism, according to which morality is something that humans are conditioned to and is therefore relative and subjective. To moral relativists, there is no innate moral ground or whispering voice that forms our conscience; rather, morality depends on the situation one is put into, and every situation is relative to another.

2

The following hypothetical scenario can put these theories into a more tangible perspective. During a robbery at a bank, the perpetrators electronically get away with an **undisclosed** amount. In the process, the bank manager becomes aware of the security system penetration as well as the methods utilized by the hackers. Before calling the police, the manager has a short window of time when she can steal five million dollars without *any* chance of being caught and without *any* chance of anyone *ever* knowing of her crime. Will she commit the crime even if she knows she could do it with **impunity**? For those with moral certainty, her decision is merely a matter of utilizing the innate morality she was born with. The psychomachia, the war in her mind, would rage between her desire for personal gain and her moral duty, but she cer-

3

tainly would know what is "right."

4   On the other hand, moral relativists would take a different stance on this bank heist scenario. A moral relativist would say that the bank manager's ethical dilemma is not triggered by any **innate** moral device, but rather it was mandated by the manager's specific moral values as shaped by her family, religion, or other social factors. To even further **solidify** the subjective character of morality, the moral relativist would weave a more complex scenario regarding the punishable character of the manager's act. What if, for instance, she were to get caught; should she be condemned in all cases? What if she stole the five million dollars not for fancy cars, dinners, vacations, diamonds, or anything for herself? What if, instead, she stole the money to donate to cancer research, and because of her donation there were a major breakthrough in the treatment of cancer? This breakthrough would save millions of lives and billions of dollars in health care. In this case, would the bank manager still be found guilty? She would have committed an apparently immoral act yet for a moral if not honorable cause.

5   Moral relativists believe that no objective morality exists; morality is induced from the outside and has to be judged by the specific circumstances of each case; it is, in essence, a set of social beliefs that becomes **codified** over time into a set of value standards. People learn moral standards along with ideas of proper behavior, **decorum**, language, style, or anything else. To substantiate their claims, moral relativists use the different cultures and traditions of the world which help explain the "relativity" of morality across the globe. Indeed, outsiders visiting planet Earth might be confused by this plurality of often contradictory norms. They may wonder, for instance, about the act of killing another human being. Why are some people who kill another human being arrested, prosecuted, and incarcerated, while others are hailed as heroes and given medals? When does killing constitute "murder"?

6   The answer to this debate between innate, God-given morality versus manmade, relative morality may lie in the most unlikely of places, Darwin's 1859 publication of the *Origin of Species*. As is well-known, Darwin used this text to promulgate his ideas of evolution and to show how mankind evolved over time, ultimately descending from apes. Evolution, therefore, would squarely support the idea that human beings construct their own social belief systems. However, a growing number of philosophers, sociologists, and cultural anthropologists have been arguing that there exists a biological "morality device" in human beings, which has evolved over time. This morality device operates like a module in the brain that triggers the need for humans to develop more complex codes of human behavior in order for them to effectively adjust to the challenges of survival. In essence, some hidden part of our brains became active at a point in the distant past, triggering the morality device. Recent books such as Harvard professor Marc Hauser's *Moral Minds* even go so far as to claim that human beings are born with a "moral grammar" hardwired into the brain, a theory that builds on notable language theorist Noam Chomsky's idea of an inherent "Language Acquisition Device" and an underlying "Universal Grammar" to prove

humans' biological predisposition to learning a language. Thus, the human species evolved physically, mentally, and *morally* at the same time, roughly 50,000 years ago.

 While it is tempting to believe that religion had it right all along or that people do have an innate sense of morality, a closer look at how scientists define morality significantly **problematizes** this quick interpretation. Many cognitive psychologists, those scientists engaged in the study of the parts of the brain in question, *do not overtly claim* that morality is innate; instead, they claim that morality developed along with other cognitive functions as part of larger social systems. As early man banded together for his own protection, he needed a more developed social system that would allow for greater cooperation, survival, procreation, and expansion of the species. In this way, morality was part of the process of developing stronger social bonds between individuals and their communities. Morality wasn't necessarily about strict notions of right and wrong; it was merely and primarily concerned with ways of establishing specific parameters for human survival; so, for instance, these parameters may coincide with peaceful coexistence and cooperation among humans while other times "war" may be proclaimed as "necessary" or morally "justifiable." Morality, then, could be seen as part of a human need for organization and structure. This differentiation in definitions may seem minor, yet it helps explain a great deal of human behavior. 7

 With this definition in hand, it becomes obvious that humans may have a predisposition for morality but not necessarily a specific morality. There is no innate set of specific behavior rules that everyone is born with, for there are far too many cultural distinctions among the world's peoples for that to be true. At the same time, however, people are biologically encoded with a predisposition for rules of **governance** in social interaction. In this way, we can see that morality is not about good or evil, right or wrong; morality is about the individual's relationship with his/her community. 8

 In the end, judging people by a distinct and inflexible set of moral codes is unhelpful or even unrealistic because people's actions and moral values differ from culture to culture and situation to situation. Perhaps morality is not about finding an innate value system implanted by an unknown creator. It is rather about humans'— as individuals and as members of a community— constant **negotiation** with an existing value system. During times of relative peace, individuals may break their "moral contract" with the community, and for that there are consequences to be suffered. During times of instability in a community, moral lapses or crimes are far more likely to be committed by even average citizens because the social pact, the common and assumed agreement between individuals and society, has broken down or is in need of adjustment to changing circumstances. In both cases, however, morality is a luxury afforded to the human species but not necessarily in absolute ways. 9

Discussing and Writing About The Text

Discussing Issues:

In class discuss the hypothetical scenario of the bank robbery proposed by the authors. Organize different debate groups each supporting a different side based on specific arguments and evidence. Try to also think of similar scenarios.

Writing about the Text:

In a well-developed and organized essay, respond to the reading; be sure to support your views with pertinent examples drawn from your own experience and observations, as well as readings.

Topic 1: According to the authors, how is the issue of human morality approached by various theories? To what extent—if at all—do you agree with these views?

Topic 2: Analyze specific examples from the American or world history to prove or disprove the validity of moral relativism.

Developing Vocabulary:

The words below may appear as part of your online quizzes. Please refer to the introduction for study strategies for learning vocabulary.

1. to embezzle
2. undisclosed
3. impunity
4. innate
5. to solidify
6. codified
7. decorum
8. to problematize
9. governance
10. negotation

Understanding the Text

Answer the following questions by carefully reviewing the authors' arugments in the short essay.

1. How does religion view human morality?

2. What are the principles of moral relativism?

3. What can the theory of evolution contribute to the definition of human morality?

4. What is the authors' approach to human morality?

Analyzing Writing

Answer the following questions by carefully reviewing the authors' aruments and writing strategies from the short essay.

1. Examine the use and effectiveness of definition in the text.

2. Find the focus of each paragraph, and write it in the margin next to each paragraph. Is each paragraph organized around a specific focus or not?

3. Examine the role and effectiveness of rhetorical strategies in the text.

63   The Fear Effect

Lest anyone become too comfortable or too happy in life, members of the Bulletin of Atomic Scientists announced in January of 2007 that the "Doomsday Clock" would be advanced to five minutes to midnight. Founded in 1947 by scientists concerned with the possibility of nuclear war, this metaphorical clock was established to indicate humanity's proximity to absolute disaster and the destruction of civilization. Right now, the clock is awfully close to the witching hour because of the real threats of nuclear war and climate change. But if these are insufficient reasons to be scared, one need only watch the host of television shows on PBS, CBS, ABC, or The Discovery Channel to recognize that anything and everything might **extinguish** our frail human existence. The airing by ABC of the program "The Last Days of the Earth" is typical of this trend. In this program, the anchor categorizes the top seven threats to humanity and the planet based on a poll of participating scientists. Number seven in the list is a Black hole, which may—over millions or billions of years—suck in every last bit of our galaxy and grind it to dust. If the Black hole doesn't destroy us, a large meteor like the one that killed the dinosaurs sixty-five-million years ago might do so by triggering 3,000 foot tall tsunamis and **catapulting** the earth into a thousand-year ice age. Of course, humanity might die out before the ice chills our fingers through a killer virus genetically engineered by artificially intelligent computers. If we are lucky, however, global warming might **offset** the effects of a nuclear winter.

1

For those who believe, the Book of Revelations in the *Bible* foretells the end of the world, so it should come as no real surprise that **apocalypse** is on its way even if we haven't seen the horses yet. But the end of the world is not all that people have to fear. The nightly news screens like a list of potential horrors one ought to fear, one more gruesome than the next. Newscasters alert the public to the danger of child molesters, burglars, tornadoes, E-coli bacteria, avian flu, flesh-eating bacteria, terrorists, car-wrecks, airplane crashes, car bombs. Less catastrophic but still hazardous might be snakebites, killer bees, shark attacks, slipping on ice, or lightning strikes. Of course, this is not to minimize the personal harm that might befall a victim of any of these occurrences, for it is no laughing matter if it happens to you, but many people experience fear of potential harm without consider-

2

ing the real and **minute** possibility of harm actually befalling them.

3   The problem is that people in the U.S. tend to mostly fear all the wrong things while avoiding thinking about the dangerous life choices that have a much higher statistical likelihood of affecting them. Looking at the 2003 data set for American deaths (the most recent data set available), we see that two people died from snakebite, forty-seven died from lightning strike, sixty-six died from bee-stings, none died from mad-cow disease or avian flu, and only forty-three died from salmonella. All of this occurred in a country of three-hundred million, so the statistical likelihood of any of these tragedies happening to an individual is minis-cule. The same American who dreads the last days on earth as well as snake bites ought to realize that in 2003 685,089 Americans died of heart disease, 556, 902 died from cancer, and 157,689 died from stroke (*Time*, December 4, 2006).

4   One explanation for this inability to rationalize fear can be found in our own physiology. Some scientists claim that the instinctual part of the brain that controls our response to fear, the Amygdala, doesn't have the capacity to distin-guish between *likely* and *hypothetical* danger. Based on fight or flight, the Amyg-dala discerns so-called immediate threats and fires nerve-synapses to the upper regions of the brain in order to induce a reaction. What the Amygdala doesn't do very well at all is calculate likely or long-term dangers. Thus, it may signal the brain to respond to an increased terrorist threat level even if the probable personal danger is very small. On the other hand, the Amygdala might not respond to a re-port about the increased risk of heart disease due to poor diet habits.

5   According to some scientists, the failure to respond to long-term risks is re-lated to the so-called "dread effect" whereby people fear pain and suffering more than, say, a disease that kills in a **chronic** and distributed way, like heart disease. For this reason, people's fear-response may be triggered by hearing of a brutal robbery or attack even if such an attack is quite isolated. People in New York, for instance, still remember the 1964 stabbing and murder of Kitty Genovese, whose screams for help were unanswered by thirty-eight bystanders. People still re-member the Zodiac serial killer, the BTK serial killer, Jack the Ripper, and a host of others whose horrifying crimes keep shocking audiences. Of course, peoples' dread response might be invoked by less violent examples: a car accident where children are trapped in the mangled wreckage; a child who falls down a well and is covered by debris; climbers trapped at high altitude in a snow blizzard. The list of horrors goes on and on, but the common element in nearly every case is the in-tensity and dread of the particular situation. People inevitably imagine themselves in the same situation, **empathizing** with the protagonists of these scenarios de-spite the statistical improbability of such an event befalling them. In short, peo-

ple psychologically respond to intense scenarios, but they respond much less to distributed dangers.

The awful truth is that promoting fear is profitable business as can be seen   6
by the sensationalist headlines for most news programs. According to Thomas Patterson of the Kennedy School of Government, crime stories now **dominate** the vast majority of local news coverage and additional "soft" stories, stories with a sensationalist or salacious bent, fill out the rest (*Doing Well and Doing Good*, 2000). Coverage of "hard" stories, material that is deemed important for people to consider when making policy or voting decisions, has declined significantly since the 1980s, and media executives are open and forthright about the change in news coverage from what people need to know (hard stories) to what people are interested in (soft stories). The end result is a host of melodramatic, salacious, and fear-provoking programs that cater far more to the primitive response of the Amygdala rather than the more rational aspects of the human mind.

Producing fear, once the province of haunted houses and amusement park   7
rides, has become the main staple of the media at large. But the real tragedy may still be waiting in store. The more the media caters to the sensational and fear-provoking, the less time they spend on stories and programs of substance that people need in order to make coherent and rational decisions about public policy. The irony here is that democracy itself may be the next **casualty** as Thomas Patterson **intimates**: "Democracy cannot operate effectively without a free press that performs well as watchdog and information source. In other words, the press must do its job well if democracy is to succeed" (*Doing Well and Doing Good*, 15). If the media continues to cater to our base instincts by promulgating and creating a culture of fear, our democratic society, based on an informed and rational citizenry, is not long for this world. Now, that is something to fear.

Discussing and Writing About The Text

Discussing Issues:

In groups watch an hour of TV news on different channels and record the techniques or strategies used to induce fear in the average reader. Report your findings to the rest of the class and compare them to those of other groups of students.

Writing about the Text:

In a well-developed and organized essay, respond to the reading; be sure to support your views with pertinent examples drawn from your own experience and observations, as well as readings.

Topic 1: According to the authors, how does fear affect the average American? To what extent—if at all—do you agree with this view point?

Topic 2: Make a proposal on how the average American could be educated to rationalize and counter fear.

Developing Vocabulary:

The words below may appear as part of your online quizzes. Please refer to the introduction for study strategies for learning vocabulary.

1. to extinguish
2. to catapult
3. to offset
4. apocalypse
5. minute (adj)
6. to empathize
7. dominate
8. to cater to
9. casualty
10. to intimidate

Understanding the Text

Answer the following questions by carefully reviewing the authors' aruguments in the short essay.

1. What are the "Doomsday Clock" and the seven threats to earth and civilization?

2. Why are the authors skeptical about people's common fears?

3. What is the scientific explanation to people's fears?

4. How is the average person's fear used and what dangers stem from this exploitation?

Analyzing Writing

Answer the following questions by carefully reviewing the authors' arugments and writing strategies from the short essay.

1. Examine the tone and style of the first paragraph in its role as an introduction to the essay.

2. Examine three topic sentences for how they effectively (or not) orient the reader.

3. Examine the use and type of sources used in support of the authors' arguments. Evaluate their effectiveness.

64 In Defense of Video Games

A lot of ink has been spilled in condemning video games for any number of social ills and potential catastrophic consequences. The typical portrayal of avid gamers has become commonplace: the addicted gamer, often an unsocial teenager, who remains locked in his room for hours on end, skips meals and human contact, and gradually becomes more prone to violence due to the games he engages in. Anecdotal evidence from a variety of newspapers props up this stereotype as parents seem to become increasingly concerned about the effects of video games on their children. Actually many parents could be worried given that 75% of America's youth have computers and 40% of those regularly play video games (*CQ Researcher*, Nov 2006). The press rarely has a good word to say about video games; instead, stories are written and arguments are made connecting violent video-game play to school shootings as happened with the shootings at Columbine High School in Colorado in a *BBC News* report of the period (May 2001). However, concern and condemnation are not solely the province of newspapers. According to Dr. David Walsh of the National Institute on Media and the Family, violent video games can further explain violence, for they provide a "greater arousal" of **endorphins** and adrenaline than non-violent games. In addition to possible violence, computer addiction, especially to video games, appears to be a prevalent pandemic among the population. Indeed, judging from the tone of reports like CBS's "Detox for Video Game Addiction," addiction is wide-spread and threatening to ruin our youth (*CBS*, July 3rd, 2006).

The list of video-game ills doesn't stop with the threat of increased violence or harmful addiction. According to their critics, video games may be responsible for distracting students from studying, for harming relationships, and for robbing players of real-life experiences and contact with other human beings. The problem, however, is that concrete evidence of the deleterious effects of video games is seldom, if ever offered up. Ironically, all the concerns of parents, scientists, and reporters may be entirely wrong, **fanned** into a firestorm by ignorance and supposition. In fact, most gamers are not socially isolated, for they regularly participate in sports or cultural activities, read books, and volunteer in charities to the tune of twenty-four hours per month whereas their average game play totals only about

1

2

seven hours a month (*CQ Researcher*, November 2006). Another grand misconception about video gamers is that they are mostly teens with potential identity problems—all **misanthropes** silently **hoarding** weapons in their gothically decorated rooms until they meet a violent end. On the contrary, according to an Entertainment Software Association annual sales and demographics report, 25% of gamers are over fifty, 44% are aged eighteen to forty-nine, and only 31% are under eighteen. Indeed, the average gamer is thirty-three years old and has been playing for ten to twelve years. Oh, and 38% of all gamers are women. Clearly, the public has been misinformed about the actual demographics of video game play and the dangers posed to players.

3   Ironically, certain video games may even be beneficial to players. If Prof. James Gee of the University of Wisconsin has his way, people will realize that video games actually prepare players for a competitive job market. His book, *What Video Games Have to Teach Us About Learning and Literacy* (2003), was one of the first academic texts to really confront the **conventional** wisdom that video games waste a player's time and also harm players in numerous **irrevocable** ways. Since then, other social critics and scientists have begun arguing the case for video games in the public consciousness with a recent foray launched by Stephen Johnson's book *Everything Bad Is Good for You* (2006), which argues that game play teaches kids the scientific method through hypothesis and testing.

4   Indeed, many of the most popular games (World of Warcraft, The Sims2, Guild Wars, Roller Coaster Tycoon 3, Battlefield 2, Age of Empires III, Call of Duty 2) demand far more than the automatic reflexes of a "couch potato." Instead, they require strategic thinking, interpretive analysis, active problem solving, longitudinal and short-term planning, establishment of objectives, and adaptation to change. In point of fact, these are not the same kind of games that Atari introduced back in the 1980s. These are **multi-faceted**, complicated scenarios that take hours and sometimes days to unfold. If players fail to make sound, strategic decisions along the way, then their character (known as an avatar) will fail or die. Take any of the Sims **simulations** as an example (now in their 4th version). Will Wright and Jeff Braun developed these complicated games to simulate the effects of the decision-making process of those in power on a simulated city. Players conceive, design, and build their "ideal" city, face natural calamities, balance budgets, fight smog, and manage an unruly population. Thus, if a player builds too many factories near a downtown area, traffic will crawl during rush hour, and people will complain about the smog. Too many complaints means the player loses the game for not being "reelected" mayor.

According to the American Federation of Scientists, games like SimCity 5
can even be used to reinforce the education system by emphasizing skills that employers need but the existing education system does not **foster** adequately (2006
Report). Games like SimCity prepare gamers for work environments where employees need to respond to situations objectively, strategically, and tactically. Even
war games like World of Warcraft or Age of Empires teach participants how to
manage "armies," monitor supplies, or anticipate tactics of enemy **combatants**.
Much of the time spent playing these video games revolves around planning and
supplying characters and armies, not around actual battle. As in real life, having
the right equipment and logistics makes all the difference.

Moreover, for fifteen to twenty million players a week, games are not iso- 6
lated events; they are played online with a community of other participants who
either join into teams or play against each other. With current technology (software and bandwidth), players can engage in real-time chats, instant messages, and
even video conferences to determine the best decisions. How different is this from
some of the activities that students in high schools or universities are asked to perform when working as part of a team on a large project? This training in collab-
oration not only doesn't isolate gamers, but it also trains them in negotiating in a
collaborative environment, an important feature of many job situations.

So, it seems that the uproar about video games may be just that: much ado 7
about nothing. The actual demographics show a distinctly different gaming population than what is commonly perceived of in the press. While some video games
like the incredibly violent Grand Theft Auto *may* lead to future violence (characters beat and murder people on the street), no statistics beyond the occasional anecdote have been provided, and it is certainly not true for all games. Indeed, the
most popular video games in the U. S. are primarily based on simulations and
strategy, which help hone skills players will definitely need in a competitive job
environment and in real life. Perhaps in a few years, job interviews will include
questions like "What video games do you play and for how long?"

Discussing and Writing About The Text

Discussing Issues:

Make a list of all the video games you have played; try to determine the beneficial or negative effects those games have had on your character, relationships, and overall development as a person. Compare your findings to those of your peers.

Writing about the Text:

In a well-developed and organized essay, respond to the reading; be sure to support your views with pertinent examples drawn from your own experience and observations, as well as readings.

Topic 1: According to the authors, in what ways are video games misunderstood by the public? To what extent—if at all—do you think the authors are correct about this assertion?

Topic 2: In an argument paper, try to correlate a job in a field of your interest to one or more video games you have played. Discuss whether your gaming experience has honed skills and attributes employers may value in your particular career choice.

Developing Vocabulary:

The words below may appear as part of your online quizzes. Please refer to the introduction for study strategies for learning vocabulary.

1.	endorphin	2.	to fan
3.	misanthrope	4.	to hoard
5.	conventional	6.	irrevocable
7.	multi-faceted	8.	simulation
9.	to foster	10.	combatant

Understanding the Text

Answer the following questions by carefully reviewing the authors' aruguments in the short essay.

1. What are the arguments made against video games?

2. What are the misconceptions about the average gamer?

3. In what ways do the authors believe that video games can be beneficial?

4. What are the main traits of games such as SimCity?

Analyzing Writing

Answer the following questions by carefully reviewing the authors' arugments and writing strategies from the short essay.

1. Examine the organization of the essay at the paragraph and the overall levels.

2. Examine the use and effectiveness of sources of evidence in the text.

3. Examine the use and effectiveness of counterarguments in the text.

65 Cultural Memory in a Digital Age

The profession of historian may soon be relegated to the past, for in the near future there may be no "new" history to study. No, this is not the dystopic dream inspired by George Orwell's *1984* where records of current events or even words are systematically destroyed. This is not the systematic attempt of governments or private industry to **clandestinely** shelve electronic documents and then let time eat away at magnetic disks. This is just the Internet Age where phenomenal growth in information has also meant **phenomenal** loss of content. The simple phrase "Here today, gone tomorrow" may well capture the essence of the issue.

Students today can already understand what this means. Plenty of researchers have found out the hard way that using electronic resources for any kind of project may prove quite complicated; often the website or link they found so interesting, **scintillating**, and authoritative is gone with the press of a button or the loss of funding for the server. Even standard maintenance of a website can significantly alter its content as old links and information are taken out and changed for new information. This constant updating may sound like a grand idea, for one can always have the most recent information, but what happens to the old? What is to be told to future generations about the dawn of the Internet when nothing exists from that era, for everything will have been deleted in this updating process? This may prove to be a silent, on-going, cultural **genocide** that few people have noticed is occurring at all.

Examining the legacy of two wars helps illustrate the current problem. When historian and filmmaker Ken Burns completed his famous documentary series on the Civil War, sixteen-million people watched PBS every night and were able to understand far more about the conflict that nearly destroyed the young country, engaged three-million soldiers in battle, and left 600,000 of them dead. Burns masterfully cobbled together a grand **narrative** that reached from Savannah, Georgia to Albany, New York with the help of 16,000 old photographs and thousands of letters from the period. However, Burns' monumental series (with five hundred hours of edited material) might easily have been condensed to an hour of facts taken from government statistics offices if he hadn't had access to the myriad of archival resources from the period. What could a Ken Burns say a hundred

1

2

3

or two-hundred years from now about the wars in Iraq or Afghanistan? Perhaps only little. The irony, of course, is that the conflict in Iraq is vastly publicized and reported on. There are real-time blogs posted by soldiers on the field; there are emails sent to loved ones about daily life in the country; there are thousands of webpages discussing the political implications of Iraq policy. However, it is very likely that all of these will be gone or deleted in ten years, let alone a hundred. The blogger, the webpage designer, the person who emails, all have to make a conscious effort to save these electronic documents for posterity. More than likely, however, these records will simply be lost, and there will be nothing for historians a hundred years from now to study and interpret the events and culture of the day.

4   This is a question of the survival of one's cultural history, for what is a people without any type of cultural or historical memory? When the Internet was announced in 1991, there were fifty Internet servers; now there are more than eighty-five-million servers with more coming online every day. However, what if a researcher wanted to write a history of the Internet in its first few years by viewing some of the original webpages that were posted? Well, this task would be almost impossible, for those pages have been updated, deleted, or lost. Even if researchers found archived websites from the period (the first real archival service started in 1996), they probably wouldn't have the software to view the websites to begin with. What if they found a 5 ¼" disk with a few records on it? Where could they find a disk drive to read it? The disk would most likely be **corrupted** because discs deteriorate over time. The third handicap is that researchers would not have a program to read such a disk. These are significant problems just fifteen or twenty years after the **advent** of the Internet and related programs. Would anyone have the resources to view such "historical documents" a hundred or a thousand years from now? Not likely.

5   Museums, as one expects, have been among the first to respond to this growing catastrophe. The Smithsonian, one of the world's largest museums, published its "Conservation of Digital Records Initiative" in 2006, which aims at "preservation, conservation, and appropriate management" of digital content, ranging from websites to computer programs. The publication explores the proper system for digital-record storage, which is a major decision in the preservation process. At present, there is no agreed-upon format for storing material, so every museum or even business that tries to **archive** material could have their own format that is unreadable by anyone else.

The most pressing issue may very well be the elephant in the room that no one sees. Indeed, many museums, governments, and even businesses have initiated **nascent** attempts at archiving "important" documents, despite the different formats, computer codes, and saving procedures available. On the other hand, there is only limited discussion of what should be saved. What, in fact, constitutes a "historical or cultural artifact" that might be of interest to someone a hundred years from now? It does not seem reasonable or possible to archive the millions of emails sent every day or the millions of websites updated daily. There isn't world, time, or money enough for that. Thus, archivists have to make important decisions for future historians about which content **merits** saving and which does not.

6

The average American has probably never thought of digital preservation, but its effects—if not consistently countered by both museums and average people alike—will be the loss of historical and cultural continuity. Without it, future historians may not be able to track the changes in language, culture, or way of life. Cultural anthropologists might discover a box full of degrading disks in an attic one hundred years from now, but they won't be able to even read them, let alone appreciate them. These disks will simply be more junk from the lost years of the twenty-first century.

7

Discussing and Writing About The Text

Discussing Issues:

In groups try to come up with a list of artifacts you consider worth saving and preserving for future generations.

Writing about the Text:

In a well-developed and organized essay, respond to the reading; be sure to support your views with pertinent examples drawn from your own experience and observations, as well as readings.

Topic 1: According to the authors, in what ways is the history threatened in the digital age? To what extent—if at all—do you think the authors are justified in their fears and skepticism?

Topic 2: According to your opinion, what should be the criteria for deciding what constitutes a "cultural" or "historical" artifact and why?

Developing Vocabulary:

The words below may appear as part of your online quizzes. Please refer to the introduction for study strategies for learning vocabulary.

1. clandestinely
2. phenomenal
3. scintillating
4. genocide
5. narrative
6. corrupted
7. advent
8. to archive
9. nascent
10. to merit

Understanding the Text

Answer the following questions by carefully reviewing the authors' aruguments in the short essay.

1. How has the digital age affected the way history and culture are preserved?

2. In what way is the example of Ken Burns significant for historians today?

3. What is the "Conservation of Digital Records Initiative" and what does it entail?

4. Why are the authors skeptical about the "Conservation of Digital Records Initiative"?

Analyzing Writing

Answer the following questions by carefully reviewing the authors' arugments and writing strategies from the short essay.

1. Examine the use of classification in the text.

2. Examine the paragraph organization and focus by finding the topic sentence(s) of each paragraph.

3. Examine the use and effectiveness of rhetorical techniques in the text.

66 Shooting into the Blogosphere

Does the name "Jorn Barger" ring any bells? The name may mean nothing to you, but the term "blog," which was coined by her back in 1997, probably rings many or rather millions of bells. No, a "blog" is not a new alien species in George Lucas's Star Wars series. Short for "weblog," it can be generally defined as a series of consecutive narratives posted to a website and read by the public in reverse chronological order, with the most recent submission often being read first. Now, despite Barger's **prescient** turn of phrase in coining the term that would one day be on everyone's tongue, as recently as 2003 very few people even knew what a blog was, let alone how to access the one million blogs in existence then. If only one knew how much change the intervening years would bring! Indeed, according to Technorati, a leading search engine for blogs, as of 2007 the number of registered blogs has not only ballooned to 71 million, but it has been doubling every six months. So, even though many traditional word processors still don't recognize the word "blog," the latter's prevalence on the Internet has led to the coining of another term: "blogosphere." From the Greek "logos" for word and "sphere" for world, the "blogosphere" labels and signifies a new "force of culture."

With as many as 120,000 weblogs being created every day, or, in other words, 1.4 blogs being registered per second, this brave new world shows no shortage of new citizens willing to participate in its rampant democracy. There is, in short, no dearth of verbiage being posted to the blogosphere, with an estimated 1.5 million posts (uploaded material) per day according to Technorati's 2007 *State of the Blogosphere* report. Interestingly, it is the political clout of blogs that seems to **capture** all the headlines. These blogs are credited, for instance, for altering the 2006 Congressional midterm elections to allow the Democratic Party to take the House and the Senate; bloggers were even afforded the same rights as traditional journalists in a 2006 California court decision, one of the **contentious** issues of public policy of late. Because of blogs' prevalence on the political scene (there are thousands of politically-oriented blogs in addition to all the political candidates' own blogs), there has developed a significant and interesting debate about the role of the citizenry in shaping and creating public policy as the numerous editorials found both online and in traditional newspapers will attest to. Even Al Gore, the former Vice President, in his new book *The Assault on Reason* (2007), holds out blogs (and the Internet in general) as the primary hope for re-engaging the populace in political discourse and distancing it from a failing Democracy.

3   Lost, however, in the conversation about the political content of the blogosphere is a phenomenon as culturally significant as the participation of citizens in the construction and regulation of their government: it is the relationship of the individual to the community. Despite the monocular vision of blogs as the future of activism of all kinds, the *vast majority* of the seventy-one million blogs available for viewing are not political or politically motivated at all; they are deeply personal in nature—like virtual diary entries submitted from ordinary people about the quotidian events in their lives. What has gone virtually unnoticed is the ongoing renegotiation of what people, specifically bloggers, consider fit for public consumption. A tour through any of a hundred popular blog spots clearly shows how the line between private and public has begun to **blur** to such an extent that it is almost unrecognizable. Intimate details about family and friends are aired online for anyone and everyone to read and what would have been considered in the past "dirty laundry" or "family secrets" to be strictly guarded with the rest of the skeletons in the closet is now openly flaunted. From cheating on boyfriends to battling cancer to committing crimes, every topic seems to be "appropriate" for one's posting pleasure.

4   This publicization of private life represents a significant change in the way people relate to each other. In the not-so-distant past, people wrote their private thoughts in diaries, hiding these sacred books away from the **prying** eyes of siblings and certainly strangers. Perhaps some of the secrets, hopes, aspirations, internal conflicts, or innermost fears might have been shared with close friends or family, but they certainly would not have been broadcasted for the world to see. Nowadays, blogging could be viewed as the equivalent of spray-painting the contents of one's journal all over the walls of the high school gymnasium: everyone welcome. Of course, the "public" only has access to what the individual blogger decides to post online. They can choose not to write anything personal at all, or they can choose to limit who has access to their blog by selecting a group of **confidants** with viewing privileges. Interestingly, however, many bloggers elect to make their intimate details available to anyone with as secret a password as an Internet connection.

5   The traces of this process of publicizing the minutiae of private life could be first traced in the public's interest in celebrities' private lives. Indeed, there has always been at least some curiosity about what celebrities are "really like" or what they do when not "performing," but the trend for more detailed access to their private lives has been accelerating since Federico Fellini coined the term *paparazzi*, meaning tabloid photographer or journalist, in 1960 in his film *La Dolce Vita*. Indeed, looking back, what was known about the personal life of Frank Sinatra during the height of his popularity? Not much. Today, on the other hand, the public has a bird's eye view of the break-up of Brad Pitt and Jennifer Aniston, the steamy romance of Brad Pitt and Angelina Jolie, the status of Tom Cruise and Katie Holmes' ultrasound device, or any of a hundred other "newsworthy" sto-

ries. Celebrities even use stories about their personal lives to strategically market themselves as can be seen with "tell-all" articles that appear whenever the rich and the famous need more publicity.

Of course, the celebrity gossip machine is simply the tip of the iceberg, for it has merely paved the way for the extreme display of personal information so rampant in blogs today. What is most bothersome, however, is the profound social implications this shift in what is considered "personal" versus "public" has had over the last fifty years. In many ways this shift in information disclosure has been privileging the "self" above the community, and has enhanced solipsism, the egoistic absorption in the self, among people, who believe that the daily details of their lives should be interesting to anyone. Furthermore, although ironically publicizing the "self" at first appears as if it **forges** stronger bonds between community members who view these blogs, in reality it simply elides any distinction between friend or acquaintance as can be seen by the number of "friends" a person can have on MySpace just by opening an account.

6

The blogger who **divulges** personal intimacies in the ear of any web browser seems to display an interesting form of narcissism that transfers the center of gravity of a relationship. While in the past this information would have privileged the most trustworthy of the circle of friends or family, now it is only exposed in order to get the attention of…anybody. While in the past this information would have been shared to strengthen a bond between people, now it is scattered unselectively for the sake of what? What could a blogger possibly expect from this audience of complete strangers, but attention to the self regardless of whether that attention is interest, sympathy, admiration, or mere salacious curiosity?

7

Besides the promotion of a new form of narcissism and the redefining of relationships, this need to publicize the self has been altering personality in other unforeseen ways. Indeed, ordinarily a person who keeps a diary designed to never be read might be more forthcoming, honest, or **introspective**. Through the process of writing and self revealing in absolute "isolation," a person may realize something about themselves that they never would have guessed or dared admit about themselves. A "diary," however, that is posted on a blog cannot significantly aid in self-discovery, for it inherently includes an element of performance; by definition, such a blog-diary is **conceived** and written with an audience in mind which defeats the purpose of keeping a diary. And even though one could claim that many diary holders secretly crave an audience, ultimately, such shooting into the blogosphere of so much personal information about oneself actually limits the process of discovery of the self and fails to connect people in deep, significant, and meaningful ways.

8

Discussing and Writing About The Text

Discussing Issues:

Find and examine the characteristics of personal blogs that you can find online. Make a list of these characteristics and discuss your findings with your peers. Also, compare your assessment of these blogs to the arguments of the authors.

Writing about the Text:

In a well-developed and organized essay, respond to the reading; be sure to support your views with pertinent examples drawn from your own experience and observations, as well as readings.

Topic 1: According to the authors, what are the implications inherent in today's personal blogs? How valid and/or accurate do you consider the authors' concerns?

Topic 2: Analyze the ways in which blogs could function as a beneficial or detrimental force in today's society.

Developing Vocabulary:

The words below may appear as part of your online quizzes. Please refer to the introduction for study strategies for learning vocabulary.

1. **prescient**
2. **to capture**
3. **contentious**
4. **to blur**
5. **prying**
6. **confidant**
7. **to forge**
8. **to divulge**
9. **introspective**
10. **to conceive**

Understanding the Text

Answer the following questions by carefully reviewing the authors' aruguments in the short essay.

1.   What is a blog and how significant is it in today's society?

2.   What are the different kinds of blogs that affect culture?

3.   According to the authors, in what ways do personal blogs affect personality?

4.   According to the authors, in what ways do personal blogs affect relationships?

Analyzing Writing

Answer the following questions by carefully reviewing the authors' aruguments and writing strategies from the short essay.

1. Examine the use and effectiveness of definition in the text.

2. Underline five or more rhetorical devices that the authors use and discuss their effectiveness. Then try to replace them with alternative ones.

3. Find the focus-theme of each paragraph, and write it in the margin next to each paragraph. Is each paragraph organized around a specific focus or not?

CHAPTER
NINE

Relationships

67 Is Philanthropy a Bad Idea?

It might seem an oxymoron or even **hubris** to argue that **philanthropy** is a bad idea, for what more noble humanitarian aid can one offer to one's fellow denizens on earth than to give money towards their welfare? Giving away money, even when you are rich, is never easy. Philanthropists who have separated themselves from their hard-earned money should be lauded and applauded for their generosity; it must have been gut-wrenching for Bill and Melinda Gates to donate thirty billion (yes, with a "B") dollars when they established their Foundation or for Warren Buffett, famed for his savvy stock trades, to announce he was giving roughly thirty-one billion ("B" again) to the Gates' **treasure-trove**. Almost overnight, the Gates Foundation turned into a company the size of Disney, Dell, or Honda whose major auspice is to spread charity throughout the world.

1

There is no denying how important the work is that philanthropic institutions do or how important is the money that the rich give to them; there is no denying the lives that are saved or altered in the process of **doling out** large grants and donations; and there is no denying the generosity of normal people in the United States who in 2005 gave a total of 62.7 billion dollars to the top four-hundred charities alone (*Chronicle of Philanthropy*, Jan 2007). There is no denying that philanthropies fill an important social role by providing seed money for hospitals, schools, AIDS research, global health care, and even food for the hungry. Bravo!

2

The problem does not lie with the sixty-eight thousand philanthropies that exist in the U.S. alone; it lies with the government institutions and policies that require them to exist in the first place; it lies with the laws and tax shelters that allow such inequities to persist to the point that before establishing his Foundation, Bill Gates could have given ten dollars to *every person on earth* and still have ten billion left over. Our modern capitalist system—global in scale—has produced a world total of 7.7 million millionaires who control over thirty trillion dollars (with a "T") worth of assets (*CNN*, June 9th, 2005). CNN attributes the increase in millionaires to "strong economic growth, low interest rates, and tax relief." In the U.

S. in particular, tax loopholes and pro-business laws have put more and more of the tax burden on the common man while creating fertile ground for the rich to get richer.

3   It's not that the rich get richer and hoard all their cash as greedy **misers**. The rich do give to charity, especially if they see such giving as part of their social duty to those less fortunate. However, charitable giving is just that—charity. It is not obligatory, and it isn't a tax. Donors can choose to give however much they want, if they want. Thus, while columnists compose encomiums for Gates, Buffett, and a host of other affluent donors, they don't realize that these individuals do not have to give a single dime to anyone; this happened, for instance, in 2005 when the gifts from the richest donors dropped from ten billion to 4.3 billion. Thus, charities cannot really estimate how much money they might have from year to year because they rely almost exclusively on those who may or may not donate.

4   What all this means is that there is a breakdown in the social contract. No man or woman should be allowed to own so much while nearly 25% of the world's population struggles to get by on one dollar a day. The inequitable system of laws, the perverse system of globalization, the ability of corporations to utilize tax loopholes, the steady decline of real wages, and the governments that only marginally care for the average citizen, all contribute to making philanthropies absolutely necessary. Because governments, especially the U.S. government, have declined their obligations to their citizenry and have by and large supported corporations, there are currently forty-eight-million Americans who don't have health care, there is 12% of the population living in poverty (about forty million people), while the burden for the limited social system falls more on the middle class than on any other group.

5   Unlike government institutions that are legally obligated to care for their citizens regardless of their race, ethnic identity, sexual orientation, or religious backgrounds, philanthropies have no such obligation. Since they are private institutions, usually set up by a founding member with a distinct political or social agenda, they can choose to benefit a specific cause through philanthropic enterprises. Thus, Bill and Melinda Gates set up their Foundation with a focus on world health, a very worthy goal. However, they just as easily could have set up their foundation to promote Jewish identity, homosexual acceptance, or a particular religious interpretation of the *Bible*. If they had been so inclined, they could have

set up a foundation that offered help to people who would worship them as deities. In fact, according to Joel Fleshman's book *The Foundation: A Great American Secret* (2007), foundations from Carnegie to Rockefeller supported eugenics experiments into the 1930s.

Philanthropies are too often tied to specific belief systems and agendas, 6 which in and of themselves may not be negative; however, in order for a person to receive the help they need, they have to pay lip-service to the **agenda** of the philanthropy. Take, for example, some of the food banks or homeless shelters run by Christian churches. Undoubtedly, these churches occupy an important role in the community by providing essential services to the most needy. However, these services, even in their most **benign** form, come with the cost of possible pressure **to convert** to a certain belief system. This may seem, for many people, entirely acceptable, for belief in God is considered as important as the saving of the flesh. Yet should someone in need of food have to convert?

At any rate, this is the case of "acceptable" philanthropies. What of un- 7 acceptable ones? What if local churches refused to serve needy African Americans, Jews, Whites, Asians, or any other group they deemed unworthy? What if a new local philanthropy, The Church of the **Immaculate** Devil, came into being and its volunteers handed out food baskets and offered beds to the homeless? The only catch would be to listen to how the Devil makes life so interesting and that through the Devil their situation in the world could be changed by simply behaving in a more "evil" manner. Would any object to this less "acceptable" philanthropy?

Philanthropies have become an integral part of the social support system 8 in the U. S. because the government is not fulfilling its social obligations. Instead, tax laws and codes systematically excuse corporations and the rich of much of their responsibility for a healthy body politic. So, into this vacuum steps a myriad of foundations, charities, and philanthropies founded by grants from the very wealthy and the donations of simple citizens. The difference is that they choose to give part of their fortunes, which keeps the **decrepit** system operating as is. What would happen if they simply did not donate their billions?

Discussing and Writing About The Text

Discussing Issues:

In your class, design a possible philanthropy institution for your school or your community.

Writing about the Text:

In a well-developed and organized essay, respond to the reading; be sure to support your views with pertinent examples drawn from your own experience and observations, as well as readings.

Topic 1: Why do the authors doubt the role of philanthropy in society? To what extent—if at all—do you agree with the authors' concerns and suggestions?

Topic 2: According to your opinion, how could governments take up the role of philanthropy?

Developing Vocabulary:

The words below may appear as part of your online quizzes. Please refer to the introduction for study strategies for learning vocabulary.

1. hubris
2. philanthropy
3. treasure trove
4. to dole out
5. miser
6. agenda
7. benign
8. to convert
9. immaculate
10. decrepit

Understanding the Text

Answer the following questions by carefully reviewing the authors' aruguments in the short essay.

1. What is the role of philanthropy in society today?

2. What are the authors' objections to philanthropy?

3. What should the role of government be in terms of philanthropy and its causes?

4. What are the authors' suggestions for the system of philanthropy?

Analyzing Writing

Answer the following questions by carefully reviewing the authors' arugments and writing strategies from the short essay.

1. What is the role of the second paragraph of the essay in the authors' construction of argument(s)?

2. Examine the role and effectiveness of statistics and data examples in the essay.

3. Examine the role of exaggeration and humor in the claims the authors make.

68 Respect Versus Courtesy

In my younger days in graduate school, I attended a class on cross-cultural communication which aimed at exploring different cultural formulations of relationships and perceptions. One class seminar examined the position of the elderly in various cultures throughout the world. In near unison, the seminar participants **enunciated** how old age warrants absolute respect from the young and how the young need to pay homage to the older generations for their invaluable contributions to the culture. Tempted by this unanimous admission, I decided to play the Devil's Advocate and brazenly announced my disagreement; after getting over the first wave of shocked stares, I elaborated that in my life I had met plenty of older people from whose life experience I had learned very little, if anything at all. Many of these people were simply ignorant, stagnant in their ways, unwilling to listen to others, carried badges of numerous foolish decisions, and were generally unpleasant to be around. There were others, I added, whose experience or advice had no bearing in the modern world. How, I wondered, were they worthy of my respect? My classmates, I maintained, were confusing respect with courtesy. Undoubtedly, all people deserve courtesy, proper and friendly treatment due to every human being; not all people, however, deserve respect, the abiding sentiment or esteem held for another person due to their experience, skills, knowledge, or actual deeds. Of course, I was to soon find out that apparently I was not old enough to be wise enough to edit my speech, for after this short vocalization I was more or less treated as the class barbarian.

1

express

Despite my ostracized status, however, I did not convert to the majority's beliefs. Certainly, in many cultures throughout the world, the elderly (those above and beyond the age of seventy) are deeply respected to the point of reverence. They are considered as the **repositories** of wisdom, the speakers of law, and the eyes to the past. In many cultures, particularly the ones that have had little or no contact with Westerners, elders hold the key to survival. In many Australian Aboriginal and African villages, the elderly remember the creation stories, keep faith alive, retain the connection to the ancestors, know the right time to plant and to harvest, the right time to slaughter the animals, the right time to be. The elderly in these communities are those participants whose knowledge and experience hold a

2

reserve

key to the past and to the future. These individuals certainly deserve appreciation for their contribution to and maintenance of the community, for their knowledge and abilities are in direct correlation with the community's survival.

3   However, the direct relevance to "the community" is far more complicated and difficult to assess in the Westernized, industrialized world, often character-ized by vast generation gaps. In more primal cultures such as with the Aborigines or certain African tribes, there is a real continuity among the generations. The collective experience of the old will probably be very similar to that of the young; only time's slow march through bone and skin differentiates the generations. In Western, industrialized countries there is a distinct divide among generations so that elders have far less relevance to contemporary young adults. An older person today grew up in a time without computers, satellites, frequent phone usage, or even television. The gap between this grandparent and a teenage grandchild who has been growing up with a cell phone in one hand and an Ipod in the other is, therefore, enormous. The elderly, objectively, are much closer to the Iron Age than the Information Age, and in today's fast-evolving society, the gap among gen-erations living in the industrialized world is ever-increasing.

4   This is not, of course, to deny any contribution that the elderly may offer or to **discredit** their total life experience. Rather the issue is that given today's cul-ture their ability to act as storehouses of wisdom in aiding the youth in today's world is limited. One could argue, of course, that despite these gaps, the elderly might have life-lessons to teach about good people, tricky people, and overall about human nature with its **diachronic** themes of life, death, love, and the pur-suit of happiness. However, even in this field human interactions have changed so much in the last fifty years, since World War II, that it seems we no longer in-habit the same universe as the grandmother or grandfather whose advice may eas-ily appear antiquated. What kind of advice can, for instance, a kindly grandmother offer a granddaughter who faces definite social disdain from her peers if she does not have sex with her boyfriend? In the grandmother's day, holding hands with a boy was a **scandalous** event. What, realistically, can the grandfather, who re-tained the same job until he retired, tell his grandson about professional prospects when the average employee today will change jobs seven or more times in the span of his work life?

5   Furthermore, these are the sympathetic elderly who make a serious effort to experience and learn from events in their lives. In any culture—even primal ones—there may be foolish, lazy, or ignorant older people who failed to learn much while growing older. Indeed, blowing out more candles every year on a birthday cake doesn't mean that a person **accrues** greater wisdom and experience.

disrespect

covered with how something develops

improper

accumulate

They should not be afforded more or any respect merely because they were able to survive long enough by breathing on a regular basis. They certainly deserve courtesy; they deserve a seat on a crowded bus; they deserve proper medication; they do not automatically deserve respect for their supposed wisdom and experience exclusively based on age.

What this essay shows, perhaps more than anything else, is the lens of the industrialized Western world in viewing people of all ages, especially the old. Our social and cultural relationships are based on individualism to a large degree, which means that we tend to make value judgments about people, be they acquaintances, friends, or family members. Even family members have to "measure up" in some way and by certain criteria; even parents or grandparents have to prove themselves on an individual basis; otherwise, the older generation simply becomes the "clueless," "out of it," "nice but boring" entities who have to be visited on certain occasions and who provide gifts every once in a while. Our **rampant** individualism requires that our social relationships offer something of value; otherwise, these relationships become more duty than anything else, an impediment to the individual's goals and aspirations.

6

unchecked

In other cultures around the world, especially Eastern ones, the social and cultural lens tends to be far more community-based, subduing much of the individualism prevalent in the West. In these cultures, the elderly are respected and revered as the direct link with the past. For this awarded privilege, the old do not have to prove their **efficacy**, their connection with modern times, or their particular use to the young. Their position within the community is secured not through their individual value, their wisdom, or their accumulated experience, but through the social **legacy** of their community. Respect is not an issue to be examined ad hoc; it is a social **mandate** to be doubted only by those who wish to be treated as outcasts, barbarians.

7

ability to produce intended results

legacy - heritage

mandate - authority to carry out an action

Discussing and Writing About The Text

Discussing Issues:

In groups, try to construct a list of criteria for evaluating an older person. Examine whether and to what extent these criteria coincide with those of other groups of students, of your parents, grandparents, or other groups of people. Discuss your findings with your peers.

Writing about the Text:

In a well-developed and organized essay, respond to the reading; be sure to support your views with pertinent examples drawn from your own experience and observations, as well as readings.

Topic 1: How does the author view the correlation between old age and respect? To what extent, if at all, do you share his views?

Topic 2: According to your opinion, how does the society you live in evaluate people? Do you agree and to what extent with the existent criteria for evaluating a person?

Developing Vocabulary:

The words below may appear as part of your online quizzes. Please refer to the introduction for study strategies for learning vocabulary.

1. **to enunciate** declare
2. **a repository** reserve
3. **to discredit** disgrace
4. **diachronic** concern with how something develops
5. **scandalous** discreditable
6. **to accrue** accumulate
7. **rampant** unchecked
8. **efficacy** ability to produce desired results
9. **legacy** heritage
10. **(a) mandate** authority to carry out a policy or action

Understanding the Text

Answer the following questions by carefully reviewing the authors' aruguments in the short essay.

1. What was the issue that the author disagreed on with his peers in the graduate seminar?

   That not all elders deserve respect but they do deserve courtesy for being human

2. In what way is respect different from courtesy?

3. In which cases are the elder's contributions valuable?

4. How has the Western perspective affected the author's thesis?

Analyzing Writing

Answer the following questions by carefully reviewing the authors' aruguments and writing strategies from the short essay.

1. Examine the use of comparison/contrast in the essay.

2. Find the examples the author provides and examine their thoroughness and effectiveness.

3. Examine the use of rhetorical questions and try to replace them with declarative sentences while retaining the same meaning.

69 Friends for Life, Not Likely!

Say goodbye to your friends while you still can, for in five or ten years you probably won't have any contact with most of them. Now, you might be ready to defend the truth and depth of your friendship with a baseball bat and a bag full of promises, but it still doesn't matter. The same friends to whom you have told your deep secrets, with whom you have shared something forbidden (cigarettes, alcohol, etc), laughed till you cried, or at whom you yelled till you exploded a blood vessel in your face, are mostly…transitory. However, this does not, in any way, devalue their current contribution to your life or the depth of your feelings for them. Indeed, high school and college friends have a great impact on the formation of personality as well as the way a person interacts with the world. But the sad truth is that what most people, especially the young, perceive of as friendship is merely based on associations of convenience with like-minded individuals who most of the time happen to be around.

1

Proximity friendships, as the name implies, **flourish** because of frequent close contact. These are the friends you happen to see in the halls of your dormitory or in the quad of the school. By chance, you might be invited to lunch, dinner, a concert, a late-night volleyball game, or a club session. There can be virtually any kind of reason for getting together, but once the reason for proximity is no longer present, the likelihood of the friendship continuing wanes remarkably. You might have had a great time with your proximity friend when you went to the Future Farmers of America (FFA) Regional Cattle Auction (your friend's idea, not yours), but where is this friend now? Actually, most dormitory relationships could be classified as proximity or convenience friendships that are struck up in classes one attends or in dorm halls where one lives.

2

Another type of friendship is based on the activities one participates in because of a shared interest. For instance, after playing basketball at the local **recreation** center for a few weeks, you steadily meet all the regular players, know their names, and even go out after the game for a cold beer or a diet Pepsi, in case you are still under-age. These people can prove to be great buddies, but only as long as you are interested in basketball and you mostly **confine** your conversations to sports. These activity friends will often not share similar interests beyond the

3

shared commitment to basketball. So, what if you study to become a doctor while your new basketball buddies only aspire to keep working at the neighborhood deli for the rest of their lives? While nothing is wrong with being a store clerk, their goals are very different from yours, which may cause conflict. You cannot talk to them about the stresses of studying, midterm examinations, or tuition costs. They probably won't understand why you can't just hang out and watch basketball all weekend with them; likewise, you probably won't really **agonize** about the issues involved with stocking the shelves with potato chips. Your ability to relate to your activity friends will invariably revolve around the activity itself. You might even discuss sports games that you recently saw on TV or the best dunk of the night. If you break your leg in a car accident, how likely is it that you will hang out with your friends from the basketball pick-up games? Will they visit you in the hospital and talk about the nature of life and the pitfalls of driving recklessly? Once you are unable to participate in or lose interest in an activity, your activity friends disappear.

4   Are you still ready to sign that high school or college yearbook with "Best Friends For Life XOX"? What of friends that you really have a lot in common with and whom you trust absolutely? Well, unfortunately, the person you are today is likely to change in the next five or ten years. Most high school and college-aged young adults undergo significant personality changes during their late teens and twenties. Through life experiences, education, and new jobs, personalities become more cemented and permanent during this period. This means that though there are some core personality characteristics that are unlikely to alter much, other aspects of character undergo significant further **refinement** and change during the twenties. It is often in this period when important decisions about career, family, and living location are made.

5   So, what happens with your friend from high school when you undergo an amazing transformation during college? You decide to participate in an Education Abroad Program (EAP) to some foreign country where you are able to see much more of the world. Upon your return, you meet a wonderful mate, whom you decide to marry even while you pursue a Masters degree. Because of all these intense experiences, you change and have less in common with your friend from high school who never went to college or traveled outside the state. Of course, you can still remain friends with your high school buddy, but the friendship will far more likely revolve around the past than the future. Gatherings might very well be based on "the good old days" and the memories from the past rather than the present and future aspects of your lives. Interests diverge and friendships fade.

There is a strange notion quite prevalent in American culture that friends   6
ought to be friends for life and that the decay of friendship over time is **distressing**. Why? It would be far more distressing if people didn't transform or develop and friendships became **stagnant**. Some friendships may last a lifetime, and these are few and far between; these are the ones where people grow in the same direction, still have similar interests, and whose characters are still compatible after years have passed. This is the kind where you might not have contact for a year, but when you do get together, there is so much to talk about. This kind of friendship is rarer among younger people because they have so much development and change ahead of them. So, even while our modern age allows us to easily keep contact with people through the telephone, cell phone, instant messages, emails, video conferences, there may very well be no reason to call, IM, email, or conference because people's paths **diverge**. This technology facilitates proximity and activity-based friendships, to be sure, but will there be a reason to communicate once you have moved on in life?

What you need to learn is that many of the people you bond with today will   7
not be there tomorrow. This is a fact of life. Therefore, before getting a red-ink tattoo on your arm that says "Jim and Joe: Friends for Life," think twice; this name may not look as good on **sagging** skin, especially if the only place you can find this buddy is on your arm.

Discussing and Writing About The Text

Discussing Issues:

Make a list of your friends and categorize these friendships according to the authors' criteria or other you deem appropriate. Compare your list to those of your peers and discuss the similarities or differences.

Writing about the Text:

In a well-developed and organized essay, respond to the reading; be sure to support your views with pertinent examples drawn from your own experience and observations, as well as readings.

Topic 1: Why do the authors support that friendships do not last forever? To what extent—if at all—do you find this assertion valid?

Topic 2: Analyze the essential components of a friendship that would have the potential to survive through many years of a person's life.

Developing Vocabulary:

The words below may appear as part of your online quizzes. Please refer to the introduction for study strategies for learning vocabulary.

1. **proximity** nearness
2. **to flourish** increase
3. **recreation** enjoyment
4. **to confine** enclose
5. **to agonize** worry
6. **refinement** improvement
7. **distressing** cause pain
8. **stagnant** still
9. **to diverge** seperate
10. **sagging** slump

Understanding the Text

Answer the following questions by carefully reviewing the authors' aruguments in the short essay.

1. What is the authors' thesis on everlasting friendship?

2. What are proximity friends, and what is the likely conclusion of such friend-ships?

3. What are activity friends, and what is the likely conclusion of such friendships?

4. Why are friendships among young people likely to change more than those among adults?

Analyzing Writing

Answer the following questions by carefully reviewing the authors' aruguments and writing strategies from the short essay.

1. Examine the use of classification in the text.

2. Examine the tone used in the text and its effectiveness.

3. Examine five word choices that seem interesting and effective.

70 Hookin' Up

It is pretty certain that there is something stirring in the air, and it has nothing to do with rising smog levels and CO_2 emissions. The change concerns an omnipresent human theme: sex and more specifically the sexual patterns among the youth of today. Certainly, the media has gone a long way in promoting the idea that young people today are running riot on college campuses across the country with the **titillating** tales of those who engage in "reckless" activities that may be entertaining but which may result in sexually transmitted diseases, pregnancy, or abortion. Is it true? For many years, the evidence has been anecdotal and piecemeal about the changes in relationship patterns and sexual liaisons among college students. But beginning in 2000 with the publication of a study by Professor of Psychology, Elizabeth Paul, many researchers have been admitting that "something" has actually been happening to change the social dynamics of sex among young people, specifically college-aged teenagers. Far beyond pre-marital sex or one-night stands, this initial study concluded that over 78% of the student body had had at least one "hook up" in their time at college, a statistic clearly showing a wider change in social dynamic.

1

While there is no absolute consensus on its definition, for most people using the term "hooking up" entails two people who come together for a sexual encounter with no expectations of long-term ties, romantic involvement, or even the **aspiration** to see each other again. Contrary to popular belief, hooking up does not *necessarily* include sex, which may be one of the reasons for its ambiguity among young people; a hook-up could include kissing, petting, oral sex, or actual sex, depending on the parties involved. In its benign sense, a hook-up becomes a release of sexual energy by two **consenting** individuals in the form of contact that avoids all the fuss, muss, and mess of what many sociologists call "meaningful relationships." Indeed, for some college students, hooking up is the best solution for their particular stage in life. They realize that adventures, further education, and jobs are all likely to take them to some other part of the country, far from any potential long-distance relationship partner. Some have even cited increased competition in the professional field as a reason for hooking up instead of establishing a long-term relationship, for such a relationship might impede their future career

2

prospects.

3   Because hooking up is so prevalent among college-aged students (and possibly younger teens), the trend can no longer be **relegated** into the category of "loose moral standards" or for those who are simply "incapable of forming relationships." In a way, hooking up can be viewed as part of the changing dynamics of mating, courtship, and relationships, which has been going on since World War II. While marriage is still the predominant form of relationship (95% of Americans get married at least once)— the rising rates of divorce (hovering at 50%), **cohabitation** arrangements, and the fact that young people wait on average until they are twenty seven or older to marry—there is a steady transformation in the way relationships are perceived. Furthermore, family units have undergone significant changes in the last fifty years as evidenced by the number of step parents, step children, adopted children, single parents, gay and lesbian couples, and older singles. In short, the myriad ways of organizing relationships and family structures have fundamentally affected young people's perception of relationships.

4   On the other hand, what has caught most sociologists off-guard is that hooking up has very little to do with traditional **courtship** or mating behavior, the model that has been used for many years to understand and interpret relationships. In this model, young people congregate and use the tools at their disposal to attract possible mates. These tools might include personality, physical appearance, class, or the ability to provide a stable economic base. Modeled in many ways on the animal kingdom, the primary focus in male/female interaction is to **procure** a mate, and sex is just one of the strategies adopted. However, many sociologists seem to be genuinely puzzled by this new form of behavior; such is their confusion that a knee-jerk reaction of disapproval is produced, as epitomized in the 2001 study "Hooking Up, Hanging Out, and Hoping for Mr. Right" where the authors' underlying assumption is that sex and sexual practices *should be* connected to establishing meaningful relationships that lead to marriage.

5   A more recent book, *Unprotected* (2006), authored by a psychologist at UCLA, primarily discusses the dangers of hooking up. These include the increased risk of sexually transmitted diseases (STDs), unwanted pregnancy, and a lack of fulfillment among the participants, especially girls who are often left depressed. The book turns into a series of case files of hooking up gone bad. *Unprotected* is not alone in its suspicion of teenage sexual practices. Articles in *Time* and *Newsweek* share a "concerned tone" for unprepared teens engaging in activities "beyond their years." Other entities such as the Institute for American Values or AmericanValues.org argue that hooking up is dangerous, foolish, and possibly immoral.

The dangers inherent in hooking up do exist, so they should not be denied.   6
It is certainly possible to contract an STD, to unwillingly become pregnant, and
even for one partner to be hurt by a misunderstanding in the specific "social contract." It also may be too far to go, as many sociologists have done, to worry that
a hooking-up culture may lead to an inability for people to form meaningful, lasting relationships. Instead, what is most interesting about the hooking-up phenomenon is not that it is happening. Its rise could clearly be foretold with the
lack of homogenous family or relationship structures. What is most interesting is
the negative reaction of most adults since hooking up so **blatantly** contradicts the
social norms prevalent for so many years. The condemnatory tone used in most
writing about the subject indicates more about the expectations for relationships
of the past than those likely to occur in the future.

     Far beyond a one-night stand, hooking up represents a serious change in   7
the courtship and mating patterns in our society, and it may be the tip of the iceberg. We seem to be **on the verge** of completely redefining relationships in our
society away from courtship that must inevitably lead to marriage and procreation. Ironically, parents themselves may be partially to blame, for the young
have been told again and again by their parents that they must be prepared for a
hectic work environment. In order to survive in this world, they need to be flexible. They need to be willing to change jobs and careers seven to ten times in
their lifetime. They need to stay focused on their goals and themselves. Perhaps
this same **motto** has been applied to relationships as can be seen by the vastly different family units that now exist. Hooking up may be simply an indicator of
what is to come—a move toward a more individualistic society where relationships, like jobs, will change based on the need (a night, a month, a year). In this
new world, "permanent" relationships, as seen with aged married couples, may be
relegated to the past. This is not to say that relationships will not be "meaningful
and full"; they may simply not be long-lasting. Hooking up is another product of
our changing society and relationship patterns; it is not necessarily evidence of immoral youth gone wild.

Discussing and Writing About The Text

Discussing Issues:

Interview a person of a previous generation about the norms and customs of courtship. Compare them to those existing among students at your school or other contemporaries. Discuss your findings with your peers.

Writing about the Text:

In a well-developed and organized essay, respond to the reading; be sure to support your views with pertinent examples drawn from your own experience and observations, as well as readings.

Topic 1: According to the authors, what does "hooking up" reveal about the youth of today and about society? To what extent—if at all—do you agree with their interpretation of this phenomenon?

Topic 2: What is your opinion of the "hooking-up" phenomenon and its effects on human relationships?

Developing Vocabulary:

The words below may appear as part of your online quizzes. Please refer to the introduction for study strategies for learning vocabulary.

1. **titillating** arousing sexual interest
2. **aspiration** desire
3. **to consent** agree to do something
4. **to relegate** downgrade
5. **cohabitation** living together
6. **courtship** love, romance
7. **to procure** obtain
8. **blatantly** unshammed matter
9. **on the verge** brink
10. **motto** a phrase

Understanding the Text

Answer the following questions by carefully reviewing the authors' aruguments in the short essay.

1. How is "hooking up" defined and what does it involve?

2. What are the social implications of the "hooking up" phenomenon?

3. Why are the analysts of "hooking up" skeptical?

4. What is the authors' interpretation of this phenomenon and the reactions to it?

Analyzing Writing

Answer the following questions by carefully reviewing the authors' aruguments and writing strategies from the short essay.

1. Examine the use of definition in its various types in the text.

2. Examine the use and role of counterarguments in the text.

3. Examine the type of sources and the effectiveness in supporting the authors' arguments.